JESUS
VS
PAUL
ON CHRISTIANITY

DR. PETER ZHAO

MILTON & HUGO L.L.C.
4407 Park Ave., Suite 5
Union City, NJ 07087, USA

Website: *www. miltonandhugo.com*
Hotline: *1- 888-778-0033*
Email: *info@miltonandhugo.com*

Ordering Information:
Quantity sales. Special discounts are granted to corporations, associations, and other organizations. For more information on these discounts, please reach out to the publisher using the contact information provided above.

Library of Congress Control Number:		2024919778
ISBN-13:	979-8-89285-287-6	[Paperback Edition]
	979-8-89285-288-3	[Hardback Edition]
	979-8-89285-286-9	[Digital Edition]

Rev. date: 09/16/2024

CONTENTS

Acknowledgments vii

Preface ix

Introduction xvii

Part 1   PROVED CANONICITY OF THREE NEW
          TESTAMENT BOOKS... 1

Chapter 1 Introduction to the New-Testament Canon 3

Chapter 2 The Timeline of Herod the Great 6

Chapter 3 The Timeline of Yeshua...14

Chapter 4 Daniel's Prophecy: the 69th Week.............................. 26

Chapter 5 Daniel's Prophecy: The First Half of the 70th Week 34

Chapter 6 Ezekiel's Prophecy: Jerusalem Twice Destroyed 41

Chapter 7 Yeshua's Prophecy on His Burial and Resurrection...... 44

Chapter 8 Yeshua's Prophecy on Destruction of the Temple.........55

Chapter 9 Yeshua's Prophecies on His First-Century Return........61

Chapter 10 Jeremiah's Prophecy on 17 Shekels of Silver.................76

Chapter 11 Canonicity of the Epistles of John............................81

Part 2   UNPROVED CANONICITY OF SOME NEW
          TESTAMENT BOOKS...87

Chapter 12 Noncanonicity of Some New-Testament Books 89

Chapter 13 Luke's Error on Appearances of the Risen Yeshua........92

Chapter 14 Luke's Error on the Time of Yeshua's Resurrection 96

Chapter 15 Luke's Error on the Year of Yeshua's Crucifixion 98

Chapter 16 Other Errors in the Gospel of Luke............................101

Chapter 17 Errors in the Book of Acts 111

Chapter 18 Error in the Second Epistle of "Peter".........................119

Part 3   PAUL'S APOSTLESHIP AND DOCTRINE........123
Chapter 19 Paul's Apostleship 125
Chapter 20 Teachings of Yeshua or His Disciples vs Paul.............127
Chapter 21 Two Gospels and Two Laws 134
Chapter 22 Paul's Teachings vs the Old-Testament Scriptures 142
Chapter 23 Luke's Accounts vs Paul's Doctrine............................148
Chapter 24 Mr. Scott Nelson's Arguments: Paul's Apostleship 156
Chapter 25 Yeshua's Teachings on Anti-messiah 160
Chapter 26 Paul's Christianity 169

Part 4   TRUE FAITH IN YESHUA MESSIAH 177
Chapter 27 True Nature of the Messiah 179
Chapter 28 Yeshua Messiah: Recognized by Few Jews 192
Chapter 29 Should We Worship the Messiah? 197
Chapter 30 True Faith in Yeshua Messiah 201
Chapter 31 Birthday of Yeshua Messiah 215
Chapter 32 Daniel's Prophecy: The Last Half of the 70th Week....227

Index of Scriptures 231

ACKNOWLEDGMENTS

I acknowledge two special people in the writing of this book and the previous book: *Perfectly Fulfilled Prophecies and the Destiny of Mankind*. First, I am very grateful to my wife, Grace Chao, who has been my faithful companion physically and spiritually for over 20 years. During the last five years, she has been very patient with me while I spent so many hours in front of my computer. Because of my busy schedule, we have not had much family quality time together. She has fully supported my commitment to writing these two books. Second, I would like to thank my son, Joshua who is the first reader of the two books and has spent many hours in proofreading this book.

I would also like to thank Dr. Pieder Beeli for numerous discussions on the teachings of Paul and John the Apostle before I started to write this book. I am also grateful to a few Christian friends (e.g., Kevin Jaw and Judy Xu) who are quite open-minded on the controversial topics in this book.

PREFACE

Having been a firm atheist before I came to the United States in 1988, I started to believe in the God of Abraham, Isaac, and Jacob, and Yeshua Messiah (Jesus Christ) in 1993 when I was convinced by some Biblical prophecies. I received my Ph.D. in Physics from University of Zürich in 1997 under the supervision of Alex Müller who received the Physics Nobel Prize in 1987. Since 2002, I have been a physics professor in the field of condensed matter physics. I have published over 110 physics papers in highly reputed journals, including two *Nature* magazine articles (first author) and 12 invited book chapters.

Prior to 2014, I had never seriously tried to write a book outside Physics. During my sabbatical leave in that year, I had planned on writing a scientific book on the microscopic mechanism of high-temperature superconductivity, the subject I had studied for many years. But during dinner one day, a few Bible verses I had previously read about the resurrection of Yeshua struck me. I jumped up and told my wife that the Bible was wrong!! I explained to my startled wife that the most important prophecy about the resurrection of Yeshua, which was foretold by Yeshua himself, was not fulfilled at all. I was experiencing **a crisis of faith**!

We have been told that Yeshua was crucified in the afternoon on Friday, buried just before sunset, and rose again before sunrise on Sunday. According to this, from the time of his burial to the time of his resurrection, there would have been only 36 hours at most. This is totally inconsistent with Matthew 12:38-40, "Then certain of the scribes and of the Pharisees answered, saying, master, we would see a sign from you. But he answered and said unto them, 'An evil and adulterous generation seeks after a sign; and there shall no sign be given to it, but the sign of the prophet Jonah: For as Jonah was **three days and three nights** in the whale's belly; so shall the Son of Man be **three days and three nights** in the heart of the earth.'"

Yeshua's own words clearly prophesized that he would be **three days and three nights** (72 hours) in the grave just as Jonah was **three days and three nights** in the fish's belly. If this crucial prophecy were not fulfilled, Yeshua would not be the Messiah and the foundation of Christianity would completely collapse.

My heart for seeking the truth motivated me to investigate this issue thoroughly. I then started to search the Internet for any discussion on this issue. Indeed, I found numerous discussions, and the majority have attempted to maintain the traditional Friday crucifixion and Sunday resurrection. Few have raised objections to the traditional view with the proposition of a Wednesday crucifixion and Saturday resurrection. After I carefully studied the Gospels and the Old Testament Scriptures for many hours, I eventually solved the mystery. I found that this prophecy was in fact fulfilled perfectly, and that the traditional view of Yeshua's crucifixion day was wrong and unbiblical. Since then, I have diligently and critically studied the Scriptures. Instead of writing my book on high-temperature superconductivity, I spent hours upon hours each day studying Biblical prophecies, the world's chronology and history, astronomy, and cosmology.

Perhaps I was moved by the Spirit of God to study numerical prophecies in the Bible. The numerical prophecies are special prophecies with clearly stated numbers, such as prophetic periods. If all the numerical prophecies were fulfilled perfectly, they must have come from the true God who is the most powerful and above all things. There are several reasons for the superior credibility of numerical prophecies. First, no human, under any circumstance, has his own power to predict any future event to happen at an exact time. Only the most-high God would have the power to guarantee the perfect fulfilment of his own words foretold by his prophets. A prophecy from a less powerful god or deity would be made void by the most-high God. Second, a numerical prophecy can have only one correct interpretation. Third, the probability for perfect fulfilments of several numerical prophecies is nearly zero if these prophecies were not from the most-high God. In contrast, number-free descriptive prophecies are less credible. This is because the interpretations to the descriptive prophecies are quite subjective and could vary significantly with interpreters. These descriptive prophecies could even be fulfilled apparently in fabricated stories by someone attempting to establish a false religion. For these reasons, only the prophecies containing numerical information can be used to prove or disprove whether a religion comes from the most-high God.

For almost four years, I have diligently studied Biblical prophecies and chronology, as well as the history of the Middle East, of Europe, and of China. I have also investigated the Hebrew, Babylonian, Islamic, and Chinese calendars, as well as Enoch's calendar. I have been able to determine the true Biblical chronology that aligns perfectly with historical records and other secular chronologies such as the Chinese chronology. I have precisely reconstructed the Chinese chronology back to 2716 BC by taking advantage of the astronomical phenomena recorded concurrently with the corresponding historical events. With an uncertainty of less than 6 months, the Chinese chronology I have constructed aligns perfectly with all the astronomical phenomena. One remarkable discovery is that the year of Noah's flood in our Biblical chronology is the same as that of China's "great flood," which took place in the 61st year of Emperor Yao.

With these accurate chronologies in hand, I can clearly show that all the Biblical numerical prophecies have been perfectly fulfilled. I have also unveiled the prophecies that are yet to be fulfilled by making an end-time chronology. The true destiny of the world can be found from these end-time prophecies that are based solely on the Bible. Based on this deep and extensive study, I have written and published a book: *Perfectly Fulfilled Prophecies and the Destiny of Mankind*.

The perfect fulfilments of these numerical prophecies tell us that Yehowah, the most-high God of the Hebrew Bible, is the most-high God of the universe, orchestrating the history of the whole world. The direction of the whole world has been and will continue to be influenced by most-high God.

In addition to studying the Biblical prophecies and chronology, I also found some discussions on the Internet concerning the doctrine of Christianity and the teachings of Paul several years ago. To my big surprise, some Christians even questioned the authenticity of the apostleship of Paul. Some even call him a false apostle and say that his teachings are heretical against both the Hebrew Bible and Yeshua's teachings. Although I previously found some contradictions between the teachings of Yeshua and of Paul, I had never thought that Paul should have been a false apostle.

After I have studied this issue very seriously for about two years, I indeed find that Paul's teachings contradict the teachings of Yeshua and his disciples on many critical issues and that these contradictions cannot be resolved with any reasonable logic. Paul's gospel is different from the gospel of Yeshua's twelve disciples. My findings have saddened me greatly. If these contradictions cannot be compromised, then what would happen to mainstream Christianity? I cannot openly discuss these controversial issues with my general Christian friends and/or "spiritual fathers" because they would rather ignore the contradictions to maintain the infallibility of every New-Testament book.

I am not a theologian nor have obtained a theological degree from a prestigious seminary. I am only a physicist with strong analytical, logical, and critical thinking skills. Most Christians believe that one cannot use man's wisdom to resolve theological controversies. If one tries to use his/her own wisdom to overthrow a well-established doctrine, he/she may be thought to be very arrogant. Such a person may be accursed by his/her friends, family members, and peers.

According to Paul, anyone who preaches a gospel different from his, let him **be accursed** (Galatians 1:9). 2 Peter 3:15-16 says: "and consider that the longsuffering of our Lord is salvation—as also our beloved brother Paul, according to the wisdom given to him, has written to you, as also in all his epistles, speaking in them of these things, in which are some things hard to understand, which untaught and unstable people twist to **their own destruction**, as they do also the rest of the Scriptures." Paul also told Timothy (1 Timothy 4:1-3): "Now the Spirit expressly says that **in latter times** some will depart from the faith, **giving heed to deceiving spirits and doctrines of demons**, speaking lies in hypocrisy, having their own conscience seared with a hot iron, forbidding to marry, and commanding to abstain from foods which God created to be received with thanksgiving by those who believe and know the truth."

If the above passages were the inspired words of God, then anyone who dares to say something against Paul would be an untaught and unstable person or even a demon-possessed person.

On the other hand, Yeshua warned his disciples (Matthew 20:16), "So the last will be first and the first last, for **many are called, but few chosen**." He repeated this again in Matthew 22:14, "**For many are called, but few are chosen**." In the earlier time, Yeshua spoke a similar message in Matthew 7:13-14, "**Enter by the narrow gate; for wide is the gate and broad is the way that leads to destruction, and there are many who go in by it. Because narrow is the gate and difficult is the way which leads to life, and there are few who find it.**"

The total number of mainstream Christians has been so **many** since the first century AD, **but few are chosen** according to Yeshua's words. At present there are about 2.42 billion Christians in the world (see the webpage: https://en.wikipedia.org/wiki/ List_of_Christian_denominations_by_number_of_members), about one third of the total global population. There are approximately 41,000 Christian denominations and organizations all over the world (see the report at https://www.learnreligions.com/christianity-statistics-700533).

Almost all the Christian denominations and organizations accept Paul as the most important apostle of Yeshua and his 14 epistles to be the inspired words of God. Almost no Christian has ever raised any doubt about Paul's apostleship since the first century AD although the evidence for his apostleship is unsustainable based on the standard prescribed by Yeshua in the New Testament and Moses in the Old Testament.

In the Bible, Paul was referred to as an apostle for 22 times, and only twice he was referred to as an apostle by someone other than himself. The two instances didn't come from Yeshua or any of the original apostles but from Paul's close traveling companion and disciple, Luke, who was not an apostle of Yeshua. He was a Gentile and didn't have a chance to directly witness Yeshua's words and deeds. The two instances where Luke referred to Paul as an apostle are found in the book of Acts (Acts 14:4,14). No one else in the Bible has ever recognized his apostleship.

According to Yeshua (Matthew 18:16) and Moses (Deuteronomy 19:15), by the mouth of two or three witnesses every word may be established. Paul could not be a witness to testify for himself. Just as a friend would not be qualified to serve as jury, Luke could not be a witness either because he was Paul's friend or follower. A disciple of Paul could honestly write down Paul's words and deeds, but he/she could not prove Paul's apostleship. Any person in Luke's books could not prove Paul's apostleship either. Therefore, there is no single reliable witness in the Bible to testify for Paul's apostleship.

On the other hand, Paul tried to use the signs, wonders, and mighty deeds he performed to prove his apostleship (2 Corinthians 12:12). This proof is not tenable either. Yeshua foretold that false prophets would show great signs and wonders to deceive, if possible, even the elect (Matthew 24:24). Yeshua also said (Matthew 7:22-23), "Many will say to me in that day, 'Lord, Lord, have we not prophesied in your name, cast out demons in your name, and done many wonders in your name?' And then I will declare to them, 'I never knew you; depart from me, you who **practice lawlessness!**'" Yeshua's teaching is consistent with Moses' in Deuteronomy 13:1-5. Both Yeshua and Moses tell us that the signs, wonders, and mighty deeds cannot be used to prove the authenticity of a prophet or an apostle.

Since Paul's apostleship has not been testified by any reliable witness in the New-Testament Scriptures or by any prophet of God in the Hebrew Bible, how could mainstream Christians blindly accept his 14 epistles to be the inspired words of God?

I write this book to present detailed comparisons: 1) between the teachings of Yeshua/his disciples and those of Paul; 2) between Paul's teachings and the Old-Testament Hebrew Scriptures; and 3) between Paul's doctrine and Luke's accounts. I will also prove that **the Gospel of Matthew, the Gospel of John, and the book of Revelation are the truly inspired words of God** by demonstrating that all the numerical prophecies of Yeshua recorded in these books and some Old-Testament prophecies about Yeshua were perfectly fulfilled and that they are consistent with each other.

I hope that readers will carefully and objectively study my detailed comparisons and arguments without judging me. It is up to the readers to agree or disagree with the view presented in the book. If my view represents the true doctrine of Christianity, this book shall be of great value to the readers who are seeking a true faith. If my view is partially incorrect, please forgive me for my misunderstanding of some Scriptures. I present these controversial issues not to bring down the true Christian faith but to seek the solutions of these contradictory issues for the purpose of strengthening faith.

INTRODUCTION

Christianity is a religion based on the story of Yeshua (Jesus) of Nazareth. Yeshua's believers are called Christians who believe that Yeshua is the Messiah (Christ), the Son of God, and the Savior of the entirety of humanity. Christians also believe in the God of Abraham, Jacob, and Isaac in the Hebrew Bible, which has been called the Old Testament.

The main contents of the faith are as follows: 1) Yeshua came to the world about 2000 years ago by virgin birth; 2) he preached the kingdom of God for about three years; 3) he died on the cross for the sins of all the world; 4) he resurrected the third day and then ascended to heaven; 5) he will come back in the end times to establish the everlasting kingdom of God; and 6) anyone who believes in him shall be saved and enter the everlasting kingdom of God. The life and teachings of Yeshua are recorded in the books of four Gospels. These Gospels and some writings of Yeshua's direct disciples along with Pauline writings were put together to form the canon of the New Testament in the 4th century AD.

The foundation of the mainstream Christian faith is the Holy Bible that contains 39 books in the Old Testament and 27 books in the New Testament. These 66 books are believed to be the inspired words of God. Although over 40 authors with different backgrounds wrote these books during different times (a time span of about 1,500 years), the true author of the Holy Bible is believed to be the most-high God who is the Creator and Sustainer of the universe.

How do we know that the Holy Bible is the true Word of the Creator? It is by faith! This is probably the most common answer you hear. How do you trust your faith? It is by the Holy Spirit. How do you prove that the spirit you have received is the Holy Spirit from God? All these questions have no definitive answers.

If you are not so serious about your faith, you could just have a blind faith without a need to verify the authenticity of your faith. But if you are a very serious about your faith and are devoting your life to it, you should have taken times to think about the foundation of your faith. There are so many different faiths in the world. Why do you only choose Christianity? Why not Judaism, Islam, or Buddhism?

As a physicist, I have a natural tendency to prove or disprove things. I believe that any physical law, principle, or widely accepted theory must be verified by reliable experimental data. A theory must be rejected or modified if it is inconsistent with a single reliable and repeatable experiment. A theory must be self-consistent and obey basic logic.

Can we prove whether the god of the Bible is the only true God and Creator of the universe and whether all the books in the Bible are the inspired words of God? No one had ever tried to answer this extremely difficult question before I partially answered the question in my book: *Perfectly Fulfilled Prophecies and the Destiny of Mankind.* In this book, I prove that the god of the Old Testament is the true Creator and God of the universe by demonstrating:

1. All the past Biblical numerical prophecies foretold by the true prophets of God were perfectly fulfilled in the time frames specified in the prophecies.
2. The historical events recorded in the Old Testament are consistent with reliable extra-biblical historical records and astronomical phenomena.
3. The Biblical chronology agrees perfectly with the accurate Chinese chronology, which is reconstructed based on the concurrently recorded historical events and astronomical phenomena.
4. God's perfect number of 7 and its multiples are coded in the orbital motions of the Moon and the Earth. The number 7 has also been coded in the history of the world. The age of the universe in terms of the human clock is almost exactly equal to 7^{12} years, which is constructed from the two perfect numbers of 7 and 12 in the Bible. In contrast, the age of the universe in

terms of God's clock is less than 6000 years. Moses perfectly prophesized the two different clocks in Psalm 90:4.

5. God of the Old Testament has directed world history.
6. The science presented in the Old Testament agrees with the confirmed physical laws.
7. The words of God do not contradict themselves.

The numerical prophecies are the special prophecies that contain well-defined numerical numbers without the possibility of multiple interpretations. If all the numerical prophecies in the Old Testament were perfectly fulfilled within the time frames specified by God, there is no doubt that this most-high God governs every aspect of the universe. Everything must be under His control so that every prophecy going forth from His mouth must be 100% fulfilled. A partial fulfilment or unfulfillment of a prophecy should violate the unique requirement for the prophecy originating from the most-high God.

Since I have proved that the Masoretic text of the Old Testament is the inspired Word of God, the canonicity of the New-Testament books must be verified by the Old Testament. Any New-Testament book that contradicts the teachings in the Old Testament should not be included in the canon of the New Testament.

Yeshua himself claimed to be the Son of God, the Son of Man, and the Messiah according to the Gospel of Matthew. The Gospel of John and the book of Revelation tell us that Yeshua is the incarnation of the Word of God who was with God in the beginning even before the creation of the world. According to mainstream Christianity, the Son is also God and has the same power, authority and glory as God the Father, and that he deserves worship just as the Father. To prove Yeshua to be the true Messiah, the Gospels and some writings of his own disciples must agree with the Old-Testament Scriptures.

In Part I of this book, I will show that all the numerical prophecies of Yeshua recorded in **the Gospel of Matthew, the Gospel of John, and the book of Revelation** were fulfilled perfectly and that some Old-Testament prophecies about Yeshua were also fulfilled exactly in the accounts of these books. These three books were written by two of the twelve disciples of Yeshua, and the stories recorded in these books do not contradict each other. Based on these facts, we conclude that at least these three books are truthful and inspired by God just as the Old-Testament books. Since the contents of Part I are mostly (about 80%) copied from my previous book: *Perfectly Fulfilled Prophecies and the Destiny of Mankind*, readers could skip this part if they have read my previous book. For completeness, I put these chapters in Part I of this book to prove the canonicity for **the Gospel of Matthew, the Gospel of John,** and **the book of Revelation.** If the readers are already convinced of the canonicity of these three books, they could initially skip Part I and directly jump to Part II.

In Part II of this book, I will show that the important story about Yeshua's post-resurrection appearances recorded in the Gospel of Luke plainly contradicts those recorded in the Gospels of Matthew and John. In addition to this crucial error (relative to the three books of Yeshua's disciples), we find many other errors in the Gospel of Luke and the book of Acts. Since Luke was the disciple of Paul whose epistles were included in the New Testament, the irrefutable errors in Luke's books raise a serious question as to whether Paul's teachings are truly inspired by God. Most Pauline teachings appear to be consistent with the teachings of Yeshua. Nevertheless, the differences between Yeshua's and Paul's teachings are significant, which will be addressed in Part III of the book. Paul's teachings are also different from those of Yeshua's direct disciples like John and James. Many of Paul's teachings contradict those of the Old-Testament Scriptures.

In Part IV, I will also discuss the true nature of the Messiah and the doctrine of Christianity from the teachings of Yeshua and his disciples. These teachings are consistent with each other as well as with the Masoretic Hebrew Scriptures.

The Biblical verses quoted in this book are mostly from the New King James Version (NKJV) unless specified. We have changed some upper-case letters into the lower-case ones according to our own understanding of the nature of the Messiah. In most cases, we have also changed "the LORD" back to "Yehowah" according to the original Hebrew Bible and the correct pronunciation of God's name by the Karaites, a sect of the Jews. We have also changed "Jesus" to "Yeshua" and "Christ" to "Messiah" according to the original Hebrew Gospel of

Matthew. An angel of God, who appeared to Joseph in a dream, called our Messiah "Yeshua" while Matthew simply called him "Yeshu," the Galilean pronunciation or a short version of "Yeshua." The Chinese Bible correctly translates both the names of God and the Messiah while the pronunciation of "Jesus" in the English Bible is well off from the original pronunciation.

PART

I

PROVED CANONICITY
OF THREE NEW
TESTAMENT BOOKS

CHAPTER

1

Introduction to the New-Testament Canon

The canon of the New Testament is the set of books that must be divinely inspired by God. The 27 New-Testament books in the Christian Bible may have been used by Origen by the early third century AD. In 367 AD, Athanasius, Bishop of Alexandria, regarded the 27 books as the canon of the New Testament. In 382 AD, the Catholic Church provided a conciliar definition of the New-Testament canon at the council of Rome. The first council that accepted the present canon of the New Testament may have been the Synod of Hippo Regius in North Africa in 393 AD. From the 4th century AD, the West Church appeared to accept the New-Testament canon quite unanimously and by the fifth century AD, the Eastern Church had come to accept Revelation as the canonized book. Nonetheless, the Canon of Trent in 1546 AD made a full dogmatic articulation of the canon for Roman Catholicism. The same action was not taken until the Gallic Confession of Faith in 1559 AD for Calvinism, the Thirty-Nine Articles in 1563 AD for the Church of England, and the Synod of Jerusalem in 1672 AD for the Greek Orthodox.

From the development of the New-Testament canon, we can clearly see that the Roman Catholic bishops canonized these 27 books into the Holy Bible. What are the criteria to choose these books? We need to be certain that the persons who canonized these books were completely under guidance from God in order for us to believe that the selected

3

books are truly inspired words of God. Nobody can prove that their opinions and judgments are from God without human bias or error. Moreover, most of the bishops who canonized the New-Testament books were from the Roman Catholic Church, which was not supposed to be the true church of God according to most Protestants. Then, how can Protestants trust the opinions and judgments made by the Roman Catholic bishops? Therefore, the acceptance of all the 27 New-Testament books as the inerrant words of God is not an intellectual decision, but a blind faith. Even in our modern world where knowledges and information are so readily available on the Internet, most Christians still firmly believe that all these books are inspired by God simply because they are in the Holy Bible and because of what preachers and pastors have said.

Mainstream Christianity is based on the foundation that all the 27 New-Testament books are the inspired words of God. We are taught that Christians are not supposed to challenge the canonicity of these books. If someone finds contradictory teachings from different books, he/she is not allowed to raise any objection to these books. Christian leaders would simply say that the contradictions are caused by the misunderstanding of the Scriptures, instead of the errors of the Scriptures themselves. At most, they would accept that there could be a few minor typos.

Is it possible for someone to prove or disprove canonicity of the New-Testament books? Our answer is yes. We have proved that the five books of Moses, the book of Jeremiah, the book of Isaiah, the book of Ezekiel, the book of Daniel, the book of Zechariah, and the book of Amos in the Hebrew Bible are the inspired words of God. We prove the canonicity of these books by demonstrating that all (over 10) numerical prophecies recorded in these books were perfectly fulfilled (see *Perfectly Fulfilled Prophecies and the Destiny of Mankind*). In the same way, we can also prove the canonicity of some New-Testament books by showing that all the numerical prophecies of Yeshua recorded in these books were perfectly fulfilled and that all the numerical prophecies on Yeshua recorded in the Hebrew Bible were completely fulfilled in the writings of these books. In addition to the perfect fulfilments of these numerical prophecies, there should be no contradiction among the writings of these books.

We first focus on the Gospel of Matthew, the Gospel of John, and the book of Revelation because these books were written by Yeshua's direct disciples who had followed him for over three years. If the teachings of these three books agree with the Old-Testament Scriptures and all the numerical prophecies of Yeshua recorded in these books were fulfilled completely, these books must be truthful and inspired by God just as the Hebrew Scriptures. Then, these books should be included in the canon of the New Testament. When this conclusion has been well established, we can make unbiased judgments on the canonicity of other books. Any writing that is not consistent with the teachings in these three books should not be included in the canon.

We will show that the 70-week prophecies in Daniel 7:26-27 were perfectly fulfilled in Yeshua (Chapters 4 and 5). We will also show that Ezekiel's prophecy on the second destruction of Jerusalem was also fulfilled exactly in Yeshua (Chapter 6). In Chapters 7-9, we will demonstrate that all the numerical prophecies of Yeshua recorded in these three books were fulfilled completely. In Chapter 10, we will show that Jeremiah's prophecy on 17 shekels of silver was absolutely fulfilled in the story recorded in the Gospel of Matthew. The perfect fulfilments of these prophecies are the foundation of the canonicity of these three books.

DISCLAIMER

If readers do not need proof for the canonicity of these three books: Matthew, John, and Revelation, they could skip Chapters 2-11 and directly jump to Part II of this book. Chapters 2-11 are very interesting but potentially difficult to comprehend. Readers could always refer to these chapters after finishing the other parts or when in doubt.

CHAPTER

2

The Timeline of Herod the Great

In order to accurately establish when Yeshua started to minister and when he was crucified, it is necessary to construct the accurate timeline of Herod, whose story was recorded in the Gospel of Matthew.

Herod, also known as Herod the Great, was the Roman client king of Judea which was referred to as the Herodian kingdom. The accurate determination of the Herod's timeline is crucial to the construction of the accurate timeline of Yeshua. The accurate timeline of Yeshua is necessary for us to prove whether Yeshua is the true Messiah.

Timeline of the reign of Herod the Great

Details about Herod's life were recorded in *The Antiquities of the Jews* by Josephus. Herod also appeared in the Gospel of Matthew as the ruler of Judea who ordered the Massacre of the Innocents at the time of the birth of Yeshua. Moreover, Herod's temple was mentioned in the Gospel of John.

We will use the historical records of Josephus, astronomical information, lunisolar calendar information, and other historical evidence to uniquely determine the date of the first year of Herod's reign. According to Josephus, Herod took Jerusalem in the day of the appointed third month's fasting in the 185th Olympiad (*Antiq.*, bk. 14, ch. 16, sect. 2-4). There is no third month's fasting according to Zechariah 8:19, "Thus says the LORD of hosts; the fast of the fourth month, and the fast of the fifth, and the fast of the seventh, and the fast of the tenth, shall be to the house of Judah joy and gladness, and cheerful feasts; therefore love the truth and peace." Currently, the Jews observe the solemnity of the fast on Tammuz 17/18 (fourth month), Av 9/10 (fifth month), Tishri 3/4 (seventh month), and Tebet 10/11 (tenth month), in agreement with Zechariah 8:19.

Since there is no fasting day in the third month of Hebrew calendar, did Josephus make a mistake about this? No, he did not. In fact, his record is correct if we understand that he uses the Babylonian calendar to describe the historical events.

We know that the first month of the Babylonian calendar always falls on or after the Vernal Equinox while the first month of the Hebrew calendar starts before or after the Vernal Equinox (see *Perfectly Fulfilled Prophecies and the Destiny of Mankind*). In Table I, we present the Hebrew lunisolar calendar of 38 BC, which is constructed from the true astronomical moon-phases and the main rules of "postponement" (see Chapter 2 in *Perfectly Fulfilled Prophecies and the Destiny of Mankind*). The lunisolar calendar is superimposed on the Julian solar calendar to save space. The first day of each lunar month is indicated with **bold face** and the 15th day of the month with ***bold italic face***. The name of a lunar month is on the left side in alignment with the first day of the month while the name of a Julian solar month is on the right side aligned with the first day of the month.

In 38 BC, the first day of the third Babylonian month was on June 11, while the first day of the fourth Hebrew month was also on June 11 too (see Table I). In the summer of 38 BC, which was also in the 185th Olympiad, the Jews should have fasted on June 27, which was on Tammuz 17 in the Hebrew calendar and in the third month of the Babylonian calendar. The day of June 27 in 38 BC perfectly matches the account of Josephus. Thus, Herod the Great must have taken Jerusalem on June 27 of 38 BC.

But modern historians believe that Herod would have taken Jerusalem in the summer of 37 BC. This conclusion contradicts Josephus' account. In 37 BC, the first day of the third Babylonian month was on May 31 which was also the first day of the third Hebrew month (see Table II). This means that in 37 BC the fourth Hebrew month (the fasting month) could not have corresponded to the third Babylonian month and that Herod could not have took Jerusalem in the summer of 37 BC.

Josephus also told us that Herod died after a lunar eclipse and before the Passover (*Antiq.*, bk. 17, ch. 6-9). This information allows us to narrow down the year and month Herod died. From 10 BC to 1 AD, there were only two lunar eclipses observable in Jerusalem during the spring season. In 4 BC, a partial lunar eclipse with a magnitude of 1.43 took place on March 13 and the Passover was on April 11. This eclipse is consistent with Josephus' description. In 5 BC, a total lunar eclipse occurred at 20:21 of March 23, one day after the Passover on March 23. This eclipse is inconsistent with Josephus' account. Therefore, Herod must have died between Adar 15 and Nisan 15 of 4 BC. It is likely that he died on Adar 29 (March 27) of 4 BC just before the new year possibly because of a divine judgment.

According to Josephus, Herod had reigned 34 years after he took Jerusalem (*Antiq.*, bk. 17, ch. 8, sect. 1). From June 27 of 38 BC to March 27 of 4 BC, there were 33 years + 9 months, which were rounded to 34 years, in perfect agreement with Josephus' direct statement.

It has been generally accepted that the first year of Herod was in 37 BC because the fall of Jerusalem occurred when Marcus Agrippa and Caninius Gallus were consuls of Rome (*Antiq.*, bk. 14, ch. 16, sect. 4), which was in 37 BC according to the accepted chronology for the consuls of Rome. This is in contradiction with 38 BC inferred above from Josephus' account. If we believe Josephus' account, we must accept that the chronology for Roman consuls may have an uncertainty of one year.

In Rome, Herod was unexpectedly appointed king of the Jews by the Roman Senate. Josephus put this in the year of the consulship of Calvinus and Pollio, which would have been 40 BC according to the accepted chronology for the consuls of Rome. On the other hand, Josephus tells us (*Antiq.*, bk 17, ch. 8, sect. 1): "Herod reigned 37 years since he was appointed by the Romans." Since Herod died in the spring of 4 BC, he should have been appointed king of the Jews by the Roman Senate in 41 BC. Therefore, the currently accepted chronology for the consuls of Rome should be shifted backward by one year to be consistent with all the accounts of Josephus.

The date of Herod's reconstruction of the holy temple

Having established the accurate timeline of Herod's reign, we can now determine the date of Herod's reconstruction of the holy temple. The month and year in which the rebuilding of the temple began can be inferred from Josephus historical record. He wrote: "Now Herod, in the eighteenth year of his reign, and after the acts already mentioned, undertook a very great work, that is, to build of himself the temple of God." (*Antiq.* **bk. 15, ch. 11, sect. 1).** Herod started his public speech, announcing his intention to rebuild the temple. He promised not to begin the actual rebuilding process until everything was prepared. The preparations should have taken some time, and the actual rebuilding should have begun during Herod's eighteenth year. That is why Josephus emphasized the eighteenth year.

To establish the exact time the temple began to be built during his eighteenth year, it is necessary to backdate from the completion of the Holy of Holies. Josephus wrote, "The temple itself was built by the priests in a year and six months.... They feasted and celebrated this rebuilding of the temple,... for at the same time with this celebration for the work about the temple, fell also the day of the king's inauguration." (*Antiq.* **bk. 15, ch. 11, sect. 6). The month that fell a year and six months before the anniversary of Herod's inauguration should have been the month of Nisan (the first** Hebrew month) because his inauguration took place in the month of Tishri (the 7th month) of 38 BC, soon after he took Jerusalem in the summer time of 38 BC. Therefore, Herod should have announced his intention to rebuild the temple probably in the beginning of his 18th year (in Tishri of 21 BC) and started to rebuild it in Nisan of 20 BC (in the middle of his 18th year). The construction of the Holy of Holies should have been finished in Tishri of 19 BC and in the 20th anniversary of Herod's inauguration.

Table I: Hebrew Lunisolar Calendar of 38 BC (The first day of each lunar month is indicated with **bold face**. The lunar month's name is on the left side.)

	1	2	3	4	5	6	7	January
(11) Shebet	8	9	10	11	12	13	**14**	
	15	16	17	18	19	20	21	
	22	23	24	25	26	27	**28**	
	29	30	31	1	2	3	4	February
	5	6	7	8	9	10	11	
(12) Adar	12	**13**	14	15	16	17	18	
	19	20	21	22	23	24	25	
	26	**27**	28	1	2	3	4	March
	5	6	7	8	9	10	11	
(1) Nisan	12	13	**14**	15	16	17	18	
	19	20	21	22	23	24	25	
	26	27	**28**	29	30	31	1	April
	2	3	4	5	6	7	8	
(2) Iyar	9	10	11	12	**13**	14	15	
	16	17	18	19	20	21	22	
	23	24	25	26	**27**	28	29	
	30	1	2	3	4	5	6	May
(3) Sivan	7	8	9	10	11	**12**	13	
	14	15	16	17	18	19	20	
	21	22	23	24	25	**26**	27	
	28	29	30	31	1	2	3	June
	4	5	6	7	8	9	10	
(4) Tammuz	**11**	12	13	14	15	16	17	
	18	19	20	21	22	23	24	
	25	26	27	28	29	30	1	July
	2	3	4	5	6	7	8	
(5) Av	9	**10**	11	12	13	14	15	
	16	17	18	19	20	21	22	

	23	*24*	25	26	27	28	29	
	30	31	1	2	3	4	5	August
(6) Elul	6	7	8	*9*	10	11	12	
	13	14	15	16	17	18	19	
	20	21	22	*23*	24	25	26	
	27	28	29	30	31	1	2	September
(7) Tishri	3	4	5	6	*7*	8	9	
	10	11	12	13	14	15	16	
	17	18	19	20	*21*	22	23	
	24	25	26	27	28	29	30	
(8) Heshvan	1	2	3	4	5	*6*	7	October
	8	9	10	11	12	13	14	
	15	16	17	18	19	*20*	21	
	22	23	24	25	26	27	28	
	29	30	31	1	2	3	4	November
(9) Kislev	*5*	6	7	8	9	10	11	
	12	13	14	15	16	17	18	
	19	20	21	22	23	24	25	
	26	27	28	29	30	1	2	December
(10) Tebet	3	4	*5*	6	7	8	9	
	10	11	12	13	14	15	16	
	17	18	*19*	20	21	22	23	
	24	25	26	27	28	29	30	
	31							

Table II: Hebrew Lunisolar Calendar of 37 BC (The first day of each lunar month is indicated with **bold face**. The lunar month's name is on the left side.)

(10) Tebet		1	2	3	4	**5**	6	January
	7	8	9	10	11	12	13	
	14	15	16	17	18	*19*	20	
	21	22	23	24	25	26	27	
(11) Shebet	28	29	30	31	1	2	**3**	February
	4	5	6	7	8	9	10	
	11	12	13	14	15	16	*17*	
	18	19	20	21	22	23	24	
	25	26	27	28	29	1	2	March
(12) Adar	3	**4**	5	6	7	8	9	
	10	11	12	13	14	15	16	
	17	*18*	19	20	21	22	23	
	24	25	26	27	28	29	30	
(1) Nisan	31	1	*2*	3	4	5	6	April
	7	8	9	10	11	12	13	
	14	15	*16*	17	18	19	20	
	21	22	23	24	25	26	27	
(2) Iyar	28	29	30	1	**2**	3	4	May
	5	6	7	8	9	10	11	
	12	13	14	15	*16*	17	18	
	19	20	21	22	23	24	25	
(3) Sivan	26	27	28	29	30	**31**	1	June
	2	3	4	5	6	7	8	
	9	10	11	12	13	*14*	15	
	16	17	18	19	20	21	22	
	23	24	25	26	27	28	29	
(4) Tammuz	**30**	1	2	3	4	5	6	July
	7	8	9	10	11	12	13	
	14	15	16	17	18	19	20	

	21	22	23	24	25	26	27	
(5) Av	28	**29**	30	31	1	2	3	August
	4	5	6	7	8	9	10	
	11	*12*	13	14	15	16	17	
	18	19	20	21	22	23	24	
(6) Elul	25	26	27	**28**	29	30	31	
	1	2	3	4	5	6	7	September
	8	9	10	*11*	12	13	14	
	15	16	17	18	19	20	21	
(7) Tishri	22	23	24	25	**26**	27	28	
	29	30	1	2	3	4	5	October
	6	7	8	9	*10*	11	12	
	13	14	15	16	17	18	19	
(8) Heshvan	20	21	22	23	24	25	**26**	
	27	28	29	30	31	1	2	November
	3	4	5	6	7	8	*9*	
	10	11	12	13	14	15	16	
	17	18	19	20	21	22	23	
(9) Kislev	**24**	25	26	27	28	29	30	
	1	2	3	4	5	6	7	December
	8	9	10	11	12	13	14	
	15	16	17	18	19	20	21	
(10) Tebet	22	23	**24**	25	26	27	28	
	29	30	31					

3

The Timeline of Yeshua

The timeline of Yeshua can be constructed based on the Gospel of Matthew, the Gospel of John, and the book of Revelation. These books are believed to be written by two of Yeshua's twelve disciples. The authenticity of Yeshua's story in these books can be verified by the self-consistency of the timeline and the perfect fulfilment of the numerical prophecies foretold by Yeshua himself and by the Old-Testament prophets.

From these Gospels, we can consistently determine that the length of Yeshua's ministry was about three years. In particular, the Gospel of John explicitly recorded Yeshua's ministry during the first, third, and fourth Passover. John the Apostle also recorded a story which took place in a spring between the first and third Passover. Below we will describe them in detail.

First Passover

Yeshua's first Passover (John 2:13) was the one that immediately followed declaration of the Lamb of God by John the Baptist (John 1:29-36) and the first miracle he performed in Cana of Galilee (John 2:1-11). According to the law (Exodus 12:3), a Passover lamb must be selected on Nisan 10. If Yeshua is the Passover Lamb of God, he must be selected by God on Nisan 10. John the Baptist (a prophet of God) declared that Yeshua was the Lamb of God when he saw Yeshua coming toward him (John 1:29-34). This declaration should have been made on Nisan 10 in order for Yeshua to be the true Passover Lamb of God. Forty days before John's declaration, Yeshua was baptized (anointed by God Father) and "then was Yeshua led up by the Spirit into the wilderness to be tempted by the devil. And when he had fasted forty days and forty nights, he was afterward hungry." (Matthew 4:1-2). Here, we assume that Yeshua went to John right after he had fasted 40 days and nights.

During Yeshua's first Passover the Jews asked for a sign, and he responded, "'Destroy this temple, and in three days I will raise it up.' The Jews therefore said, 'It took forty-six years to build this temple, and will you raise it up in three days?' But he was speaking of the temple of his body." (John 2:19-21). These passages provide an important clue to establishing the year of Yeshua's first Passover.

What did Yeshua mean by "temple" and how did the Jews interpret his meaning? Yeshua referred to his own body as a temple or shrine as he was standing in the front of the main temple. The Jews thought that he was referring to the physical temple and not to his body. They thought that if Yeshua were to destroy the physical temple, it would not be possible for him to build it again in three days. They responded to Yeshua with the same word "temple," which had taken forty-six years in building. They confronted Yeshua with the impossibility of rebuilding it in three days in contrast to forty-six years in rebuilding their physical temple. The Jews knew when the physical temple had begun to be rebuilt but did not understand the spiritual implication of Yeshua's words.

In Chapter 2, we have shown that Herod started to rebuild the holy temple in the spring of 20 BC. From the spring of 20 BC to the spring of 27 AD, 46 years had elapsed (please note that 20 BC means year –19 because of no zero year). This suggests that Yeshua's first Passover was in the spring of 27 AD. From the calendar of 27 AD (see Table III), we see that Nisan 10 of 27 AD was on 5 April and 40 days before that day was February 24. Yeshua started his earthly ministry in the daytime of Nisan 11 (John 1:35-42), which was on April 6 of 27 AD. On Nisan 12, Yeshua found Philip and Nathanael (John 1:43-51). After sunset of Nisan 12 (on Nisan 13), there was a wedding in Cana of Galilee (John 2:1).

According to the calendar in Table III, we find that the wedding day was on April 8 (Tuesday). During the wedding, Yeshua performed the first miracle: water turned to wine (John 2:7-11).

Tuesday is the best day for wedding according to the page: https://www.chabad.org/library/article_cdo/aid/476754/jewish/Approved-Dates-for-a-Wedding.htm. In this webpage, it is said:

> In recounting the story of Creation, the third day, Tuesday, is the only day when the Torah says twice, "And God saw that it was good." The Sages interpreted this to mean that this day is doubly good— "Good for Heaven, and good for the creations."

Yeshua and his family and disciples attended this special wedding in Cana, which took place on Tuesday, the doubly good day in a week.

Table III: Hebrew lunisolar calendar of 27 AD (The first day of each lunar month is indicated with **bold face**. The lunar month's name is on the left side.)

				1	2	3	4	January
	5	6	7	8	9	10	11	
	12	13	14	15	16	17	18	
	19	20	21	22	23	24	25	
(11) Shebet	26	**27**	28	29	30	31	1	February
	2	3	4	5	6	7	8	
	9	*10*	11	12	13	14	15	
	16	17	18	19	20	21	22	
(12) Adar	23	24	25	**26**	27	28	1	March
	2	3	4	5	6	7	8	
	9	10	11	*12*	13	14	15	
	16	17	18	19	20	21	22	
(1) Nisan	23	24	25	26	**27**	28	29	
	30	31	1	2	3	4	5	April
	6	7	8	9	*10*	11	12	

	13	14	15	16	17	18	19	
(2) Iyar	20	21	22	23	24	25	**26**	
	27	28	29	30	1	2	3	May
	4	5	6	7	8	9	*10*	
	11	12	13	14	15	16	17	
	18	19	20	21	22	23	24	
(3) Sivan	**25**	26	27	28	29	30	31	
	1	2	3	4	5	6	7	June
	8	9	10	11	12	13	14	
	15	16	17	18	19	20	21	
(4) Tammuz	22	23	**24**	25	26	27	28	
	29	30	1	2	3	4	5	July
	6	7	*8*	9	10	11	12	
	13	14	15	16	17	18	19	
(5) Av	20	21	22	**23**	24	25	26	
	27	28	29	30	31	1	2	August
	3	4	5	*6*	7	8	9	
	10	11	12	13	14	15	16	
(6) Elul	17	18	19	20	21	**22**	23	
	24	25	26	27	28	29	30	
	31	1	2	3	4	*5*	6	September
	7	8	9	10	11	12	13	
(7) Tishri	14	15	16	17	18	19	**20**	
	21	22	23	24	25	26	27	
	28	29	30	1	2	3	*4*	October
	5	6	7	8	9	10	11	
	12	13	14	15	16	17	18	
(8) Heshvan	19	**20**	21	22	23	24	25	
	26	27	28	29	30	31	1	November
	2	*3*	4	5	6	7	8	
	9	10	11	12	13	14	15	
(9) Kislev	16	17	**18**	19	20	21	22	

	23	24	25	26	27	28	29	
	30	1	*2*	3	4	5	6	December
	7	8	9	10	11	12	13	
(10) Tebet	14	15	16	**17**	18	19	20	
	21	22	23	24	25	26	27	
	28	29	30	*31*				

The third Passover

John 6:4-14 records another story of Yeshua in the third Passover:

> Now the Passover, a feast of the Jews, was near. Then Yeshua lifted up his eyes, and seeing a great multitude coming toward him, he said to Philip, "Where shall we buy bread, that these may eat?" But this he said to test him, for he himself knew what he would do. Philip answered him, "Two hundred denarii worth of bread is not sufficient for them, that every one of them may have a little." One of his disciples, Andrew, Simon Peter's brother, said to him, "There is a lad here who has five barley loaves and two small fish, but what are they among so many?" Then Yeshua said, "Make the people sit down." Now there was much grass in the place. So the men sat down, in number about five thousand. And Yeshua took the loaves, and when he had given thanks he distributed them to the disciples, and the disciples to those sitting down; and likewise of the fish, as much as they wanted. So when they were filled, he said to his disciples, "Gather up the fragments that remain, so that nothing is lost." Therefore they gathered them up, and filled twelve baskets with the fragments of the five barley loaves which were left over by those who had eaten. Then those men, when they had seen the sign that Yeshua did, said, "This is truly the prophet who is to come into the world."

This story of feeding the five thousand was also recorded in the Gospel of Matthew (Matthew 14:13-21). This story took place after John the Baptist was beheaded by Herod the Tetrarch (Matthew 14:1-12). After this story, both John and Matthew recorded the crucifixion and resurrection of Yeshua during the fourth Passover. Thus, John the Baptist was beheaded about one year before Yeshua's crucifixion.

The fourth and last Passover

The last Passover of Yeshua's ministry is the most documented Passover of all. John 11:55 records, "And the Jews' Passover was near at hand: and many went out of the country up to Jerusalem before the Passover, to purify themselves."

All the Gospels recorded that Yeshua and his disciples had the Passover supper in the beginning of the preparation day (Nisan 14). It seems very difficult to understand why they celebrated the Passover one day earlier than the Pharisees. This mystery can be naturally resolved if Yeshua's disciples were Essenes who followed Enoch's solar calendar. We know that the first day of the first Enoch's month is always on the Wednesday of the week within which the Vernal Equinox falls.

In 30 AD, the Essenes' Passover was on April 5 (see the calendar in Table IV), which was on the fifteenth day of the first Enoch's month. April 5 was one day before the Pharisees' Passover on April 6. In other years around 30 AD, the Essenes' and Pharisees' Passover fell in different weeks. Consequently, 30 AD was the only year in which Yeshua and his disciples could have observed the Essenes' Passover exactly one day before the Pharisees' Passover, and he himself be the Passover Lamb of God in the preparation day of the Pharisees' Passover. Therefore, Yeshua was crucified on 5 April 30 AD (Wednesday).

Table IV: Hebrew lunisolar calendar of 30 AD (The first day of each lunar month is indicated with **bold face**. The lunar month's name is on the left side. "I" marks the beginning of the 1st month in Enoch's solar calendar.)

	1	2	3	4	5	6	7	
	1	2	3	4	5	6	7	January
	8	9	10	11	12	13	14	
	15	16	17	18	19	20	21	
(11) Shebet	22	**23**	24	25	26	27	28	
	29	30	31	1	2	3	4	February
	5	**6**	7	8	9	10	11	
	12	13	14	15	16	17	18	
(12) Adar	19	20	21	**22**	23	24	25	
	26	27	28	1	2	3	4	March
	5	6	7	**8**	9	10	11	
	12	13	14	15	16	17	18	
(1) Nisan	19	20	21	I 22	**23**	24	25	
	26	27	28	29	30	31	1	April
	2	3	4	5	**6**	7	8	
	9	10	11	12	13	14	15	
(2) Iyar	16	17	18	19	20	21	**22**	
	23	24	25	26	27	28	29	
	30	1	2	3	4	5	**6**	May
	7	8	9	10	11	12	13	
	14	15	16	17	18	19	20	
(3) Sivan	**21**	22	23	24	25	26	27	
	28	29	30	31	1	2	3	June
	4	5	6	7	8	9	10	
	11	12	13	14	15	16	17	
(4) Tammuz	18	19	**20**	21	22	23	24	
	25	26	27	28	29	30	1	July
	2	3	**4**	5	6	7	8	
	9	10	11	12	13	14	15	
(5) Av	16	17	18	**19**	20	21	22	
	23	24	25	26	27	28	29	
	30	31	1	**2**	3	4	5	August
	6	7	8	9	10	11	12	

(6) Elul	13	14	15	16	17	**18**	19	
	20	21	22	23	24	25	26	
	27	28	29	30	31	*1*	2	September
	3	4	5	6	7	8	9	
(7) Tishri	10	11	12	13	14	15	**16**	
	17	18	19	20	21	22	23	
	24	25	26	27	28	29	*30*	
	1	2	3	4	5	6	7	October
	8	9	10	11	12	13	14	
(8) Heshvan	15	**16**	17	18	19	20	21	
	22	23	24	25	26	27	28	
	29	*30*	31	1	2	3	4	November
	5	6	7	8	9	10	11	
(9) Kislev	12	13	14	**15**	16	17	18	
	19	20	21	22	23	24	25	
	26	27	28	*29*	30	1	2	December
	3	4	5	6	7	8	9	
(10) Tebet	10	11	12	13	14	**15**	16	
	17	18	19	20	21	22	23	
	24	25	26	27	28	*29*	30	
	31							

In Chapter 7, we will show that Yeshua resurrected at sunset on 8 April (Saturday) of 30 AD. From the day (5 April 27 AD) he was declared to be the Lamb of God to the day (5 April 30 AD) of his crucifixion, there are **exactly three solar years.**

After he resurrected in the beginning of Sunday (April 9), he revealed to Marys right after his resurrection (Matthew 28:9; John 20:14-17). He revealed to his disciples in Galilee (Matthew 26:32; Matthew 28:10,16) in the evening of a Sunday (John 20:19). Because it took at least 4 days for Yeshua's disciples to travel from Jerusalem to Galilee on foot, it was impossible for Yeshua to meet his disciples in Galilee on April 9 (shortly after his resurrection). Therefore, Yeshua's first post-resurrection appearance to his disciples must have taken place in the following Sunday evening, which was on April 16 (after sunset of April 15). After he stayed with his disciples for 40 days (Acts 1:3), he then ascended to heaven on 26 May 30 AD (after sunset of May 25), right on the feast day of Pentecost. Before he ascended to heaven, he gave a great commission to his disciples (Matthew 28:19): "Go therefore and make disciples of all the nations." Yeshua's disciples would bear witness of him and make disciples of all the nations because they had stayed with him from the beginning (John 15:27). Those who believe in Yeshua through the words of his disciples will be in perfect union with the Father and the Son (John 17:20-21).

It is convenient to use the Julian day (JD) numbers to calculate a period. The JD numbers for 26 May 30 AD and 6 April 27 AD are JD 1732161 and JD 1731015, respectively. From 6 April 27 AD to 26 May 30 AD, there were 1,732,161–1,731,015 = 1,146 days. Since Yeshua spent three days and three nights in the grave, the total length of his ministry on the earth in his first advent was 1,146 − 3 = 1,143 days. The length of his ministry was over three years.

The spring between the first and third Passover

John the Apostle recorded Yeshua's ministry in the first, third, and fourth Passover. There appeared to be no direct record of Yeshua's work in the second Passover. Instead, John recorded a story in the spring between the first and third Passover (John 4:31-38):

> [31]In the meantime his disciples urged him, saying, "Rabbi, eat." [32]But he said to them, "I have food to eat of which you do not know." [33]Therefore the disciples said to one another, "Has anyone brought him anything to eat?" [34]Yeshua said to them, "My food is to do the will of Him who sent me, and to finish His work. [35]Do you not say, 'There are still four months and then comes the harvest'? Behold, I say to you, lift up your eyes and look at the fields, for they are already white for harvest! [36]And he who reaps receives wages, and gathers fruit for eternal life, that both he who sows and he who reaps may rejoice together. [37]For in this the saying is true: 'One sows and another reaps.' [38]I sent you to reap that

for which you have not labored; others have labored, and you have entered into their labors."

Verse 35 implies that the story happened at the time when the fields Yeshua and his disciples passed had already whitened for harvest and there would have been about 4 months until the major harvest. If we know the harvest seasons of Israel, we can pin down the time of the story.

The agricultural year in Israel begins in the fall (after the harvest Festival of Tabernacles) with plowing and sowing. Harvests in Israel begin in the spring in the month of Adar (February/March). The harvest times in the ancient Israel are listed in Table V, which is obtained from the website: http://www.joybysurprise.com/harvest_times_in_israel_. html.

From Table V, one can see that the harvest season in ancient Israel began in Adar (Feb/March) and continued by stages into the fall. The barley harvest begins in the first month Nisan (March-April). The major wheat harvest completes in the 4th month.

Yeshua said that the fields were already white (John 4:35). The color of the barley seeds is white when they are ripe. The color of flax seeds is dark brown or light brown when they are ripe. Therefore, we can conclude that this story should have taken place in the month of Nisan (possibly in the Passover) when the barley harvest began. After about 4 months in the 4th/5th lunar month, the major harvests (wheat and grape harvests) were complete.

Table V: Harvest Times in Ancient Israel

Months	Weather	Crops & activity
Tishri 7th month (Sep/Oct)	First rains	Plowing begins
Heshvan 8th month (Oct/Nov)		Plowing / grain planting
Kislev 9th month (Nov/Dec)		Grain planting continues
Teveth 10th month (Dec/Jan)	Main rains	
Sebat 11th month (Jan/Feb)		
Adar 12th month (Feb/Mar)	Spring rains	Almond in bloom / flax harvest
Nisan 1st month (Mar/Apr)		Barley harvest begins
2nd month (Apr/May)		Barley harvest completed
3rd month (May/Jun)	Dry season	Wheat harvest begins
4th month (Jun/Jul)		Wheat harvest completed / first figs
Av 5th month (Jul/Aug)	Summer heat	Vintage (grape harvest) begins
Elul 6th month (Aug/Sep)		Date harvest / summer figs

Therefore, John recorded Yeshua's ministry in 4 consecutive Passover Festivals, indicating that the total length of his ministry was indeed over three years.

John the Baptist was beheaded by Herod Antipas in 29 AD, one year before Yeshua's crucifixion in 30 AD. Matthew 14:3-4 tells us that Herod put John in prison for the sake of Herodias because John rebuked him of unlawfully marrying Herodias, his brother Philip's wife. According to Josephus (*Antiq.* bk. 18, ch.5, sect. 4), Herod married his brother Philip's wife when Philip was still alive. Since Philip died in 34 AD, the story in Matthew 14:3-4 must have taken place before 34 AD. The year of 29 AD when John was put in prison and beheaded was indeed before 34 AD. Therefore, this account of Matthew is historically accurate.

CHAPTER

4

Daniel's Prophecy: the 69th Week

One of the famous numerical prophecies of Daniel is about 70 weeks, which was recorded in Daniel 9:24-25:

> [24]**Seventy weeks** are determined for your people and for your holy city, to finish the transgression, to make an end of sins, to make reconciliation for iniquity, to bring in everlasting righteousness, to seal up vision and prophecy, and to anoint the Most Holy. [25]"Know therefore and understand, that from the going forth of the command to restore and build Jerusalem until Messiah the Prince, there shall be seven weeks and sixty-two weeks; the street shall be built again, and the wall, even in troublesome times.

These two verses tell us that the length of 70 weeks is determined for the destiny of the holy people (the Israelites), for the holy city (Jerusalem), and for anointing the most holy who is the Messiah and the Prince of the nation of Israel. According to the prophecy, the Messiah, should have appeared in the 69th week from the time when the command to restore and rebuild Jerusalem was issued. The last day of the 69th prophetic week (one prophetic day is equivalent to one solar year) should correspond to the 483rd year (697 = 483) from the time of issuing the command.

In order to check whether this prophecy was fulfilled, we need to know exactly which year the command to restore Jerusalem went forth and which year the Messiah appeared. As we have already shown that Yeshua was proclaimed by God to be His Son when John the Baptist baptized him on 24 February 27 AD (see Chapter 3). He was declared to be the Lamb of God on Nisan 10 (April 5 of 27 AD) and started his ministry on April 6 of 27 AD which lasted for 3 years. If Yeshua is indeed the Messiah, the command to restore and rebuild Jerusalem must have been issued in the spring of 457 BC. This is because the 483rd year from the spring of 457 BC is the year from the spring of 26 AD to the spring of 27 AD (please note that 457 BC = −456 because year 0 does not exist). We will show below that the spring of 457 BC was the time when Ezra received a command from King Artaxerxes I in his 7th year of reign. We will also prove that this command has a component of rebuilding the city of Jerusalem, which perfectly matches the prophecy.

Detailed explanations

Two clear commands were described in the book of Ezra. Cyrus king of Persia in the first year of his reign proclaimed the first command (Ezra 1:1-4). Artaxerxes I issued the second command in the seventh year of his reign (Ezra 7:6-26). In the 20th year of Artaxerxes I, the governor Nehemiah asked the king to send him to Jerusalem to repair broken wall (Nehemiah 2:1-6). After the request was granted, Nehemiah asked the king to write two letters (Nehemiah 2:7-8). One letter was addressed to the governors of the region beyond the River so that they permitted Nehemiah to pass through their region. The second letter was given to Asaph the keeper of the king's forest. In this letter, Asaph was asked to provide timber to make beams for the temple gates and the city wall. It is apparent that these two letters were not the commands to restore and rebuild Jerusalem, but only served to help Nehemiah in his work of repairing the city wall. Therefore, only one of the two commands recorded in the book of Ezra was the command to rebuild the city.

Now let us check which command is relevant to the one mentioned by Daniel. In the first year of Cyrus king of Persia, the king issued a decree to rebuild the temple and to allow the exiled Jews to return to

Jerusalem. Since Cyrus' decree was only to rebuild the temple but not the city, the returned Jews began to rebuild the temple and lay its foundation (Ezra 3:10-11) while the city remained in ruin (Ezra 4:11-12).

The adversaries of the Jews despised the sanctuary and this holy people who knew God's law. Chapter 4 of the book of Ezra clearly recorded how the adversaries tried to oppose rebuilding the temple and the city with several strategies during a long period from the days of Cyrus to the reign of Artaxerxes I. Some events in this chapter happened after the events described in later chapters, which may confuse readers. But if one reads the book carefully, one should be able to understand why the author did not write these events sequentially. The author clearly wanted to describe all of the schemes of Israel's adversaries together.

The schemes of the adversaries include the following (Ezra 4) : 1) They gathered to oppose it, 2) they tried to join (infiltrate) so they could manipulate and hinder the process, 3) they wrote an accusation against the Jews to Artaxerxes I, "they are building a rebellious and evil city and will excite sedition," and 4) they asked Artaxerxes I to issue a command to stop rebuilding the city.

Because of the adversaries, the early progress to rebuild the temple in Jerusalem was discontinued until the second year of Darius (Ezra 4:24). In this year, Yehowah spoke to the prophet Haggai concerning the temple. With the encouragement of the prophet, the Jews again started to work by laying the foundation of the temple. The temple was finally finished on the third day of the month of Adar, which was in the sixth year of Darius (Ezra 6:15) and in the spring of 516 BC.

The Jews started to rebuild the city of Jerusalem in the days of Xerxes I (Ezra 4:6) after Darius helped rebuild the temple in 516 BC. However, in the days of both Xerxes I and Artaxerxes I, the adversaries wrote accusations against the Jews who were rebuilding the city (Ezra 4:6-23). During the earlier reign of Artaxerxes I, the adversaries wrote Artaxerxes I in Aramaic script, accusing the Jews of rebuilding a rebellious and evil city. Then Artaxerxes I commanded the Jews to stop rebuilding the city wall. The king also ordered that this city could not resume its reconstruction until he gave a new command (Ezra 4:21).

The king's reply was a great victory for the adversaries who went immediately to the Jews in Jerusalem and compelled them by force to stop their work (Ezra 4:23). Then Yehowah raised up Ezra who was a ready scribe in the law of Moses. The king granted Ezra **all his requests** because the hand of Yehowah was upon him (Ezra 7:6). Because the king had previously issued the command to temporarily suspend the reconstruction of Jerusalem, it is natural that one of Ezra's requests should have been a reversal of the king's previous cessation command. Apparently, the king granted Ezra all his requests and sent him to investigate Judah and Jerusalem according to the Law of Moses (Ezra 7:14). King Artaxerxes I provided more than enough gold and silver to beautify the temple of God in Jerusalem. The king also said that any silver and gold that was left over may be used for whatever Ezra and his colleagues felt was the will of their God (Ezra 7:18). Since the king had withdrawn his previous cessation decree and issued a new decree to restore Jerusalem, Ezra may have used the rest of the gold and silver to rebuild Jerusalem. This can be seen in the prayer of Ezra in Ezra 9:9. Ezra thanked God for not forsaking them but extending mercy unto them in the sight of the kings of Persia, and giving them revival and the wall in Judah and in Jerusalem. Ezra's prayer implies that the Persian king had granted them the permission and provided enough gold and silver to rebuild the house of their God, to repair its ruins, and to rebuild the wall in Judah and in Jerusalem.

In the adversaries' efforts to thwart Jerusalem's reconstruction, they apparently knocked down the rebuilt sections of the wall and burned the gates. This was where Nehemiah came into the picture (Nehemiah 1:3). In the 20th year of Artaxerxes I, Nehemiah heard the sad news that the attempts to rebuild Jerusalem were frustrated again. Nehemiah 1:3 implies that the Jews must have been given permission to rebuild Jerusalem from Artaxerxes I in his decree issued in his 7th year.

Because of the bad news, Nehemiah spoke to Artaxerxes I, who gave him permission to go back and repair the broken wall in Jerusalem (Nehemiah 2), which was rebuilt previously. If Artaxerxes I had not given the Jews the permission to rebuild Jerusalem in his 7th year, there would have been no rebuilt wall in Jerusalem to be knocked down by the adversaries in the 20th year of Artaxerxes I (Nehemiah 1:1-3). If Artaxerxes I had not given the Jews the permission to rebuild Jerusalem in his 7th year, he would not have let Nehemiah go back to repair the broken wall in Jerusalem in his 20th year. Therefore, Artaxerxes's command in his 7th year must have had a component of rebuilding the city of Jerusalem.

With the two letters Nehemiah received from Artaxerxes I in his 20th year, the wall was put up successfully without much trouble (Nehemiah 6:15). Daniel predicted that the street and the wall would be built again in troublesome times after the command to rebuild Jerusalem was issued. Because Nehemiah did not go back to rebuild the street but only to repair the broken wall, the king's letters in his 20th year could not have included the component of rebuilding the street. Thus, the street must have been rebuilt after Ezra received the command of Artaxerxes I in the spring of his 7th year.

In summary, only the decree of Artaxerxes I to Ezra was the command to restore and rebuild both the temple and Jerusalem while the command of Cyrus was only to allow the Jews to rebuild the temple of God. The street and the wall were rebuilt after Ezra received the command of Artaxerxes I in his 7th year. Then some sections of the wall in Jerusalem were destroyed again by the adversaries in the 20th year of Artaxerxes I. Nehemiah and his colleagues finally finished repairing the wall within 52 days in 25 Elul of 444 BC (Nehemiah 6:15).

Now back to the subject concerning the issuing time for the decree of Artaxerxes I. According to Ezra 7:8, Ezra left Babylon on Nisan 1 and arrived in Jerusalem on the first day of the fifth month in the 7th year of Artaxerxes I. Since Ezra left Babylon on the first day of the month of Nisan, the command must have been issued on or before that day.

Artaxerxes I began to reign on 12 October 464 BC (see Chapter 8 in *Perfectly Fulfilled Prophecies and the Destiny of Mankind*). Thus, the 7th year of Artaxerxes I was from 12 October 458 BC to 11 October 457. Since Ezra left Babylon on Nisan 1 and arrived in Jerusalem on the 1st day of the fifth month, in the 7th year of Artaxerxes I, the day that Ezra left for Jerusalem must have been on 1 Nisan (26 March) of 457 BC (see Table VI).

Table VI: Hebrew lunisolar calendar of 457 BC (The first day of each lunar month is indicated with **bold face**. The lunar month's name is on the left side.)

		1	2	3	4	5	6	January
	7	8	9	10	11	*12*	13	
	14	15	16	17	18	19	20	
(11) Shebet	21	22	23	24	25	26	**27**	
	28	29	30	31	1	2	3	February
	4	5	6	7	8	9	***10***	
	11	12	13	14	15	16	17	
	18	19	20	21	22	23	24	
(12) Adar	25	**26**	27	28	29	1	2	March
	3	4	5	6	7	8	9	
	10	**11**	12	13	14	15	16	
	17	18	19	20	21	22	23	
(1) Nisan	24	25	**26**	27	28	29	30	
	31	1	2	3	4	5	6	April
	7	8	*9*	10	11	12	13	
	14	15	16	17	18	19	20	
(2) Iyar	21	22	23	24	**25**	26	27	
	28	29	30	1	2	3	4	May
	5	6	7	8	*9*	10	11	
	12	13	14	15	16	17	18	
(3) Sivan	19	20	21	22	23	**24**	25	
	26	27	28	29	30	31	1	June
	2	3	4	5	6	*7*	8	
	9	10	11	12	13	14	15	
	16	17	18	19	20	21	22	
(4) Tammuz	**23**	24	25	26	27	28	29	
	30	1	2	3	4	5	6	July
	7	8	9	10	11	12	13	
	14	15	16	17	18	19	20	

(5) Av	21	**22**	23	24	25	26	27	
	28	29	30	31	1	2	3	August
	4	*5*	6	7	8	9	10	
	11	12	13	14	15	16	17	
(6) Elul	18	19	20	**21**	22	23	24	
	25	26	27	28	29	30	31	
	1	2	3	*4*	5	6	7	September
	8	9	10	11	12	13	14	
(7) Tishri	15	16	17	18	**19**	20	21	
	22	23	24	25	26	27	28	
	29	30	1	2	*3*	4	5	October
	6	7	8	9	10	11	12	
(8) Heshvan	13	14	15	16	17	**18**	19	
	20	21	22	23	24	25	26	
	27	28	29	30	31	***1***	2	November
	3	4	5	6	7	8	9	
	10	11	12	13	14	15	16	
(9) Kislev	**17**	18	19	20	21	22	23	
	24	25	26	27	28	29	30	
	1	2	3	4	5	6	7	December
	8	9	10	11	12	13	14	
(10) Tebet	15	**16**	17	18	19	20	21	
	22	23	24	25	26	27	28	
	29	30	31					

It is interesting to note that Nisan 1 just coincided with the Vernal Equinox in 457 BC, suggesting that this year is special and significant. This day was also the new-year day in both the Hebrew and Babylonian lunisolar calendars. Ezra should have left for Jerusalem immediately after the king issued the command because he prepared his heart to seek the law of God, to follow it, and to teach it in Israel (Ezra 7:9). If he left on the same day, the command should have gone forth on Nisan 1 of 457 BC and on the day of the Vernal Equinox.

Daniel 9:25 is literally translated as, "Know therefore and understand, that from the going forth of the command to restore and build Jerusalem until Messiah the Prince, weeks 7 and weeks 62; the street shall be built again, and the wall, even in troublesome times." Here, the phrases "weeks 7" and "weeks 62" have an unusual word order that may express an idea of counting weeks. If this is the case, the number "7" and "62" in Daniel 9:25 should be understood as ordinal numbers and the Messiah should have been anointed in the 483rd year from the time of issuance of the command to restore and rebuild Jerusalem. The 483rd year from the issuance of the command was the year between the Vernal Equinoxes of 26 AD and 27 AD. Yeshua was baptized by John the Baptist on 24 February 27 AD, which was exactly four weeks before the Vernal Equinox (March 23) of 27 AD. The day when Yeshua was baptized and anointed was indeed in the 483rd year from the time of issuing the command. This cannot be a coincidence. It provides clear evidence that Yeshua is the Messiah anointed by God in the early spring of 27 AD.

CHAPTER

5

Daniel's Prophecy: The First Half of the 70th Week

Yeshua was proclaimed to be the Son of God by the heavenly Father during his baptism on 24 February 27 AD, which was towards the end of the 483rd year (the 69th prophetic weeks) from the time (26 March 457 BC) of the issuance of the command to rebuild Jerusalem. This fulfills the prophecy of Daniel 9:25, "Know therefore and understand, that from the going forth of the commandment to restore and rebuild Jerusalem unto the Messiah, the Prince, shall be seven weeks, and threescore [60] and two weeks."

In Chapter 4, we provided detailed evidence that this prophecy was fulfilled in Yeshua on the assumption that the 69 weeks from 26 March 457 BC passed without interruption. However, the 69 weeks in Daniel 9:25 had two separated periods: a 7-week period and a 62-week period.

Why did Daniel separate the 69 weeks into two periods? One possible explanation is that there was a gap between the first continuous period of 7 (17) weeks and the last continuous period of 63 (97) weeks. There should have been no gap from one week to another within the 7-week or the 63-week period. This gap idea can help unlock the prophecy of the 70th week, which should have also been separated into two periods with a gap according to Daniel 9:27 (our modified translation based on the interlinear Bible):

And he shall strengthen a covenant with many for one week; but in the middle of the week, he shall cause sacrifice and offering to fail. And on the extremity of abominations, [it shall] be desolated even until the consummation. And [that] being determined is poured out on [the one] being desolated.

Daniel 9:27 tells the prophecy of the 70th week during which the Messiah shall strengthen covenant with many but in the middle of the week, he shall cause sacrifice and offering to fail. If this prophecy was fulfilled in Yeshua, the 70th week should have started on 6 April 27 AD when he began his ministry. If this was the case, the 62nd week of the 63-week period should have ended on 6 April 27 AD and the 63rd week of the 63-week period should have started on the same day. Then the beginning time of the 63-week period (434 solar years) was on April 9 of 408 BC. Since the first 7-week period started on 26 March 457 BC, the ending time of this period should have been on 26 March 408 BC. Hence, there was a small gap of 14 days between 26 March 408 BC and 9 April 408 BC, which justifies the assumption of 69 continuous weeks in the previous chapter.

The second part of verse 27 says that in the middle of the week (the 70th week), he should cause sacrifices and offerings to fail. Here, the Hebrew word "תִבֵּשׁ (shabath)" means "cause to cease" or "cause to fail." In the middle of the 70th week, which was between 30 and 31 AD, the Jews did not cease the sacrifices and offerings after Yeshua was crucified and ascended to heaven in 30 AD. The prophecy would not have been fulfilled in Yeshua if the word "תִבֵּשׁ (shabath)" were translated into "cause to cease." On the other hand, if we translate this word into "cause to fail" or "cause to be ineffective," the prophecy was fulfilled in Yeshua. Indeed, the sacrifices and offerings of the Jews were not accepted by God after 30 AD, as seen from the following statements of the Jews in *the Jerusalem Talmud* or *the Babylonian Talmud*.

In the centuries following the destruction of the temple in Jerusalem (70 AD), the Jewish people began writing two versions of Jewish thought, religious history, and commentary. One was written in Palestine and became known as *the Jerusalem Talmud*, and the other was written in Babylon and was known as *the Babylonian Talmud*.

The Jerusalem Talmud reads: "Forty years before the destruction of the temple, the western light went out, the crimson thread remained crimson, and the lot for Yehowah always came up in the left hand. They would close the gates of the temple by night and get up in the morning and find them wide open." (Jacob Neusner, *The Yerushalmi*, p.156-157).

A similar passage in *the Babylonian Talmud* states: "Our rabbis taught: During the last forty years before the destruction of the temple the lot ['For Yehowah'] did not come up in the right hand; nor did the crimson-colored strap become white; nor did the western most light shine; and the doors of the Hekel [Temple] would open by themselves." (Soncino version, *Yoma* 39b).

Both passages tell us that God did not accept their sacrifices and offerings between 30 and 70 AD. Before that time, the crimson thread should have been changed into white whenever God had accepted their offerings and forgiven their sins. It was the Messiah who caused their sacrifices and offerings to be ineffective after he ascended to heaven. Solomon in Proverb 15:8 said, "The sacrifice of the wicked is an abomination to Yehowah, but the prayer of the upright is His delight." Because the Jews continued to reject the teachings of the Messiah through his disciples and even persecuted them, their sacrifices and offerings were abominable to Yehowah.

In the Mosaic sacrifice law, sacrifices and offerings can atone the sins unintentionally committed while intentional sins cannot be atoned by the animal sacrifices. Then, how shall the intentional sins be forgiven? In Psalm 40:6-8, David said, "Sacrifice and offering You did not desire; My ears You have opened. Burnt offering and sin offering You did not require. Then I said, 'Behold, I come; In the scroll of the book it is written of me. I delight to do Your will, O my God, and Your law is within my heart.'" Even before the Messiah came, God did not desire and require burnt offering and sin offering. What He really desires is that we delight to do His will, put His law in our heart, and observe it. Sacrifice and offering cannot change our heart.

Yeshua who was the Passover Lamb of God was killed and his blood can redeem our lives (Isaiah 53:4-6,8,10). It is the grace of God! When the Israelites came out of Egypt, all the lives of the Israelites and foreigners (even the Egyptians) could be saved from the wrath of God if the blood of the Passover lamb was on the lintels and the two doorposts of their home. The Passover Lamb of God shed his blood for our sins (Isaiah 53:4-6,8,10) and can redeem us to serve God.

Most Biblical scholars have misunderstood Daniel 9:27. They mistakenly referred to "he" as the anti-messiah who would confirm the covenant with Israel in the 70th week and break it after three and a half years. According to the Hebrew grammar, "he" must refer to a person previously defined. No anti-messiah was mentioned in any previous sentence. A Hebrew language expert has clearly proved that "he" in verse 27 refers to the Messiah (see a YouTube video at https://www.youtube.com/watch?v=3EX830ATa2A).

From the context of Daniel 9:24, it is apparent that seven weeks were decreed for the holy people (the Israelites), for Jerusalem, and for the Messiah to bring everlasting righteousness. Therefore, the seventy weeks are always related to the Messiah and the destinies of the Israelites and Jerusalem. The 70th week is all about the ministry of the Messiah while at the end of the 69th week, God prepared the way for Messiah's ministry via the ministry of John the Baptist. John preached the message of repentance in the wilderness of Judea (Matthew 3:1), baptized the Jews who were willing to repent of their sins, anointed Yeshua, and declared him to be the Lamb of God.

Now we discuss the prophecy of Daniel 9:26, "And after the threescore and two [62] weeks shall Messiah be cut off, but not to himself." Here, the 62 weeks refer to the 62 weeks of the second 63-week period. After the 62 weeks (the 69th week), which was in the 70th week, the Messiah shall be cut off. Yeshua was cut off on Nisan 14 of 30 AD, which was in the 70th week. But to him, he was not cut off because he resurrected and would see his seeds and prolong his days (Isaiah 53:10). He was cut off for three days and three nights to bear the iniquities of God's people and justify many (Isaiah 53:11). God shall share a portion with him (Isaiah 53:12) because he was so obedient that he was willing to die for many according to the will of God. Here, the prophecy of Daniel 9:26 was also fulfilled in Yeshua.

Daniel 9:26 further tells us that after the Messiah was cut off, the Messiah himself would destroy the holy temple and Jerusalem with a Gentile prince. LXX Septuagint correctly translated the original

Hebrew word "עם" into "with" before the Masoretic Hebrew text was used (while the Masoretic Hebrew word "עַם" with a short line below ע means "people"). Indeed, 40 years after the Messiah was crucified, the Romans destroyed Jerusalem and the temple by the will of God and the Messiah.

How about the prophecy about the second period of the 70th week? In Chapter 3, we have shown that the length of Yeshua's ministry in his first advent (in the first half of the 70th week) was 1,143 days. Yeshua shall have to minister for an additional 1,413 days to fulfill the prophecy of the whole 70th week (1,143 days + 1,413 days = 2,556 days = 7×365.143 days = 7 years). Therefore, he should come back to the earth to finish his ministry assigned in the second period of the 70th week, which should start on 12 May 2027 AD (see *Perfectly Fulfilled Prophecies and the Destiny of Mankind*).

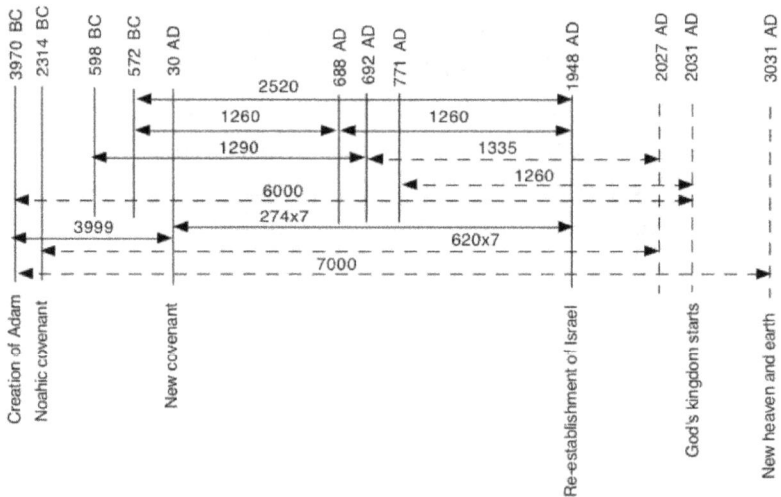

Figure 1: Schematic diagra m for the destiny of mankind.

The day of 12 May 2027 AD for Yeshua's final return is predicted based on the accurate Biblical chronology (with an uncertainty of less than 6 months) and the numerical prophecies in the books of Daniel and Revelation. Figure 1 shows a schematic diagram for the destiny of mankind, which has been obtained precisely from the books of Daniel and Revelation.

More precisely, the most likely days of these years in Figure 1 are as follows: 15 April (1 Nisan) 3970 BC, 10 June (6 Sivan) 2314 BC, 3 April (10 Nisan) 598 BC, 17 March (10 Adar II) 572 BC, 12 July (9 Av) 688 AD, 8 May (16 Iyar) 692 AD, 7 December (25 Kislev) 771 AD, 14 May (6 Sivan) 1948 AD, and 12 May (6 Sivan) 2027 AD, 25 March (1 Nisan) 2031 AD, and 17 March (1 Nisan) 3031 AD. The prophetic periods connected by solid lines were perfectly fulfilled while the prophetic periods marked by dashed lines are yet to be fulfilled. In order to intellectually judge on the correctness of the diagram, readers need to read carefully and critically the entire book: *Perfectly Fulfilled Prophecies and the Destiny of Mankind*. If the readers are convinced of the diagram, they should prepare for the final coming of Yeshua, which are imminent (within only 7 years).

According to the view of mainstream Christians, no one knows the exact day of Yeshua's final return. So, the predicted day would be false and never be fulfilled. This view comes from Matthew 24:36, "But about that day or hour [of Yeshua's final return] no one knows, not even the angels in heaven, nor the Son, but only the Father."

The verb "know" in the English translation of Matthew 24:36 is in present tense, meaning that only the Father knows the day or hour while all the others (including Yeshua himself) will never know them. On the other hand, Yeshua said: "Remember therefore how you have received and heard; hold fast and repent. Therefore if you will not watch, I will come upon you like a thief, and you will not know what hour I will come upon you." (Revelation 3:3). This verse implies that if we remain vigilant, we might be able to know the hour so that his coming might not be like a thief. This appears to contradict his own words in Matthew 24:36. By carefully examining the Greek texts, one can readily discover that the tenses of the verbs are present perfect. Therefore, the correct English translation of Matthew 24:36 (as Young Literal Translation) should be: "But about that day and hour no one has known, not even the angels in heaven, nor the Son, but only the Father." This means that before Yeshua was crucified, no one, including himself, had known the day and hour except for the Father.

Yeshua's statement at that time agrees with what Daniel stated in Daniel 12:9-10: "He replied, 'Go your way, Daniel, because the words are rolled up and **sealed until the time of the end**. Many will be purified, made spotless and refined, but the wicked will continue to be wicked. None of the wicked will understand, but those who are wise will understand.'" Daniel's prophecies about the end times were sealed by God at the time they were written. The end-time prophecies were sealed until the time of the end during which the wise will understand the prophecies and keep themselves pure and spotless. Revelation 3:3 warned his saints to be alert before his coming in the last days. Otherwise, Yeshua's return would be like a thief, and no one would know the day and the hour.

Yeshua also said that his coming would be like the days of Noah. God told Noah that the flood would come in seven days. Noah knew the day and hour, but no other man knew about the flood until it came and swept them all away. To the wicked, the calamities will come like the coming of a thief. But God may reveal the time to the wise by unlocking the sealed prophecies, as written in Daniel 12:9-10.

Only in the last days shall our knowledge increase rapidly (Daniel 12:4) so that we are able to unveil the sealed end-time prophecies if we study the Scriptures diligently and objectively. Thus, unlocking the end-time prophecies right before the coming of the Messiah is not heretical. In contrast, it is perfectly aligned with the teachings of Yeshua Messiah and the prophets in the Hebrew Bible.

The predicted exact day of Yeshua's return in Figure 1 is not based on a conjecture of the author or his own prophecy (he is not a prophet of God). He has consistently unlocked all the numerical prophecies in Daniel, Revelation, and other Old-Testament Scriptures. Just like solving complicated mathematical equations with many variables, he has attempted to solve very complicated puzzles with many inputs of the numerical prophecies in the Bible. It happens that the puzzles are solved, and the solutions have no numerical error. Readers should be able to figure out themselves the probability for the solutions being wrong. Having figured this out, then they can decide whether they should believe the prediction and change their lives for preparation of Yeshua's return soon (within 7 years).

CHAPTER

6

Ezekiel's Prophecy: Jerusalem Twice Destroyed

Ezekiel prophesized about the destruction of the city of Jerusalem. The detailed prophecy was recorded in Ezekiel 4:1-6:

> ¹You also, son of man, take a clay tablet and lay it before you, and portray on it a city, Jerusalem. ²Lay siege against it, build a siege wall against it, and heap up a mound against it; set camps against it also, and place battering rams against it all around. 3Moreover take for yourself an iron plate, and set it as an iron wall between you and the city. Set your face against it, and it shall be besieged, and you shall lay siege against it. 4Lie also on your left side and lay the iniquity of the house of Israel upon it. According to the number of the days that you lie on it, you shall bear their iniquity. ⁵For I have laid on you the years of their iniquity, according to the number of the days, **three hundred and ninety [390] days**; so you shall bear the iniquity of the house of Israel. ⁶And when you have completed them, lie again on your right side; then you shall bear the iniquity of the house of Judah **forty [40] days**. I have laid on you a day for each year.

Ezekiel's prophecy is about the siege and destruction of Jerusalem as seen from Ezekiel 4:1-3. The verses in Ezekiel 4:4-5 tell us that the prophet must lie on his left side for 390 days to bear the iniquity of the house of Israel for 390 years (one day for one year). Similarly, the prophet had to lie on his right side for 40 days to bear the iniquity of the house of Judah for 40 years.

A possible interpretation of this prophecy is that 390 and 40 years refer to two independent periods and that at the end of each period, Jerusalem would be besieged and destroyed. Jerusalem would be destroyed twice due to the iniquity of the house of Israel and the iniquity of the house of Judah.

Ezekiel did not provide any information about the starting point of the 390-year prophetic period. No one would be able to figure out what event should be related to the starting point of the 390-year prophetic period before finding out the starting point for the second 40-year prophetic period. It is well known that Jerusalem was destroyed in the 9th day of the fifth lunar month of 70 AD, forty years after the crucifixion of Yeshua in 30 AD. Yeshua referred to his own body as the temple and prophesized that his body would be destroyed and raised up in three days. This implies that the resurrected body of Yeshua is the temple of God, which was built after his resurrection, in agreement with Revelation 21:22, "But I saw no temple in it, for Yehowah God Almighty and the Lamb are its temple."

For the 40-year prophetic period, the starting point was from the building of a true temple of God, which was the resurrected body of Messiah Yeshua. By analogy, the starting point of the 390-year prophetic period should have been the time when the physical temple began to be built. Indeed, it is proved (see Chapter 11 of *Perfectly Fulfilled Prophecies and the Destiny of Mankind*) that there were 390 years plus about 100 days from the beginning of the construction of Solomon's temple to the first destruction of Jerusalem in the 10th day of the fifth lunar month of 587 BC.

Yeshua also prophesizes the destruction of Jerusalem in Matthew 23:37-39; 24:1-2. Yeshua's prophecy about his own crucifixion and resurrection is recorded in Matthew 12:38-41:

> [38]Then some of the scribes and Pharisees answered, saying, "Teacher, we want to see a sign from You." [39]But

he answered and said to them, "An evil and adulterous generation seeks after a sign, and no sign will be given to it except the sign of the prophet Jonah. [40]For as Jonah was three days and three nights in the belly of the great fish, so will the Son of Man be three days and three nights in the heart of the earth. [41]The men of Nineveh will rise up in the judgment with this generation and condemn it, because they repented at the preaching of Jonah; and indeed a greater than Jonah is here.

Yeshua foretold that after being buried he would resurrect three days and three nights just as the prophet Jonah was in the belly of the great fish for three days and there nights. He also told the scribes and Pharisees that he is greater than Jonah. Jonah prophesized that Nineveh would be destroyed within 40 days. The people of Nineveh believed Jonah's warning and turned away from their evil ways, so God relented from the disaster that He would have brought upon the city. Yeshua foretold that the men of Nineveh would rise to judge this generation and condemn it because they repented at the preaching of Jonah while this generation did not repent in the 40-year grace period at the preaching of Yeshua who is even greater than Jonah. From this, Yeshua knew that God would not spare the holy city because of the evils that the leaders of His people committed. God gave Nineveh the grace period of only 40 days, but to His own people, He granted a grace period of 40 years in hopes of their repentance.

CHAPTER

7

Yeshua's Prophecy on His Burial and Resurrection

When was Yeshua crucified, buried, and resurrected? This question has not been answered since the beginning of Christianity. Almost all Christians have just followed the Roman Catholic Good Friday-Easter Sunday tradition, accepting that Yeshua was crucified on a Friday afternoon, buried just before sunset of that Friday, and resurrected on the following Sunday morning. This timeframe includes Friday night, the daylight portion of Saturday, and Saturday night. The time interval is clearly two nights and one day—**not three days and three nights**, as Yeshua promised as his only sign: "Then some of the scribes and Pharisees answered, saying, 'Teacher, we want to see a sign from you.' But he answered and said to them, 'An evil and adulterous generation seeks after a sign, and no sign will be given to it except the sign of the prophet Jonah. For as Jonah was **three days and three nights** in the belly of the great fish, so will the Son of Man be **three days and three nights** in the heart of the earth.'" (Matthew 12:38-40).

Yeshua's own words suggest that he would be **three days and three nights** in the grave just as Jonah was **three days and three nights** in the whale's belly. How long did Jonah stay inside the whale's belly? The Scripture says: "Now Yehowah had prepared a great fish to swallow up Jonah. And Jonah was in the belly of the fish **three days and three nights.**" (Jonah 1:17). The Scripture continues to say: "Then Jonah prayed unto Yehowah his God out of the fish's belly, ... And Yehowah

44

spoke unto the fish, and it vomited out Jonah upon the dry land." (Jonah 2:1-10).

These verses tell us that Jonah was inside the fish for three days and three nights plus a short time of Jonah's prayers. In other words, Yeshua might rise slightly over three days and three nights after he was buried. This is consistent with what the chief priest and Pharisees said about Yeshua's resurrection, "Sir, we remember while he was still alive, how that deceiver said, 'After three days I will rise.'" (Matthew 27:63). Here, "after three days" could also mean "three days after his crucifixion."

Yeshua himself also said, "Behold, we are going up to Jerusalem, and the Son of Man will be betrayed to the chief priests and to the scribes; and they will condemn him to death and deliver him to the Gentiles to mock and to scourge and to crucify. And the third day he will rise again." (Matthew 20:18-19). Here, Matthew tells us that Yeshua would rise again the third day by directly quoting Yeshua's own words.

According to our current understanding of the language, "three days and three nights" and "the third day" are not the same. How could the same author write the same thing using apparently contradictory wordings? Did Matthew or Yeshua say something contradictory to each other? If this would be the case, how would this Gospel be inspired by the Almighty God and how would Yeshua be the Son of God and the Messiah?

Understanding of "the third day"

Did Matthew make such an obvious mistake? Absolutely not! It is important to note that like the Romans, the Jews counted day and year exclusively, following Babylon's way during the second temple period. For the Jews, a day starts and ends from one sunset to next. For example, if today is Wednesday, "in the first day" means the day between today's sunset and Thursday's sunset, and "in the third day" means the day between sunset of Friday and sunset of Saturday. "The third day" without the preposition "in" means the end of the third day (see below). Therefore, if Yeshua was buried at or right before sunset of Wednesday and rose just at or right before sunset of Saturday, it is correct to say that he resurrected the third day. If Yeshua was buried at sunset of Wednesday and resurrected at sunset of Saturday, he had stayed in the grave for three days and three nights, just as what Yeshua said in Matthew 12:38-40. According to Matthew's account, Yeshua was indeed buried at sunset of his crucifixion day (Matthew 27:57). The fact that Yeshua was crucified during the daytime of that Wednesday and rose at or right before sunset of that Saturday is indeed consistent with Matthew 27:63, "Sir, we remember while he was still alive, how that deceiver said, '**After three days** I will rise'" and with Matthew 20:19, "…And **the third day** he will rise again." "The third day" provides a definitive time for his resurrection: He rose in the end part of that Saturday (at or right before sunset).

Yeshua's own words confirm that the Jews at his time followed the Babylonian counting of hour, day or year. Yeshua teaches us how to count the hour in Matthew 20:1-16:

> [1]"For the kingdom of heaven is like a landowner who went out early in the morning to hire laborers for his vineyard. [2]Now when he had agreed with the laborers for a denarius a day, he sent them into his vineyard. [3]And he went out **about the third hour** and saw others standing idle in the marketplace, [4]and said to them, 'You also go into the vineyard, and whatever is right I will give you.' So they went.[5]Again he went out about the sixth and the ninth hour, and did likewise. [6]And **about the eleventh hour** he went out and found others standing idle, and said to them, 'Why have you been standing here idle all day?' [7]They said to him, 'Because no one hired us.' He said to them, 'You also go into the vineyard, and whatever is right you will receive.' [8]So **when evening had come**, the owner of the vineyard said to his steward, 'Call the laborers and give them their wages, beginning with the last to the first.' [9]And when those came who were hired **about the eleventh hour**, they each received a denarius. [10]But when the first came, they supposed that they would receive more; and they likewise received each a denarius. [11]And when they

had received it, they complained against the landowner, [12]saying, 'These last men have worked only one hour, and you made them equal to us who have borne the burden and the heat of the day.' [13]But he answered one of them and said, 'Friend, I am doing you no wrong. Did you not agree with me for a denarius? [14]Take what is yours and go your way. I wish to give to this last man the same as to you. [15]Is it not lawful for me to do what I wish with my own things? Or is your eye evil because I am good?' [16]So the last will be first, and the first last. **For many are called, but few chosen."**

This passage tells us that a daytime is divided into twelve hours. The passage also implies that if the Sun rises at 6:00 am and sets at 6:00 pm, then "the first hour" of the day is at 7:00 am, "the third hour" at 9:00 am, "the ninth hour" at 3:00 pm, "the eleventh hour" at 5:00 pm, and "the twelfth hour" at 6:00 pm. Those who came at the eleventh hour worked only one hour toward the end of the day at the twelfth hour (verses 9 and 12).

Therefore, the Scriptures clearly teach us that "the third hour" means the time at which exactly three hours have passed from the beginning of a day. "The third hour" without the preposition "in" means exactly three hours counted from the beginning of a day. Here, there appears to be a concept of "zero hour" at the beginning of a day. By analogy, "the third day" means the day exactly three days after a new day starts, that is, **at the end of the third day** according to our modern human mind.

The Gospel of John recorded the detailed events day by day in John 1:28-51 and John 2:1-2. From these events, we can clearly see the meaning of "the third day." John 1:28 tells us that the testimonies of John the Baptist took place in the Jordan river. After this verse, John 1:29 recorded: "**The next day** John saw Yeshua coming toward him, and said, 'Behold! The Lamb of God who takes away the sin of the world!'" John testified that Yeshua was the Lamb of God **the next day**, which was in the first day, relative to the day in John 1:28. Then verses 35 and 36 say: "**Again, the next day**, John stood with two of his disciples. And looking at Yeshua as he walked, he said, 'Behold the Lamb of God!'"

John introduced Yeshua the Lamb of God to two of his disciples in the second day. In the third day, Yeshua found Philip in Galilee, as recorded in John 1:43, "**The following day** Yeshua wanted to go to Galilee, and he found Philip and said to him, 'Follow Me.'" In the same day, Yeshua also found Nathanael (see verses 45-51). Then John 2:1 says, "**The third day** there was a wedding in Cana of Galilee, and the mother of Yeshua was there." The wedding in Cana of Galilee should have started just at sunset of the same day when Yeshua met Philip and Nathanael in Galilee. At or right before sunset, Yeshua and his companions just arrived in Cana to attend the wedding ceremony. At this moment, the old day ended, and a new day started, so John the Apostle uses the phrase "the third day" to tell us that the wedding should have started exactly at sunset of that day. From the day when John the Baptist made the testimonies in the Jordan river to the evening of the wedding ceremony, three days and three nights had passed.

During the first Passover right after Yeshua performed the first miracle (changing water to wine) at Cana, he said to the Jews, "Destroy this temple, and in three days I will raise it up." (John 3:19). Here, Yeshua spoke of the temple of his body, which will be raised up in three days (three days later) after it is destroyed.

Therefore, all these verses in the Gospels of Matthew and John consistently suggest that Yeshua resurrected exactly three days and three nights after his burial or three days and three nights after he was crucified. In contrast, most Biblical scholars believe and teach a false idea that Yeshua was only buried for half that time. *Clarke's Commentary*, in explaining Matthew 12:40, follows this false tradition, established as early as the mid-second century AD. "One day and two nights" cannot mean "three days and three nights" despite many attempts of scholars and theologians to "prove."

Even with our current understanding of the day and night, there **cannot** be "three days and three nights" from Friday's crucifixion to Sunday's resurrection. A partial day on Friday + a full day on Saturday + a partial day on Sunday could be three days according to our current understanding. A full night between sunset of Friday and sunrise of Saturday + a full night between sunset of Saturday and sunrise of Sunday are two nights exactly. Thus, there are at most three days and two nights from Friday afternoon to Sunday morning, which cannot harmonize "three days and three nights" Yeshua clearly prophesized for the time interval of his staying in the grave.

Yeshua's crucifixion and burial

Yeshua's crucifixion took place on the 14th day of Nisan, the first month of a year assigned by God, which is the preparation day of the Passover (John 19:14). Yeshua was nailed on the cross around the sixth hour (John 19:14), in agreement with Matthew 27:45, "Now from the sixth hour there was darkness over all the land unto the ninth hour." The darkness should have started right after Yeshua was nailed on the cross.

Yeshua died around 3:00 pm (the ninth hour) (Matthew 27:45-50). With Governor Pilate's permission, Joseph of Arimathaea procured the body, wrapped it in linen (John 19:40), and placed it in the sepulcher. By evening (just before or at sunset) of that day, the burial was complete (Matthew 27:57). The burial took place on **the preparation day** of the Passover, shortly before or at sunset. The **preparation day** preceded the Feast of Unleavened Bread, which was also called the Feast of Passover. The first day of the Feast was called a high Sabbath or "high day" (John 19:31), which is held annually to memorialize the day in which the Almighty God brought the Israelites out of Egypt. The midnight of Nisan 15 is the Passover of Yehowah. John 19:31 especially emphasizes that the next day after Yeshua's crucifixion was a special Sabbath that is different from the weekly Sabbaths (in plural form in Greek). It was on this special Sabbath that the high priest and the Pharisees came to Pilate to ensure that Yeshua's tomb was securely guarded and sealed (Matthew 27:62-66).

John 19:31 also tells us that Yeshua cannot be crucified on a Friday. If his crucifixion were on a Friday, the next day would be the weekly Sabbaths rather than a high Sabbath. Below we will prove that Yeshua resurrected at the end of Saturday. We have proved that the only year of Yeshua's crucifixion, which was consistent with the Gospels of Matthew and John, was 30 AD (see Chapter 3). According to the Hebrew lunisolar calendar of 30 AD (see Table IV in Chapter 3), the preparation day of the Feast of the Passover in 30 AD is indeed on Wednesday. From sunset of Wednesday to sunset of Saturday, there are exactly three days and three nights, in agreement with Yeshua's own prophecy about his resurrection.

Some Biblical scholars and theologians argued that the darkness from the sixth hour to the ninth hour during Yeshua's crucifixion, as recorded in Matthew 27:45, was related to a solar eclipse. This argument does not have any scientific foundation. First, solar eclipses only take place in either the first or the last day of a lunar month while Yeshua's crucifixion occurred in the middle of the first lunar month (Nisan 14). Second, solar eclipses last for less than 6 minutes, much shorter than 3 hours. Therefore, the darkness cannot be caused by a natural solar eclipse.

Another possibility is that God might have miraculously darkened the sky by bringing dark heavy clouds or by darkening the sun. Yeshua prophesized that the sun would be darkened, and the moon would not give its light immediately after the end-time tribulation (Matthew 24:29). This type of darkness should not happen in a dark-moon phase when a solar eclipse can take place. In the dark-moon phase, the moon does not give its light because of the special positions of the sun, the moon, and the earth, independent of whether the sun is darkened or not. The predicted miraculous darkness immediately after the end-time tribulation shall happen in a day when both the sun and the moon are supposed to be seen by the people in different parts of the world but fail to be seen in reality. If the sun had been miraculously darkened from 12:00 to 3:00 pm during Yeshua's crucifixion, the full moon in China would not have given its light from 6:00 to 9:00 pm and Chinese chroniclers would have recorded such an unusual phenomenon in the sky. However, they recorded all the natural eclipses around the year of Yeshua's crucifixion (during the reign of Emperor Guang-Wu in the Later Han Dynasty) but nothing else. This fact suggests that such a phenomenon should have never taken place during Yeshua's crucifixion. Alternatively, the darkness recorded by Matthew should have been caused by dark heavy clouds.

The Book of Later Han records two solar eclipses in the 30th day of the 9th month in the 6th year of Emperor Guang-Wu (30 AD) and in the 30th day of the 3rd month in Guang-Wu's 7th year (31 AD). These two solar eclipses are predicted to have taken place in China around 7:00 am on November 14 of 30 AD and around 9:00 am on May 10 of 31 AD, respectively. The dates of the predicted solar eclipses perfectly match the ones recorded in *The Book of Later Han* (Volume 1b). Thus, the Chinese chroniclers accurately recorded these natural astronomical phenomena but no miraculous phenomenon in the sky around the year of Yeshua's crucifixion.

The time of Yeshua's resurrection

Most Christians believe that Yeshua resurrected in the early morning of Sunday. Most English translated Bibles explicitly say that the women (several Marys) went to the tomb of Yeshua in the early morning shortly after he was raised.

If the Gospels of Matthew and John are all inspired by God, they must be consistent with each other. **John 20:1** (NKJV) says: "Now on the first day of the week Mary Magdalene went to the tomb early, while it was still dark, and saw that the stone had been taken away from the tomb."

The Greek word "prior" in John 20:1 was translated into "early," which means the early part of the first day of the week. Since a day starts from sunset to the Jews, the early part of the first day of the week could have corresponded to the time just after sunset of Saturday.

If the Greek word "prior" is translated into "early," then John 20:1 can be translated as: "Now at the early time of the first day of the week, Mary Magdalene went to the tomb, while it was yet (already) dark, and saw that the stone had been taken away from the tomb." The Greek word "ἔτι" in John 20:1 should best match the English word "yet" rather than "still." The adverb "yet" has the meanings of "now," "right now," "at this time," and "already."

The Gospel of Matthew even provides a precise time of Yeshua's resurrection. Matthew 28:1 has also been mistranslated. The original Greek text reads: "Ὀψὲ δὲ σαββάτων, τῇ ἐπιφωσκούσῃ εἰς μίαν σαββάτων (after then, the Sabbaths it being dawn towards the first day of the week)." Here, Saturday is written in the plural (sabbaton), while Sunday is written as eis mian sabbaton. These two phrases have exactly the same meaning and specify the hour that falls on the Saturday evening when the Sunday is about to begin. The first word of the phrase, opse (ὀψὲ), when it is used with a day of the week, means: "at dusk," "at nightfall," or "at evening." The word "opse" can also mean "at the end" of an event.

Now, let's take a look at the second phrase of the ancient Greek text of Matthew "epiphoskouse eis mian sabbaton (ἐπιφωσκούσῃ εἰς μίαν σαββάτων)," which is usually translated as "it began to dawn toward the first day of the week." This is where the serious misunderstanding occurs. This particular translation leads to an entirely incorrect understanding, since the modern reader thinks that it is referring to dawn (early morning). This is not the case. When the Jews used the expression "the break/light of a new day," they did not mean at daylight in the morning, but "the night of the new day has come to light." Consequently, for the Jews, the "daybreak" of the new day corresponds to the evening time. In the Gospel of Luke, Luke specifies the time of Yeshua's burial with the phrase: καὶ ἡμέρα ἦν παρασκευῆς, καὶ σάββατον ἐπέφωσκεν, i.e., "it was the day of Preparation, and Sabbath was about to begin (literally translated: it began to dawn toward the Sabbath)." (Luke 23:54). This phrase in Luke "it began to dawn toward the Sabbath" and the phrase in Matthew "it began to dawn toward the first day of the week" use the same verb "epiphosko" and specify the same time, right at sunset (at daybreak). This means that the women departed to see the tomb just after sunset of Saturday. Right after the weekly Sabbaths, the women must want to see the tomb as soon as possible because they love Yeshua so much. There is no point for them to wait a whole night and get up very early to see the tomb.

Before they arrived at the tomb, an angel of Yehowah descended from heaven, rolled back the stone from the door, and sat on it at sunset of Saturday (Matthew 28:2). After the women arrived in the tomb at the very beginning of Sunday and entered the tomb, the angel clothed with a long white robe talked to them that Yeshua had risen (Matthew 28:5). The verb "egeiró" in the Greek text is in the past tense, meaning that Yeshua had risen when the angel talked to the women. Therefore, Yeshua resurrected at or right before sunset of Saturday.

Mary Magdalene saw the empty tomb at the beginning part of that Sunday (early Sunday) when there was already darkness according to John (John 20:1). Mark 16:1 says Mary Magdalene, Mary the mother of James, and Salome brought spices to anoint Yeshua's body after the weekly Sabbaths. Mark 16:2 says that they came to tomb at the very beginning of Sunday (very early Sunday) when the sun was still shining (that is, right before the sun was completely set down). The Greek word "anatellō" in Mark 16:2 means "cause to rise," "rise," and "shine." The same Greek word in Matthew 4:16 should be translated as "shine" because this verse directly quotes Isaiah 9:2, "… upon them a light has shined." "Early Sunday" with darkness and "very early Sunday" with sun shining are only possible when the time is around sunset of Saturday.

In order to be in harmony with John 20:1, "they" in Mark 16:2 should refer to James' mother and Salome. Then Mary Magdalene came to the tomb alone a bit later than James' mother and Salome. After Mary Magdalene saw the empty tomb, she ran and came to Peter and John (John 20:2). Then they ran to the tomb, found the empty tomb, and went to their homes (John 20:4-10). Mary also returned to the tomb later and stayed there alone since Peter and John had left the tomb (John 20:11). Then she saw the risen Yeshua (John 20:14).

It is interesting that our correct translation of these verses is backed up by all the ancient translations of the New Testament, such as the Latin translation by St Jerome (Vulgata), the Syriac Peshitta, the Ethiopian, the Arabic, the Armenian translation of the fifth century, etc. They attest that Yeshua resurrected just at sunset of Saturday and Mary Magdalene and the other Mary visited the tomb afterward.

In *The Report of Pilate the Procurator Concerning Our Lord Yeshua Christ*, sent to the August Cæsar, Pilate stated:

> And the fear of the earthquake remained from the sixth hour of the preparation until the ninth hour. And on the evening of the first day of the week there was a sound out of the heaven, so that the heaven became enlightened sevenfold more than all the days. And at the third hour of the night also the sun was seen brighter than it had ever shone before, lighting up all the heaven. And as

lightnings come suddenly in winter, so majestic men appeared in glorious robes, an innumerable multitude, whose voice was heard as that of a very great thunder, crying out: "Yeshua that was crucified is risen: come up out of Hades, ye that have been enslaved in the underground regions of Hades." And the chasm of the earth was as if it had no bottom; but it was as if the very foundations of the earth appeared along with those that cried out in the heavens and walked about in the body in the midst of the dead that had risen. And he that raised up all the dead, and bound Hades, said: "Say to my disciples, 'He goes before you into Galilee; there shall you see him.'"

Pilate's letter to August Cæsar tells us that on the evening of the first day of the week there was a sound out of the heaven and that the heaven became enlightened sevenfold more than all the days. His statement is consistent with Matthew 28:2-3: "And behold, there was a great earthquake; for an angel of Yehowah descended from heaven and came and rolled back the stone from the door, and sat on it. His countenance was like lightning, and his clothing as white as snow." Pilate's report, if reliable, confirms that Yeshua resurrected around sunset of Saturday.

CHAPTER

8

Yeshua's Prophecy on Destruction of the Temple

Yeshua prophesized about the destruction of the temple of God within about 40 years in Matthew 24:1-3,34:

> [1]Then Yeshua went out and departed from the temple, and his disciples came up to show him the buildings of the temple. [2]And Yeshua said to them, "Do you not see all these things? Assuredly, I say to you, not one stone shall be left here upon another, that shall not be thrown down." [3]Now as he sat on the Mount of Olives, the disciples came to him privately, saying, "Tell us, when will these things be [ruined]? And what will be the sign of your coming, and of the end of the age?..."
> [34]Assuredly, I say to you, **this generation will by no means pass away till all these things become [ruined].**

In verse 2, **all these things** Yeshua refers to are the buildings of the temple, which shall be thrown down (ruined) completely. In verse 3, his disciples asked him three independent questions: (1) When will [all] these things be [ruined]? This question is related to the buildings of the temple, which Yeshua prophesized to be ruined completely; (2) what will be the sign of Yeshua's return; and (3) what will be the sign of the end of the age?

55

Yeshua did not answer these three questions sequentially. He answered and said to them: "Take heed that no one deceives you. For many will come in my name, saying, 'I am the Messiah,' and will deceive many." (Matthew 24:4-5).

In these verses, Yeshua told his disciples that before all these things (the buildings of the temple) were ruined, many false messiahs would come in his name and deceive many. Yeshua warned his disciples not to be deceived by the false messiahs. Here he answered the first question of his disciples.

In verses 6-14, Yeshua said:

> "And you will hear of wars and rumors of wars. See that you are not troubled; for it is necessary for them to take place, but the end is not yet. For nation will rise against nation, and kingdom against kingdom. And there will be famines, pestilences, and earthquakes in various places. All these are the beginning of sorrows. And they will deliver you up to tribulation and kill you, and you will be hated by all nations for my name's sake. And many will be offended, will betray one another, and will hate one another. And many false prophets will rise up and deceive many. And because lawlessness will abound, the love of many will grow cold. But he who endures to the end shall be saved. And this gospel of the kingdom will be preached in all the world as a witness to all the nations, and then the end will come."

In these verses, Yeshua answered the third question of his disciples: What will be the signs before the end of the age?

In verses 15-20, Yeshua said:

> "Therefore when you see the 'abomination of desolation,' spoken of by Daniel the prophet, standing in the holy place (whoever reads, let him understand), then let those who are in Judea flee to the mountains. Let him who is on the housetop not go down to take anything out of

his house. And let him who is in the field not go back to get his clothes. But woe to those who are pregnant and to those who are nursing babies in those days! And pray that your flight may not be in winter or on the Sabbath."

In these verses, Yeshua answered the first question of his disciples again. Yeshua prophesized the destruction of Jerusalem and the temple of God. The Romans (the Gentiles) standing in the holy place was an abomination to God because no foreigner who is uncircumcised in flesh and heart is allowed to enter the holy temple of God (Ezekiel 44:6-9). Yeshua foretold that the Jews could escape from the tribulation by fleeing to the mountains when they saw the Romans stand in the holy place.

In verses 21-22, Yeshua stated:

"There will indeed then be great tribulation (literally translated), such as has not been since the beginning of the world until this time, no, nor ever shall be. And unless those days were shortened, no flesh would be saved; but for the elect's sake those days will be shortened."

In these verses, Yeshua answered the third question of his disciples: What will be the signs before the end of the age?

In verses 23-28, Yeshua told his disciples:

"And if anyone says to you, 'Look, here is the Messiah!' or 'There!' do not believe it. For false messiahs and false prophets will rise and show great signs and wonders to deceive, if possible, even the elect. See, I have told you beforehand. Therefore if they say to you, 'Look, he is in the desert!' do not go out; or 'Look, he is in the inner rooms!' do not believe it. **For as the lightning comes from the east and flashes to the west, so also will the coming of the Son of Man be.** For wherever the carcass is, there the eagles will be gathered together."

Here, Yeshua provided a general guidance to identify false messiahs and false prophets in any time. Since false messiahs and false prophets had appeared before the temple was destroyed (Matthew 24:4-5) and continued to appear till the end times, this general guidance is necessary for his true believers not to be deceived. The general guidance is that Yeshua will come down from heaven with thunders and lightning flashes. Resurrected Yeshua should never appear "in the desert" nor "in the inner rooms (secret chambers)." If anyone tells you that he has seen the resurrected Yeshua in the desert and/or in the inner rooms, what he has seen is not Yeshua but a false messiah. Even if the false messiah and his prophets could perform great signs and wonders, do not believe them because they do these to deceive you, even the elect.

In verses 29-31, Yeshua said:

> "Immediately after the tribulation of those days the sun will be darkened, and the moon will not give its light; the stars will fall from heaven, and the powers of the heavens will be shaken. And the sign of the Son of Man will appear in heaven, and all the tribes of the earth will mourn, and they will see the Son of Man coming on the clouds of heaven with power and great glory. And he will send his angels with a great sound of a trumpet, and they will gather together his elect from the four winds, from one end of heaven to the other."

In these verses, Yeshua answered the third question of his disciples: What will the signs of his coming in the end times be? He also foretold his disciples that he would return with power and great glory and would first gather his true believers before he would pour out the wrath of God upon the ungodly.

In verses 32-34, Yeshua said:

> "Now learn this parable from the fig tree: When its branch has already become tender and puts forth leaves, you know that summer is near. So you also, when you see all these, know that it is near, at the doors! Assuredly, I

say to you, **this generation will by no means pass away** till all these things become (ruined)."

In these verses, Yeshua answered the first question of his disciples again: When will all these things become (ruined)?

The Greek word "Γίνομαι" (transliteration: ginomai) in verse 34 has the following meanings: come into being; come to pass; happen; **become** (signifying a change of condition, state or place). In most English translations, "ginomai" is translated as "happen" or "take place." Then verse 34 reads: "Assuredly, I say to you, this generation will by no means pass away till all these things take place." If all these things would refer to the end-time events, this prophecy of Yeshua would not be fulfilled because the end did not come one generation after his prophecy. If "ginomai" is translated as "become," verse 34 reads: "Assuredly, I say to you, this generation will by no means pass away till all these things **become** [ruined]." This verse naturally answered the first question of his disciples: When will [all] these things be [ruined]?

In these verses, Yeshua actually prophesized the time for destruction of the temple of God. He foretold that the temple would be destroyed in the summertime (verse 32) and within a generation (verse 34) from his prophecy. In Chapter 1 of the Gospel of Matthew, the author counted 14 generations from captivity of Jeconiah (Jehoiachin) into Babylon to the birth of Yeshua. It is known that Jehoiachin was taken into Babylon in the spring of 597 BC. In Chapter 31, we will show that Yeshua was born in the spring of 5 BC. Therefore, the average number of years per generation is calculated to be (597-5)/14 = 42.3. Yeshua prophesized this in the spring of 30 AD and the temple was destroyed in the summer of 70 AD. Therefore, the temple of God was destroyed about 40.5 years (slightly less than a generation) after the time of his prophecy. This prophecy of Yeshua was fulfilled perfectly.

A similar prophecy on the destruction of Jerusalem can be found in Matthew 13:41: "The men of Nineveh will rise up in the judgment with this generation and condemn it, because they repented at the preaching of Jonah; and indeed [one] greater than Jonah is here."

There is an implied prophecy in his statement. Before this statement, Yeshua prophesized that he would resurrect after he would be buried for 3 days and 3 nights just as happened to Jonah. In Matthew 13:41, Yeshua foretold God's judgment and condemnation on this generation because they did not repent at the warning of Yeshua. Jonah the prophet prophesized the destruction of Nineveh within 40 days. The men of Nineveh repented at the warning of Jonah. Yeshua who is greater than Jonah prophesized the destruction of Jerusalem within one generation. God gave a 40-day warning to the men of Nineveh through His prophet Jonah. In contrast, God gave a 40-year warning to the men of Jerusalem through His only begotten Son. Unfortunately, the Jews did not repent, and God's wrath poured out on His people, as also prophesized by Daniel (Daniel 9:26-27). The Romans destroyed Jerusalem ruthlessly in 70 AD and killed over 1 million Jews, 40 years after Yeshua's warning.

CHAPTER

9

Yeshua's Prophecies on His First-Century Return

Matthew 10: 16-23 recorded the prophecy of Yeshua on the time of his return:

> [16]"Behold, I send you out as sheep in the midst of wolves. Therefore be wise as serpents and harmless as doves. [17]But beware of men, for they will deliver you up to councils and scourge you in their synagogues. [18]You will be brought before governors and kings for my sake, as a testimony to them and to the Gentiles. [19]But when they deliver you up, do not worry about how or what you should speak. For it will be given to you in that hour what you should speak; [20]for it is not you who speak, but the Spirit of your Father who speaks in you. [21]Now brother will deliver up brother to death, and a father his child; and children will rise up against parents and cause them to be put to death. [22]And you will be hated by all for my name's sake. But he who endures to the end will be saved. [23]**When they persecute you in this city, flee to another. For assuredly, I say to you, you will not have gone through the cities of Israel before the Son of Man comes.**"

This prophecy of Yeshua suggests that his return should have taken place before his disciples had gone through all the cities of Israel. Yeshua also prophesied that his disciples would be persecuted and flee from one city to another. Before they went through all the cities of Israel or before the persecution was over, Yeshua should have returned. This is his first return he foretold his disciples. He also foretold his final return in Matthew 24:26-31.

If the prophecy of his first return would not have been fulfilled, Yeshua would not be the true Messiah and Savior. We will show that this prophecy was fulfilled in the spring of 67 AD when he returned to instruct John to measure the temple of God and to prophesy the destruction of Jerusalem in 42 months.

Just as the Spirit of God took Ezekiel from Babylon to Jerusalem (Ezekiel 8:3), the angel of God may have taken John from Patmos island to the temple of God in Jerusalem. After John was given a reed-like measuring rod, the mighty angel stood and said to John, "Rise and measure the temple of God, the altar, and those who worship there. But leave out the court, which is outside the temple, and do not measure it, for it has been given to the Gentiles. And they will trample down the holy city, forty-two [42] months." (Revelation 10:1-2).

In most English translations, the preposition "for" has been added before 42 months. When "for" is added, the prophecy would read: "And they (the Gentiles) will trample down the holy city for 42 months." Since the holy city Jerusalem has never been trampled down continuously for 42 months, most Biblical scholars believe that this prophetic event shall take place in the end times after the third temple of God is rebuilt.

Since there is no "for" in the Greek text of Revelation 11:2 and the verb is in the future indicative active mode [describing a future action (snapshot) at a particular time], we can interpret this verse alternatively. If we add "in" before 42 months, the prophecy will read: "And they (the Gentiles) will trample down (destroy ruthlessly) the holy city in 42 months." This interpretation can be justified by analogy with John 2:20. The interlinear English translation of this verse is:

> The Jews therefore said: "46 years [ago] this temple was erected [and is still under construction] and you will raise it up in three days?"

Here, the verb "οἰκοδομέω (oikodomeó)" means "erect a building" and "build a house." The verb "οἰκοδομήθη" in the above sentence is in the aorist indicative passive form. The Greek aorist tense in the indicative mood simply describes a past action (snapshot at a particular time). Therefore, the erection of the temple (the commencement of the temple's construction) is a past action relative to the time when the Jews spoke to Yeshua.

We have shown (see Chapter 2) that the temple was erected (started to be built) in the spring of 20 BC, which was 46 years before the Jews spoke to Yeshua (see Chapter 3). Since these Jews knew that the construction of the temple started 46 years ago [and was still under way], their statement can be rephrased as: "The temple has been under construction for 46 years and you will raise it up in three days?"

In the Greek text of John 2:20, there is no preposition before 46 years nor adverb after 46 years. Adding the adverb "ago" after 46 years correctly conveys the meaning of this verse: The temple was erected 46 years before the Jews spoke to Yeshua. By analogy, adding the proposition "in" before 42 months in Revelation 11:2 conveys the idea that Jerusalem will be destroyed ruthlessly 42 months after this prophecy of the mighty angel. If this interpretation is correct, the book of Revelation was written 42 months before Jerusalem was destroyed.

Who is the mighty angel of God described in Revelation 10:1-3? In Chapter 27, we will show that the mighty angel of God is Yeshua Messiah.

When was John on Patmos island? The time must have been in the period when the disciples of Yeshua were persecuted (Revelation 1:9). We know that Nero severely persecuted the Christians and the Jews between 64 and 68 AD. But most Biblical scholars believe that John was on Patmos Island around 90 AD when Domitian was the Roman emperor (81-96 AD). There is no historical record of severe persecution of Christians during the reign of Domitian.

We will use the historical records of Josephus about the Jewish war to determine the time of John's writing of the book of Revelation. Josephus told us (*Wars*, bk. 6, ch. 5, sect. 3):

> Thus were the miserable people persuaded by these deceivers, and such as belied God himself; while they did not attend nor give credit to the signs that were so evident, and did so plainly foretell their future desolation, but, like men infatuated, without either eyes to see or minds to consider, did not regard the denunciations that God made to them. Thus there was a star resembling a sword, which stood over the city, and a comet, that continued a whole year. Thus also before the Jews' rebellion, and before those commotions which preceded the war, when the people were come in great crowds to the feast of unleavened bread, **on the eighth day of the month Xanthicus [the first month], and at the ninth hour of the night [about 3 am], so great a light shone round the altar and the holy house, that it appeared to be bright day time; which lasted for half an hour. This light seemed to be a good sign to the unskillful, but was so interpreted by the sacred scribes, as to portend those events that followed immediately upon it.**

This passage tells us that before the Jewish war started (in April of 67 AD), there were two astronomical phenomena: A star resembling a sword stood over the city and a comet appeared. The Chinese astronomers also recorded these two astronomical phenomena separated by about 7 months. The separation between the revolt of the Jews (in the fall of 66 AD) and the starting of the Jewish war (in April of 67 AD) was also about 7 months. So, what Josephus tells us is that the two astronomical phenomena took place about one year before the revolt of the Jews and before the starting of the Jewish war, respectively. Since the original Greek text does not have punctuation, the English translation may read as: "Thus there were a star resembling a sword (which stood over the city) and a comet, which were a whole year before the Jews' revolt and before those commotions (which preceded the war), respectively."

The Chinese recorded a comet-like star on 29 July 65 AD: "孝明永平八年六月壬午, 长星出柳张, 三十七度, 犯轩辕, 刺天船, 陵太微, 气至上阶, 凡见五十六日去." Our English translation reads:

> On the day of *ren-wu* (the 19th day of a sexagenary cycle) in the sixth month, in the eighth year of the Yong-Ping reign-period of King Xiao-Ming (29 July 65 AD), a long star (extending 37 degrees) was seen. The head of the star was within Hydra. It falls into Leo Major, stabs towards Perseus (or Perseids), and crosses over the supreme-palace enclosure. Its halo tail reaches the upper steps of Ursa Major. The star disappeared after 56 days.

Figure 2 simulates the above description of the long star. The Chinese word "刺" (which means "stab") suggests that the long star was like a sword. The picture indeed shows that the "sword" stabs towards Perseus (or Perseids); the head of the star was within Hydra; its halo tail reaches the upper steps of Ursa Major.

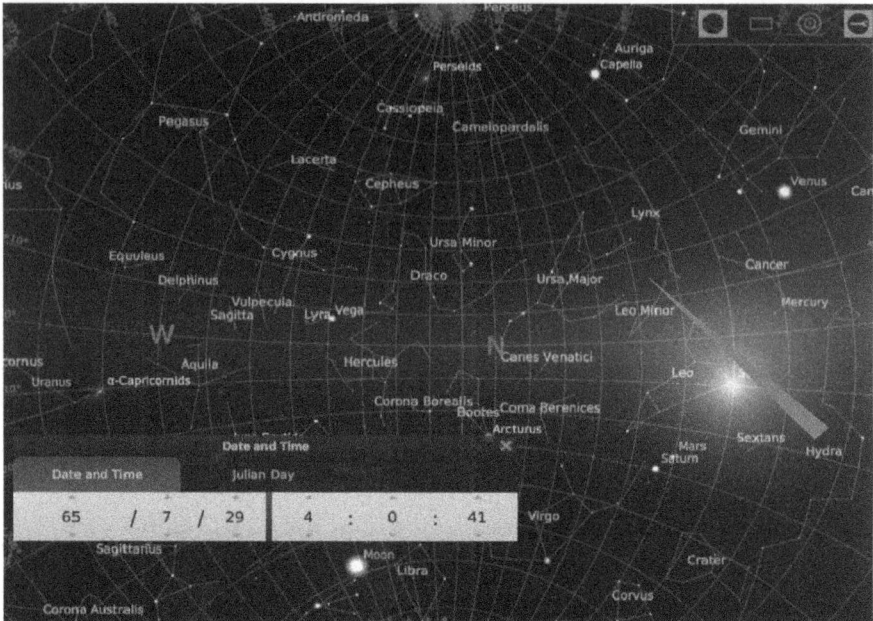

Figure 2: A comet-like long-star was like a sword, which appeared on 29 July 65 AD and was recorded by the Chinese astronomer. The "sword" stabs (points) towards Perseus (or Perseids).

Since the revolt of the Jews took place in the fall of 66 AD and the long star was seen in August and September of 65 AD, the separation of the two events was indeed about one year, in agreement with the account of Josephus.

The Chinese astronomer also recorded a comet on 20 February 66 AD: "On the day of *wu-shen* (the 45th day of a sexagenary cycle) in the first month, in the ninth year of the Yong-Ping reign-period of King Xiao-Ming, a "guest star" (comet) appeared in α-*Altair* (ninth lunar mansion) with a length of 8 feet. It went out of sight after appearing for 50 days."

This comet appeared in February, March, and in early April of 66 AD, which was also about one year before the commotions which preceded the Jewish war (in April of 67 AD).

Josephus further tells us that on the eighth day of the month Xanthicus [the first Macedonian month] of 67 AD, the Jews came in great crowds for the feast of unleavened bread. At the ninth hour of the night (about 3:00 am) in the 9th day, a great light shone around the altar and the temple for half an hour, and it appeared like the daytime due to the great light.

This miraculous event recorded by Josephus may be related to the event described in Revelation 11:2. This verse tells us that the mighty angel and John were inside the holy temple of God and the angel instructed John to measure the temple of God, the altar, and those who worshipped there. Since the face of the angel was like the sun (Revelation 10:1), the altar and the holy temple must have been brightened like the daytime at his presence. Those who worshipped there must have seen the great light. Josephus should have eye witnessed it or obtained the information from those who worshipped there. The mighty angel must have chosen this particular time to let his people witness the miraculous event and record it.

The 9th day of the month Xanthicus of 67 AD happened to be the 9th day of the month Nisan in the Hebrew calendar (see Table VII), which was on April 12 and on Sunday. Yeshua also revealed to John on Sunday according to Revelation 1:10-11 (Hebraic-Roots Version):

> [10]And I was in the spirit on the first [day] of the week. And I heard from behind me, a great voice as a shofar, [11]That said, those [things] that you see, write in a book and send to the seven assemblies: to Ephesus, and to Smyrna, and to Pergamos, and to Thyatira, and to Sardis, and to Philadelphia, and to Laodicea.

The Hebrew version of Revelation does not say "the Lord's day," but instead "the first day of the week". In contrast, the Greek version says, "the Lord's day." Since the original book of Revelation was written in Hebrew (see the proof in the beginning part of *The Hebraic-Roots Version Scripture*), the Greek translator of the book changed "the first day of the week" into "the Lord's day." This implies that the assignment of Sunday as "the Lord's day" should not have originated from God. Yeshua only said that the Son of Man is the Lord of the Sabbaths. The implication of his word is that the seventh day (Saturday) is "the Lord's day."

Table VII: Hebrew Lunisolar Calendar of 67 AD (The first day of each lunar month is indicated with **bold face**. The lunar month's name is on the left side.)

					1	2	3	January
(10) Tebet	4	5	**6**	7	8	9	10	
	11	12	13	14	15	16	17	
	18	19	*20*	21	22	23	24	
	25	26	27	28	29	30	31	
(11) Shebet	1	2	3	**4**	5	6	7	February
	8	9	10	11	12	13	14	
	15	16	17	*18*	19	20	21	
	22	23	24	25	26	27	28	
(12) Adar	1	2	3	4	5	**6**	7	March
	8	9	10	11	12	13	14	
	15	16	17	18	19	*20*	21	
	22	23	24	25	26	27	28	
(1) Nisan	29	30	31	1	2	3	**4**	April
	5	6	7	8	9	10	11	
	12	13	14	15	16	17	*18*	
	19	20	21	22	23	24	25	
	26	27	28	29	30	1	2	May
(2) Iyar	3	**4**	5	6	7	8	9	
	10	11	12	13	14	15	16	
	17	*18*	19	20	21	22	23	
	24	25	26	27	28	29	30	
(3) Sivan	31	1	**2**	3	4	5	6	June
	7	8	9	10	11	12	13	
	14	15	*16*	17	18	19	20	
	21	22	23	24	25	26	27	
(4) Tammuz	28	29	30	1	**2**	3	4	July
	5	6	7	8	9	10	11	
	12	13	14	15	*16*	17	18	

	19	20	21	22	23	24	25	
(5) Av	26	27	28	29	30	**31**	1	August
	2	3	4	5	6	7	8	
	9	10	11	12	13	*14*	15	
	16	17	18	19	20	21	22	
	23	24	25	26	27	28	29	
(6) Elul	**30**	31	1	2	3	4	5	September
	6	7	8	9	10	11	12	
	13	14	15	16	17	18	19	
	20	21	22	23	24	25	26	
(7) Tishri	27	**28**	29	30	1	2	3	October
	4	5	6	7	8	9	10	
	11	*12*	13	14	15	16	17	
	18	19	20	21	22	23	24	
(8) Heshvan	25	26	27	**28**	29	30	31	
	1	2	3	4	5	6	7	November
	8	9	10	*11*	12	13	14	
	15	16	17	18	19	20	21	
(9) Kislev	22	23	24	25	**26**	27	28	
	29	30	1	2	3	4	5	December
	6	7	8	9	*10*	11	12	
	13	14	15	16	17	18	19	
(10) Tebet	20	21	22	23	24	**25**	26	
	27	28	29	30	31			

Table VIII: Hebrew Lunisolar Calendar of 70 AD (The first day of each lunar month is indicated with **bold face**. The lunar month's name is on the left side.)

(10) Tebet		1	**2**	3	4	5	6	January
	7	8	9	10	11	12	13	
	14	15	*16*	17	18	19	20	
	21	22	23	24	25	26	27	
(11) Shebet	28	29	30	**31**	1	2	3	February
	4	5	6	7	8	9	10	
	11	12	13	*14*	15	16	17	
	18	19	20	21	22	23	24	
(12) Adar	25	26	27	28	1	**2**	3	March
	4	5	6	7	8	9	10	
	11	12	13	14	15	*16*	17	
	18	19	20	21	22	23	24	
(1) Nisan	25	26	27	28	29	30	**31**	
	1	2	3	4	5	6	7	April
	8	9	10	11	12	13	*14*	
	15	16	17	18	19	20	21	
	22	23	24	25	26	27	28	
(2) Iyar	29	**30**	1	2	3	4	5	May
	6	7	8	9	10	11	12	
	13	*14*	15	16	17	18	19	
	20	21	22	23	24	25	26	
(3) Sivan	27	28	**29**	30	31	1	2	June
	3	4	5	6	7	8	9	
	10	11	*12*	13	14	15	16	
	17	18	19	20	21	22	23	
(4) Tammuz	24	25	26	27	**28**	29	30	
	1	2	3	4	5	6	7	July
	8	9	10	11	*12*	13	14	
	15	16	17	18	19	20	21	
(5) Av	22	23	24	25	26	**27**	28	
	29	30	31	1	2	3	4	August
	5	6	7	8	9	*10*	11	
	12	13	14	15	16	17	18	

	19	20	21	22	23	24	25	
(6) Elul	**26**	27	28	29	30	31	1	September
	2	3	4	5	6	7	8	
	9	10	11	12	13	14	15	
	16	17	18	19	20	21	22	
(7) Tishri	23	**24**	25	26	27	28	29	
	30	1	2	3	4	5	6	October
	7	*8*	9	10	11	12	13	
	14	15	16	17	18	19	20	
(8) Heshvan	21	22	23	**24**	25	26	27	
	28	29	30	31	1	2	3	November
	4	5	6	*7*	8	9	10	
	11	12	13	14	15	16	17	
(9) Kislev	18	19	20	21	**22**	23	24	
	25	26	27	28	29	30	1	December
	2	3	4	5	*6*	7	8	
	9	10	11	12	13	14	15	
(10) Tebet	16	17	18	19	20	21	**22**	
	23	24	25	26	27	28	29	
	30	31						

If Yeshua prophesied the destruction of Jerusalem on 12 April 67 AD (the 9th day of the month Xanthicus or Nisan), exactly 42 lunar months after the prophecy should have been on **the 8th day of the month Gorpeius [the sixth month] (September 3) of 70 AD** or on the 9th day of the month Elul in the Hebrew calendar (see Table VII). This date can be easily figured out considering the fact that there was one embolismic year from 67 to 70 AD. It is also easy to check this by the Julian day numbers of the two dates. The Julian day number is JD 1745630 for 12 April 67 AD and JD 1746870 for 3 September 70 AD. Therefore, there are (1,746,870 − 1,745,630) days = 1,240 days = 42×29.524 days = 42 lunar months.

According to the prophecy of the mighty angel, Jerusalem should have been destroyed by the Gentles 42 months from the time of his prophecy. If this prophecy was fulfilled perfectly, Jerusalem should have been destroyed on **the eighth day of the month Gorpeius of 70 AD**. This is indeed the case. According to Josephus (*Wars*, bk. 6, ch. 10, sect. 1), "And thus was Jerusalem taken, in the second year of the reign of Vespasian [in 70 AD], **on the eighth day of the month Gorpeius.** It had been taken five times before though this was the second time of its desolation." Therefore, the prophecy of the mighty angel (Yeshua Messiah) was perfectly fulfilled.

The perfect fulfilment of this prophecy also pins down the exact time of John's writing of Revelation and the exact time of Yeshua's first return. His first return was on 12 April 67 AD (Sunday) and John wrote the book of Revelation. His first return in the spring of 67 AD perfectly fulfils the prophecy of Yeshua in Matthew 10:23: His return should have taken place before his disciples went through all the cities of Israel and before the end of Nero's severe persecution in 68 AD. Yeshua's first return in 67 AD was to prophesize and warn the pending judgment of God on His people.

His return in 67 AD also fulfilled another puzzling prophecy of Yeshua, which was recorded in the Gospel of John (John 21:21-23): "Peter, seeing him, said to Yeshua, 'But Lord, what about this man?' Yeshua said to him, 'If I will that he remains till I come, what is that to you? You follow me.' Then this saying went out among the brethren that this disciple would not die. Yet Yeshua did not say to him that he would not die, but, 'If I will that he remains till I come, what is that to you?'" This prophecy implies that John the Apostle should have been still alive at Yeshua's return, but Peter should have died. Yeshua's return in the spring of 67 AD made this prophecy perfectly fulfilled. **The fulfilment of this prophecy also proves that John the Apostle rather than John the Elder wrote the book of Revelation in the spring of 67 AD.**

His return in 67 AD also fulfilled one more puzzling prophecy of Yeshua, which was recorded in Matthew 16:28, "Assuredly, I say to you, there are **some** standing here who shall not taste death till they see the Son of Man coming in his kingdom (royal power)." Here, Greek word "βασιλεία" means "kingdom," "sovereignty," and "royal power." The best English translation of "βασιλεία" in this verse should be "royal power," because this verse is in parallel with Matthew 16:27, "For the Son of Man will come in the glory of his Father with his angels, and then he will reward each according to his works." Verse 27 talks about his final return in the glory of his Father to judge the whole world while verse 28 refs to his return in 67 AD in his royal power. In 67 AD, John, Jude, and Simon were still alive while all the other disciples of Yeshua were martyred (please see the martyrdom of the 12 disciples of Yeshua at http://www.about-jesus.org/martyrs.htm). This fact confirms the time of his return: when some of his disciples were still alive.

The perfect fulfilments of these three prophecies prove that **the Gospel of Matthew, Gospel of John, and the book of Revelation are the inspired words of God.** This also provides clear evidence for Yeshua being the true Prophet of God, as foretold by Moses in Deuteronomy 18:17-22.

Josephus also tells us (*Wars*, bk. 6, ch. 5, sect. 3):

> **At the same festival [Feast of Unleavened Bread] also, a heifer, as she was led by the high priest to be sacrificed, brought forth a lamb in the midst of the temple.** Moreover, the eastern gate of the inner [court of the] temple, which was of brass, and vastly heavy, and had been with difficulty shut by twenty men, and rested upon a basis armed with iron, and had bolts fastened very deep into the firm floor, which was there made of one entire stone, was seen to be opened of its own accord about the sixth hour of the night. Now those that kept watch in the temple came hereupon running to the captain of the temple, and told him of it; who then came up thither, and not without great difficulty was able to shut the gate again. This also appeared to the vulgar to be a very happy prodigy, as if God did thereby open them the gate of happiness. But the men of learning understood it, **that the security of their holy house was dissolved of its own accord, and that the gate was opened for the advantage of their enemies. So these publicly declared that the signal foreshowed the desolation that was coming upon them.** Besides these, a few days after that feast, on the one and twentieth day of the month Artemisius [the second month], a certain prodigious and incredible phenomenon appeared: I

suppose the account of it would seem to be a fable, were it not related by those that saw it, and were not the events that followed it of so considerable a nature as to deserve such signals; for, before sun-setting, chariots and troops of soldiers in their armor were seen running about among the clouds, and surrounding of cities. Moreover, **at that feast which we call Pentecost**, as the priests were going by night into the inner [court of the temple,] as their custom was, to perform their sacred ministrations, **they said that, in the first place, they felt a quaking, and heard a great noise, and after that they heard a sound as of a great multitude, saying, "Let us remove [the temple] hence."**

This passage implies that the temple should have been removed by the will of God and the Messiah. The word "us" in the last sentence in the above passage means at least two "Persons." Thus, it is very likely that "us" is referred to as God and the Messiah. The Messiah instructed John to measure the temple in the 9th of the first month (Nisan 9). During the Feast of Unleavened Bread (Nisan 15-21), two miraculous events happened: 1) a **heifer**, as she was led by the high priest to be sacrificed, brought forth a **lamb** in the midst of the temple; and 2) the gate of the temple was opened of its own accord and was unable to be closed anymore. On the 20th of the second month, before sunset, chariots and troops of soldiers in their armor were seen running about among the clouds and surrounding cities. On the Feast of Pentecost, the priests heard a sound as of a great multitude, saying, "Let us remove [the temple] hence." All these events suggest that God and the Messiah should have prepared to destroy the temple by opening the gate of the temple and removing the angelic protection right after the Messiah prophesized the destruction of Jerusalem. The account of Josephus indicates that the Messiah and God wanted to destroy the temple and Jerusalem by lifting up all the protections for the advantage of Jews' enemies, the Romans.

In 70 AD, Titus, the son of Emperor Vespasian besieged and captured Jerusalem, and destroyed the city and the temple. God and the

Messiah used the hands of Titus—the prince of the Roman Empire—to destroy the city and the temple. This fulfils the prophecy of Daniel 9:26, "… he [the Messiah] shall destroy the city and sanctuary with the prince who is to come." In Chapter 5, we have clearly shown that "he" in Daniel 9:26 is referred to as the Messiah.

CHAPTER

10

Jeremiah's Prophecy on 17 Shekels of Silver

Matthew 27:9-10 concludes the final story of Judas Iscariot with a quotation from the Hebrew Scripture showing how the events around his final days were predicted. In the New King James Version of the Bible it is translated as:

> [9]Then was fulfilled what was spoken by Jeremiah the prophet, saying, "And they took the thirty pieces of silver, the value of Him who was priced, whom they of the children of Israel priced, [10]and gave them for the potter's field, as Yehowah directed me."

These verses can be more literally translated as:

> [9]This fulfilled what was spoken by Jeremiah the prophet, saying, "And they took the thirty silver coins, the price of the (one) had been set, which had been set by the children of Israel, [10]and used them to buy the potter's field, as Yehowah directed me."

What Matthew means in these two verses is that the chief priests took the thirty silver coins to buy the potter's field, whose price had been set by the children of Israel in the time of Jeremiah the prophet.

In the book of Jeremiah, Jeremiah received the word from God about 17 shekels of silver, which was recorded in Jeremiah 32:6-15,

> [6]And Jeremiah said, "The word of Yehowah came to me, saying, [7]'Behold, Hanamel the son of Shallum your uncle will come to you, saying, "Buy my field which is in Anathoth, for the right of redemption is yours to buy it."' [8]Then Hanamel my uncle's son came to me in the court of the prison according to the word of Yehowah, and said to me, 'Please buy my field that is in Anathoth, which is in the country of Benjamin; for the right of inheritance is yours, and the redemption yours; buy it for yourself.' Then I knew that this was the word of Yehowah. [9]So I bought the field from Hanamel, the son of my uncle who was in Anathoth, and weighed out to him the money—**seventeen shekels of silver**. [10]And I signed the deed and sealed it, took witnesses, and weighed the money on the scales. [11]So I took the purchase deed, both that which was sealed according to the law and custom, and that which was open; [12]and I gave the purchase deed to Baruch the son of Neriah, son of Mahseiah, in the presence of Hanamel my uncle's son, and in the presence of the witnesses who signed the purchase deed, before all the Jews who sat in the court of the prison. [13]Then I charged Baruch before them, saying, [14]"Thus says the Lord of hosts, the God of Israel: "Take these deeds, both this purchase deed which is sealed and this deed which is open, and put them in an earthen vessel, that they may last many days." [15]For thus says the Lord of hosts, the God of Israel: "Houses and fields and vineyards shall be possessed again in this land."'

In this passage, the prophet tells us that he purchased a field in Anathoth from Hanamel, his uncle's son, with a price of **17 shekels of silver**. The purchase deed was sealed and kept in an earthen vessel that may have lasted for many days (verse 14). The houses, fields, and vineyards would be possessed again in this land by purchasing them according to the price of **17 shekels of silver** sealed in the original purchase deed.

Why did God instruct Jeremiah to keep the purchase deed for many days? This was because God had the foreknowledge that the chief priests in the time of the Messiah would purchase the potter's field with the price according to the original purchase deed. Since Anathoth is located about 3 miles north of Jerusalem, it is likely that the field Jeremiah purchased should have been the potter's field Matthew referred to.

What silver coins did the chief priests pay Judas Iscariot for his betrayal? According to the information in https://en.wikipedia.org/wiki/Shekel, it was customary among the Jews to annually offer a half-shekel coin to the temple treasury, for the upkeep and maintenance of the temple precincts and also on the purchase of public animal-offerings during the **second temple** period. This practice did not only apply to the Jews living in the **land of Israel**, but also to the Jews living outside the land of Israel. This information leads us to believe that the chief priests paid Judas half-shekel coins, which were offered by the Jews.

In 2008, a Judaea half-shekel coin was discovered in Horvat Ethry. The coin was minted in 67/68 AD and weighed 6.69 grams. It has "Half Shekel" imprinted in Hebrew, chalice with beaded rim, date above/ "Jerusalem is holy" in Hebrew, sprig of three pomegranates (see the page: https://en.wikipedia.org/wiki/File:JUDAEA_Half_Sheke.jpg).

What is the purity of a Judaea half-shekel coin? It was known that the Tyrian shekel coins were issued by the Tyrians between 126 BC and 56 AD. After the Roman Empire closed down the mint in Tyre, the Roman authorities allowed the Jewish Rabbani to continue minting Tyrian shekels in Palestine, but with the requirement that the coins should continue to bear the same image and text to avoid objections that the Jews were given autonomy. They were replaced by the First Jewish Revolt coinage in 66 AD. This information leads us to believe that the Judaea half-shekel coin should have the same purity as the Tyrian shekel coin, which contained about 94% of silver.

Since an ancient shekel was equal to 11 grams, one 6.69-gram Judaean half-shekel coin should have weighed 0.6082 ancient shekels.

Then 30 Judaean half-shekel coins weigh 18.245 ancient shekels. With 94% of silver in the coins, the 30 Judaean half-shekel coins should have contained 17.15 ancient shekels of silver, very close to 17 ancient shekels priced for the field in the time of Jeremiah. According to the information at https://en.wikipedia.org/wiki/Denarius, the Denarius coin between 64 and 68 AD contains 93.5% silver. Using this more accurate number for the purity, we find that the 30 Judaean half-shekel coins contain 17.06 ancient shekels of silver, in perfect agreement with the prophecy of Jeremiah.

Matthew was right about the perfect fulfilment of the prophecy of Jeremiah. However, Biblical scholars claim that the purchase of the potter's field was the fulfilment of a prophecy of Zechariah in Zechariah 11:12-13:

> [12]Then I said to them, "If it is agreeable to you, give me my wages; and if not, refrain." So they weighed out for my wages thirty pieces of silver. [13]And Yehowah said to me, "Throw it to the potter"— that princely price they set on me. So I took the thirty pieces of silver and threw them into the house of Yehowah for the potter.

Matthew usually quoted the Hebrew Bible liberally from the source materials. But the verses in Matthew 27:9-10 do not exactly match any Hebrew Bible text. The closest Hebrew Bible text is Zechariah 11:13. One immediate complication with this verse is that if it quotes Zechariah, why does the author attribute it to Jeremiah? This misattribution has been noted since the earliest days of Christianity, and a number of explanations have been given. Many scholars have accepted that this was simply a mistake on the part of the writer. Other arguments to preserve Biblical inerrancy are that Jeremiah was a shorthand to refer to any of the prophets. All these arguments are handwave and have no foundation.

Now we have proved that Matthew did not make a mistake in quoting the prophecy of Jeremiah. The correctness of Matthew concerning Jeremiah's prophecy further demonstrates that the author of the Gospel of Matthew was a true disciple of Yeshua, who was the true witness of Yeshua's ministry and recorded the words of Yeshua exactly. We have also shown that several other numerical prophecies of Yeshua recorded in the Gospel of Matthew were perfectly fulfilled in the events recorded in the Gospel of John and the book of Revelation. **All these facts prove that the Gospel of Matthew, the Gospel of John, and the book of Revelation are the inspired words of God.**

The Gospel of Matthew is the earliest Gospel written by Matthew, one of the twelve disciples of Yeshua, as demonstrated in the Acts of Barnabas. The book of the Acts of Barnabas tells us that Mark and Barnabas used the Gospel of Matthew to preach after they departed from Paul. If this book truly records the story of Barnabas, we may conclude that the Gospel of Mark was not the earliest Gospel but a short and modified version of the Gospel of Matthew.

We have found two accounts in the Gospel of Mark, which are inconsistent with those in the Gospels of Matthew and John. These inconsistencies are quite minor and may originate from later modifications made by some copyists.

CHAPTER
11

Canonicity of the Epistles of John

Authorship of the three epistles of John has been debated for about 2000 years although it is generally accepted that they all were written by the same author. Since epistles' content and conceptual style are very similar to those in the Gospel of John, all these four books should have been written by the same author. In the previous chapters, we have clearly demonstrated that the Gospel of John was written by John the Apostle. Accordingly, the author of the three epistles of John should also be John the Apostle.

At the end of the 19th century AD, Ernest DeWitt Burton wrote that there could be "no reasonable doubt" that the first epistle of John and the Gospel of John were written by the same author. Amos Wilder also said that "Early Christian tradition and the great majority of modern scholars have agreed on the common authorship of these writings, even where the author has not been identified with the apostle John."

However, other modern scholars have challenged this position. Holtzmann and Dodd have maintained that the epistles and the Gospel were written by different authors. At least two principal arguments support this view. The first is that the epistles often use a demonstrative pronoun at the beginning of a sentence, then a particle or conjunction, followed by an explanation or definition of the demonstrative at the end of the sentence, a stylistic technique which is not used in the Gospel. The second is that the author of the epistles uses the conditional sentence in a variety of rhetorical figures which are unknown to the Gospel.

The above arguments would lose foundation if the original language of these writings was not Greek, but Hebrew and/or Aramaic. In this case, the Greek translations of these writings could have different writing styles if translated by different persons. The detailed arguments for the Hebrew and Aramaic origin of these writings can be found in *Hebrew and Aramaic origin of the New Testament*.

Here we briefly summarize their arguments below (almost exactly copied from "Introduction" in *The Hebraic-Roots Version Scriptures*):

1. The language of Israel in the first century AD

   The Middle East, through all of its political turmoil, has in fact, been dominated by a single master from the earliest ages until the present day. The Semitic tongue has dominated the Middle East, from ancient times until the modern day. Aramaic dominated the three great Empires: Assyrian, Babylonian, and Persian. It endured until the seventh century, when under the Islamic nation it was displaced by a cognate Semitic language, Arabic. Even today some few Syrians, Assyrians, and Chaldeans, speak Aramaic as their native tongue, including three villages north of Damascus.

   The Jewish people, through all of their persecutions, sufferings, and wanderings, **have never lost sight of their Semitic heritage, nor their Semitic tongue. Hebrew, a Semitic tongue closely related to Aramaic, served as their language until the great dispersion** when a cognate language, Aramaic, began to replace it. Hebrew, however continued to be used for religious literature, and is today the spoken language in Israel.

   Some scholars have proposed that the Jews lost their Hebrew language, replacing it with Aramaic during the Babylonian captivity. The error of this position becomes obvious. The Jewish people had spent 400 years in captivity in Egypt, yet they did not stop speaking Hebrew and begin speaking Egyptian. Why should they exchange Hebrew for Aramaic, after only seventy years in Babylonian captivity?

Upon return from the Babylonian captivity, it was realized that a small minority could not speak "the language of Judah", so drastic measures were taken to abolish these marriages and maintain the purity of the Jewish people and language. One final evidence rests in the fact that the post-captivity books (Zechariah, Hag., Mal., Nehemiah, Ezra, and Ester) are written in Hebrew, rather than Aramaic.

Some scholars have also suggested that under the Helene Empire, Jews lost their Semitic language, and, in their rush to Hellenize, began speaking Greek. The books of the Maccabees do record an attempt by Antiochus Epiphanies, to forcibly Hellenize the Jewish people. In response, the Jews formed an army led by Judas Maccabee. This army defeated the Greeks and eradicated Hellenism. This military victory is still celebrated today as Chanukkah, the feast of the dedication of the Temple, a holiday that even Yeshua seems to have observed at the Temple at Jerusalem in the first century. Those who claim that the Jews were Hellenized and began speaking Greek at this time, seem to deny the historical fact of the Maccabean success.

During the first century, Hebrew remained the language of the Jews living in Judah, and to a lesser extent, in Galilee. Aramaic remained a secondary language and the language of commerce. Jews at this time did not speak Greek. In fact one tradition had it, that it was better to feed ones children swine, than to teach them the Greek language. It was only with the permission of authorities, that a young official could learn Greek, and then, solely for the purpose of political discourse on the National level. The Greek language was completely inaccessible, and undesirable, to the vast majority of Jews in Israel in the 1st century. Any gauge of Greek language outside of Israel cannot, nor can any evidence hundreds of years removed from the 1st century, alter the fact that **the Jews of Israel in the 1st century did not know Greek.**

The first century Jewish historian Flavius **Josephus (37-100 AD) testifies to the fact that Hebrew was the language of first century Jews.** Moreover, he testifies that Hebrew, and not Greek, was the language of his place and time. Josephus gives us the only first-hand account of the destruction of the Temple in 70 AD. According to Josephus, the Romans had to have him, translate the call to the Jews to surrender, into "their own language". Josephus gives us a point-blank statement regarding the language of his people during his time: "I have also taken a great deal of pains to obtain the learning of the Greeks, and to understand the elements of the Greek language. Although, I have so long accustomed myself to speak our own language, that I cannot pronounce Greek with sufficient exactness: for our nation, does not encourage those that learn the languages of many nations." Thus, **Josephus makes it clear, that first century Jews could not even speak or understand Greek, but spoke "their own language."**

Confirmation of Josephus's claims has been found by Archaeologists. The Bar Kokhba coins are one example. These coins were struck by Jews during the Bar Kokhba revolt (about 132 AD). All of these coins bear only Hebrew inscriptions. Countless other inscriptions, found at excavations of the Temple Mount, Masada, and various Jewish tombs, have revealed first century Hebrew inscriptions. Even more profound evidence that Hebrew was a living language during the first century, may be found in ancient Documents from about that time, which have been discovered in Israel. These include the Dead Sea Scrolls, and the Bar Kokhba letters.

The Dead Sea Scrolls consist of over 40,000 fragments of more than 500 scrolls dating from 250 BC to 70 AD. These Scrolls are primarily in Hebrew and Aramaic. A large number of the "secular scrolls" (those which are not Bible manuscripts) are in Hebrew. The Bar Kokhba letters are letters between Simon Bar Kokhba and his army, written during the Jewish revolt of 132 AD. These letters were discovered by Yigdale Yadin in 1961 and are almost all written in Hebrew and Aramaic. Two of the letters are written in Greek; both were written by men with Greek names, to Bar Kokhba. One of the two Greek letters, actually apologizes for writing to Bar Kokhba in Greek, saying, "the letter is written in Greek, as we have no one who knows Hebrew here."

The Dead Sea Scrolls and the Bar Kokhba letters, not only include first and second century Hebrew documents, but give even more significant evidence in the dialect of that Hebrew. The dialect of these documents was not the Biblical Hebrew of the Tenach (Old Testament), nor was it the Mishnaic Hebrew of the Mishna (about 220 AD). The Hebrew of these documents is colloquial; it is a fluid living language in a state of flux, somewhere in the evolutionary process, from Biblical to Mishnaic Hebrew. Moreover, the Hebrew of the Bar Kokhba letters, represent Galilean Hebrew (Bar Kokhba was a Galilean), while the Dead Sea Scrolls give us an example of Judean Hebrew. Comparing the documents, shows a living distinction of geographic dialect as well, a sure sign that Hebrew was not a dead language.

2. The scholars on the language of the New Testament

A number of noted scholars have argued, that at least portions of the New Testament were originally penned in a Semitic tongue. This argument has been asserted of the four Gospels, Acts, and Revelation.

3. Testimony of the church fathers

All of the church's fathers, both East and West testified to the Semitic origin of at least the book of Matthew. For example, Jerome (382 AD) testified:

Matthew, who is also Levi, and from a tax collector came to be an emissary; first of all evangelists, composed a Gospel of Messiah in Judea, in the Hebrew language and letters, for the benefit of those of the circumcision who had believed, who translated it into Greek, is not sufficiently ascertained. Furthermore, the Hebrew itself is preserved to this day in the library at Caesarea, which the martyr Pamphilus, so diligently collected. I also, was allowed by the Nazarenes who use this volume in the Syrian city of Borea, to copy it. In which is to be remarked that, wherever the evangelist makes use of the testimonies of the Old Scripture, he does not ... follow the authority of the seventy translators [the Greek Septuagint], but that of the Hebrew.

Pantaenus found that Bartholomew, one of the twelve emissaries, had there [India] preached the advent of our Lord Yeshua the Messiah according to the Gospel of Matthew, which was written in Hebrew letters, and which, on returning to Alexandria, he brought with him.

Having established the fact that the Gospel of John and the book of Revelation were originally written in Hebrew and/or Aramaic language, the different Greek writing styles of the two books do not disprove the same authorship of the two books. If these epistles of John were all written by the apostle John, they should be included in the canon of the New Testament.

PART

II

UNPROVED CANONICITY OF SOME NEW TESTAMENT BOOKS

CHAPTER

12

Noncanonicity of Some New-Testament Books

In Part I, we have shown that the three books: Matthew, John, and Revelation are the inspired words of God by demonstrating the perfect fulfilments of all the numerical prophecies by Yeshua himself and the Old-Testament prophets. These books are proved to be written by the direct disciples of Yeshua (see Chapter 9) and do not contradict each other. For these reasons, they should be included in the canon of the New Testament. Any writing that plainly contradicts the writings of these three books should not be included in the canon.

In Part II, we show that, relative to the three books canonized in Part I, there are some **irreputable** errors in the Gospel of Luke, the book of Acts, and in the second epistle of "Peter" (Peter II). If the contradictions or errors in a New-Testament book are **plain and irrefutable**, one should not blindly and rigidly maintain the infallibility of the book. Because of the irreputable errors in Luke's books and because Luke was not a direct disciple of Yeshua, the Gospel of Luke and the book of Acts should not be treated as the inspired words of God. At most, they could be used as less authoritative historical books provided that the author of the books was honest and had no bias. Because of the irreputable error in the second epistle of "Peter" and because the apparent author of "Peter" has not been clearly proved to be the true Peter—Yeshua's direct disciple, Peter II should not be included in the canon of the New Testament.

Since Paul called himself an apostle of Yeshua for 22 times in his epistles. Only in the book of Acts, was Paul referred to as apostle of Yeshua by Luke, his own disciple and friend. Just as a friend would not be qualified to serve as jury, Luke would not be a reliable witness for Paul's apostleship. Moreover, since Luke was not an apostle of Yeshua, his testimony in his book was not authoritative enough unless the book of Acts were infallible words of God. Since Paul's apostleship has not been proved by any reliable witness, why should mainstream Christians consider all his 14 epistles to be the inspired words of God?

Any book that has not been proved unambiguously to be authored by one of Yeshua's twelve disciples should not be in the canon. According to John 15:27, only Yeshua's direct disciples who were with him from the beginning shall bear witness for his words and deeds. The criterion for selecting Yeshua's witnesses (or his twelve apostles) in Acts 1:21 is in agreement with Yeshua's words in John 15:27. Matthias who replaced Judas the Betrayer to become one of the twelve apostles should have been with Yeshua from the beginning. When the risen Yeshua appeared to his eleven disciples, Matthias should have been present although he had not been listed as an apostle yet according to Luke. Since John in Revelation 21:14 mentioned the names of the twelve apostles, Judas the Betrayer must have been replaced by someone who walked with Yeshua from the beginning. Luke's account of the replacement, which is not found in the Gospels, is unprovable but could be true.

Paul himself confirmed that he **was not** one of the twelves (1 Corinthians 15: 3-8). He claimed himself as the least of the apostles (1 Corinthians 15: 9). According to Paul's own testimony, he was not qualified to serve as a witness for Yeshua's words and deeds because he had never walked with Yeshua in the flesh. Therefore, Paul was not qualified to replace Judas the Betrayer to become one of the twelves. His own words also testified that he was not one of the twelves. Since his name was not in one of the twelve foundations of the wall of the new Jerusalem according to Revelation 21:14, how would the Roman Catholic bishops have placed Paul's 14 epistles in the canon of the New Testament? Having accepted that the book of Revelation is the inspired words of God, how would modern Protestants still keep all the 14 Pauline epistles in the canon of the New Testament? The contradictions between Paul's epistles and the book of Revelation are plain and irreputable. That is why Martin Luther made an attempt to remove the books of Hebrews, James, Jude, and Revelation from the canon (see the page: https://en.wikipedia.org/wiki/Luther%27s_canon). He perceived them to go against certain protestant doctrines. Although his followers did not remove these books, they ordered them last in the German Luther Bible because the books were thought to be less authoritative.

In the following chapters, we will show that Luke recorded the stories he directly witnessed himself and some other stories he leaned indirectly. The errors in Luke's accounts should have originated from the errors of his indirect sources and from Paul's influence.

CHAPTER

13

Luke's Error on Appearances of the Risen Yeshua

The story of Yeshua after his resurrection was recorded in all of the four Gospels. In the previous chapters, we have shown that the Gospels of Matthew and John are truly inspired words of God. If anything in another Gospel is unambiguously shown to contradict what was recorded in these two canonized Gospels, it should be in error.

Matthew records Yeshua's words in Matthew 26:31-32, "All of you will be made to stumble because of me this night, for it is written: 'I will strike the shepherd, and the sheep of the flock will be scattered.' But after I have been raised, I will go before you to **Galilee**." Yeshua clearly told his disciples that God would strike the shepherd (Yeshua), and the sheep (Yeshua's disciples) of the flock would be scattered. He also said that after he would be raised, he would go to **Galilee** before his disciples. Since Yeshua predicted that his disciples would go back to their homes (Galilee) after he would be handled into the Jews and be killed, he told his disciples in advance that he would first go to **Galilee** to meet them after his resurrection.

John the Apostle also records Yeshua's prediction in John 16:31-32, "Do you now believe? Indeed the hour is coming, yes, has now come, that you will be scattered, each to his own [home], and will leave me alone. And yet I am not alone, because the Father is with me." Many other versions of English translation like NIV, ESV, BSB, NASB, CSB, CEV, GNT, HCSB, ISV, NB, NAS1997, and WNT add "home" after "his own." Some other versions add "place" instead of "home." According to John, Yeshua's disciples were scattered to their own homes in Galilee after he was handled into the Jews, in agreement with Matthew's account.

Matthew 28:16-17 says that Yeshua appeared to his eleven disciples in **Galilee** after his resurrection. The first meeting should have been several days after Yeshua's resurrection because it took at least four days for his disciples to travel from Jerusalem back to Galilee on foot.

In contrast, Luke's account of Yeshua's post-resurrection story in Luke 24:1,13-36 differs from the accounts of both Matthew and John.

Luke 24:1 says that the women went to the tomb of Yeshua in the early morning of Sunday. Then in the later afternoon of the same Sunday (Luke 24:13,29), Cleopas and another believer traveled to a village called Emmaus, which was seven miles from **Jerusalem** (Luke 24:13). Yeshua appeared to them when they were talking about the things which had happened (Luke 24:14-15). When Yeshua asked them, what things had happened in Jerusalem in these days (Luke 24:19), they said to him, "The things concerning Yeshua of Nazareth, who was a Prophet mighty in deed and word before God and all the people, and how the chief priests and our rulers delivered him to be condemned to death, and crucified him. But we were hoping that it was he who was going to redeem Israel. Indeed, besides all this, **today is the third day since these things happened**." (Luke 24:19-21). When the evening was approaching (Luke 24:29), they arrived in the village and Yeshua sat at the table with them, took bread, blessed and broke it, and gave it to them (Luke 24:30). After Yeshua left, the two believers immediately left the village for **Jerusalem** to see the eleven disciples there (Luke 24:33). The eleven disciples assembled in **Jerusalem** and said that the resurrected Yeshua had appeared to Simon Peter (Luke 24:34). When they said these things, Yeshua appeared to the eleven disciples (Luke 24:36).

Luke clearly tells us that Yeshua appeared to his eleven disciples in the evening of the same Sunday of his resurrection (i.e., in the beginning part of Monday) and that **the place of the meeting was in Jerusalem**. The place of Yeshua's post-resurrection appearance plainly contradicts the accounts of both Matthew and John who consistently said that

Yeshua's disciples would go to **their own homes in Galilee** after he would be delivered to the Jews for crucifixion (Matthew 26:31-32, 28:10; John 16:31-32). Here, Luke records that these disciples **stayed in Jerusalem** and Yeshua appeared to them about 12 hours after his resurrection. Matthew clearly records that these disciples indeed went to **Galilee** and Yeshua appeared to them in **Galilee** (Matthew 28:16-17).

If Yeshua's disciples had not gone to Galilee but stayed in Jerusalem, Yeshua's own prophecy would not have been fulfilled. This would make Yeshua a false prophet and a liar.

Both Matthew and Mark record that only Peter and John remained in Jerusalem to witness Yeshua's crucifixion while other disciples went away (Matthew 26:31; Mark 14:27). John also records that after Peter and John left the tomb, they also went back to their own place (John 20:10). John then says that in the evening of the first day of the week, Yeshua first appeared to the ten disciples (John 20:19,24). This was not the evening of the same Sunday when Yeshua rose because Peter and John had not arrived in Galilee yet (it took at least four days for them to walk from Jerusalem to Galilee). Some English translations suggest the first post-resurrection appearance would have happened in the same Sunday of Yeshua's resurrection while the original text simply means the evening of a Sunday. The third appearance to the disciples was recorded in John 21:1-23. John specifically stated that this was the third time Yeshua showed to his disciple after he rose (John 21:14). The last appearance was recorded in Matthew 28:18-20, when he gave a great commission to his disciples to preach the gospel to all the nations.

John 20:19-20 and John 20:21-23 recorded two separate appearances, as seen from Yeshua's two independent salutations of "Shalom" to his disciples, which should have occurred at the beginning of each meeting. The second appearance in John 20:21-23 may have been the last appearance although **this** text was placed before the third **noted** appearance in John 21:14. This is because Chapter 21 in the Gospel of John may be supplementary to the main text, which was possibly written later.

The most critical false testimony in the Gospel of Luke is that Yeshua first appeared to his disciples in Jerusalem while all other three

Gospels consistently show that he first appeared to his disciples in Galilee.

Luke (Luke 24:45-46) testified that Yeshua rose again the third day **according to the Scriptures**. Nowhere in the Old Testament prophesized that the Messiah would rise again the third day. It is Yeshua himself who prophesized that he would rise again the third day. If the Scriptures in the Old Testament had already prophesized this, why should Yeshua have prophesized this again and again? Yeshua's own prophecy about his resurrection proves that the Old-Testament Scriptures had never prophesized the time of his resurrection.

If we believe in the accounts of both Matthew and John, we have to say that Luke's account of the place and time of Yeshua's first post-resurrection appearance is in error.

CHAPTER

14

Luke's Error on the Time of Yeshua's Resurrection

In the previous chapter, we have proved that Luke's story about Yeshua's resurrection contradicts those of other three Gospels. Luke tells us that Yeshua appeared to his eleven disciples at Jerusalem about half a day after he rose in a Sunday morning. All other Gospels consistently show that Yeshua appeared to the women during the early part of Sunday (the evening of Saturday) at Jerusalem, and then appeared to the eleven disciples at Galilee in the following Saturday night, which was foretold by Yeshua before he was delivered to the Jews for crucifixion.

In Luke 24:1, Luke tells us that the women went to the tomb of Yeshua in the early morning of Sunday. They brought their prepared spices to anoint Yeshua. This must have been the women's first trip to the tomb because during this trip they found the stone rolled away from the tomb (Luke 24:3) for the first time. Then they went in and did not find the body of Yeshua (Luke 24:4). Luke used a unique Greek word "orthros" to describe the time when the women went to the tomb. Greek word "orthros" originates from the word "oros" meaning "rise" and "hill." Therefore, the meaning of the Greek word "orthros" is "early morning," the time when the sun starts to rise. Therefore, Luke plainly tells us that the women went to the tomb in the early morning of Sunday to anoint Yeshua.

Most Christians believe that Yeshua resurrected in the early morning of Sunday (the first day of the week) possibly because of this account of

Luke, which is very clear and makes other interpretations impossible. Since they believe that the Gospel of Luke is the Word of God and that Luke's account is most definitive, they simply accept the Sunday morning to be the time of Yeshua's resurrection.

Based solely on Luke's account, Yeshua resurrected in the early morning of Sunday. This conclusion contradicts the consistent accounts of Matthew and John. In Chapter 7, we have clearly shown that Yeshua resurrected around sunset of Saturday according to the accounts of Matthew, John, and Mark. Therefore, Luke's account of Yeshua's resurrection time should also be in error.

CHAPTER
15

Luke's Error on the Year of Yeshua's Crucifixion

Luke records that John the Baptist started his ministry in the 15th year of Tiberius Caesar in Luke 3:1-3,

> [1]Now in the fifteenth year of the reign of Tiberius Caesar, Pontius Pilate being governor of Judea, Herod being tetrarch of Galilee, his brother Philip tetrarch of Iturea and the region of Trachonitis, and Lysanias tetrarch of Abilene, [2]while Annas and Caiaphas were high priests, the word of God came to John the son of Zacharias in the wilderness. [3]And he went into all the region around the Jordan, preaching a baptism of repentance for the remission of sins.

When was the first year of Tiberius? Werner Eck (*Age of Augustus*, page 119-120, Blackwell publishing, 2003) wrote about the reign of Tiberius:

> Then 13 AD he celebrated his second triumph. In addition, emissaries from foreign kings were required to pay their respects to Tiberius, an unmistakable indicator of his status. And finally in the same year, 13 AD, Tiberius received an imperium equal to Augustus' own. It empowered him to act in every province, where he

could also command the troops. By this time, Tiberius was doubtless aware that Augustus had named him as his chief heir in his will, dated April 13, 13 AD. In the event of the princeps' death, the legal transfer of power had been arranged. It was also time for Augustus to put the finishing touches on the account of his deeds that had long been in preparation. Between June and August 14 AD he made the last changes in the text. Despite all the setbacks that had occurred, he could look back on a complete and fulfilled life.

This passage suggests that Tiberius may have co-reigned with Augustus in 13 AD after Augustus made his will on 13 April 13 AD. If this were the case, 13 AD may have been the ascension year of Tiberius.

If Luke had been inspired by God, he would have used the anniversary reckon method commonly used by the Old-Testament writers. Then the 15th year of Tiberius would have been from 13 April 27 AD to 12 April 28 AD (started from the time of his supposed co-regency).

If this were true, John the Baptist would have started his ministry after 13 April 27 AD. Since Yeshua started his ministry much later than John the Baptist—after John was put in prison (Luke 3:20), he would have been baptized much later than 13 April 27 AD. This contradicts the account of John in his Gospel, which unambiguously shows that Yeshua was baptized on or before 24 February 27 AD (see Chapter 3).

If Luke counted the regnal years like Roman historians, the 15th year of Tiberius should have been from 18 September 28 AD to 17 September 29 AD. If John the Baptist had started his ministry in the spring of 29 AD, Yeshua would have begun his ministry in the fall of 29 AD. If Yeshua's ministry had lasted for 3.5 years, he would have been crucified in the spring of 33 AD.

This crucifixion date of 33 AD is purely based on Luke's account and has been generally accepted for about 2,000 years. But we know that Yeshua was crucified in the spring of 30 AD, as proved by the Gospel of John and the timeline of Herod (see Chapters 2 and 3).

Therefore, if we believe in the account of John and Daniel's prophecy in Daniel 9:25 (see Chapter 4), we have to say that Luke's account of the year of Yeshua's crucifixion should be in error.

16

Other Errors in the Gospel of Luke

In the previous chapters, we have shown that Luke mistakenly accounted for the place and time of Yeshua's first post-resurrection appearance to his eleven disciples, the time of his resurrection, and the year of his crucifixion. In addition to these errors, there are several other errors, which will be addressed below.

Errors in Luke 2:1-4

In Luke 2:1-4, Luke makes errors on the original dwelling place of Joseph and on the census in the time of Yeshua's birth:

> And it came to pass in those days that a decree went out from Caesar Augustus that all the world should be registered. This census first took place while Quirinius was governing Syria. So all went to be registered, everyone to his own city. Joseph also went up from Galilee, **out of the city of Nazareth**, into Judea, to the city of David, which is called Bethlehem, because he was of the house and lineage of David,...

These verses tell us that Joseph originally dwelt in the city of Nazareth and went up to Bethlehem to be registered during the first census that took place when Quirinius was governing Syria. In contrast, Joseph should have originally lived in Bethlehem where Yeshua was born, as implied from Matthew 2:20-23 (Hebrew Gospel of Matthew by George Howard):

> [20]saying: Arise, take the boy and his mother and go to the land of Israel, because those who were seeking to kill the boy are dead. [21]So he arose, took the boy and his mother, and they **returned** to the land of Israel. [22]Then he heard that Horcanus, his name is Archelaus, reigned in Judah in the place of Herod his father, and he feared to go there. So the angel urged him in a dream that he should turn unto the land of Galilee. [23]He came and dwelt in **a city** called Nazareth, **in order to fulfil** what the prophet said: He shall be called a Nazarene.

Verse 23 implies that Joseph should not have lived in Nazareth before Yeshua was born in Bethlehem. If Joseph had originally dwelt in Nazareth, Matthew would not have written: He came and dwelt in **a city** called Nazareth. Here "**a city**" conveys an idea that Joseph had not lived in Nazareth before. In addition, Nazareth should have been Joseph's new dwelling place **in order to fulfil** the prophecy: He [Yeshua] shall be called a Nazarene. Therefore, the logical conclusion of Matthew 2:20-23 is that Joseph originally dwelt in Bethlehem and Yeshua was born there to naturally fulfil the prophecy of Micah 5:2. After they came back from Egypt, they were directed by the angel to dwell in Nazareth in order to fulfil the prophecy: He shall be called a Nazarene. If we believe the account of Matthew, we conclude that Luke's account of Joseph's original dwelling place should be in error.

Richard Carrier says that Luke flatly contradicts Matthew (https://infidels.org/library/modern/richard_carrier/quirinius. html#Conclusion):

> There is no way to rescue the Gospels of Matthew and Luke from contradicting each other on this one point of historical fact. The contradiction is **plain and irrefutable,** and stands as proof of the fallibility of the

Bible, as well as the falsehood of at least one of the two New Testament accounts of the birth of Jesus.

Although Richard Carrier is an atheist, his conclusion about the infallibility of the New-Testament books is based on solid evidence and very careful and thorough investigations. He is more honest than many Biblical apologists who try to defend the infallibility of some Biblical books with shaky and unreliable evidences.

In addition, Luke 2:1-2 has received serious criticisms from Biblical critics. These verses tell us that Caesar Augustus issued a decree for all of the [Roman] world to be registered during the time of Yeshua's nativity and that this census first happened when Quirinius was governing Syria. The Romans normally kept detailed records of such events, but Luke's census, if different from the one recorded by Josephus and the Romans, was not in their records. Moreover, Josephus provided detailed account of Herod's story near the end of his life and of the census that took place when Quirinius was governing Syria. Josephus would have mentioned another important Roman-world census near the end of Herod's life if such a census had occurred.

Quirinius started to govern Syria in the 36th year of Caesar Augustus counted from the Battle of Actium (2 September 31 BC) according to the coins issued by Quirinius (see the webpage at https://en.wikipedia.org/wiki/Quirinius). This implies that the earliest date for the starting of the census should have been on 2 September 5 AD. In other words, the earliest birth date of Yeshua would have been on 2 September 5 AD.

On the other hand, if Luke had referred to another independent census taking place in the days of Herod the Great and when Quirinius was governing Syria, Luke should have been in error for the following reasons:

1. When Augustus issued this degree, Judea was not part of the Roman province, but was a client kingdom ruled by Herod the Great. It would therefore not have been part of any Roman census.

2. Quirinius was the governor of Syria from 5/6 to 12 AD, and not during the reign of Herod the Great (before 4 BC). The

governor of Syria was Sentius Saturninus from 9 to 6/7 BC and Quinctilius Varus from 6/7 to 4 BC.

3. There is no Roman record that requires people to return to their ancestral homes.

4. There would have been no need for Joseph to take Mary with him; registration was by the male head of the house only.

5. Any reasonable person would not have taken such a risk to let Mary travel from Nazareth to Bethlehem for more than 4 days when she was on the verge of labour.

On the other hand, many Biblical scholars have attempted to defend this error because they believe that the Gospel of Luke is inerrant. There are three main arguments to defend Luke's accuracy below and we offer counter arguments:

1. Three inscriptions: the Lapis Tiburtinus; the Lapis Venetus; and the Antioch Stones supposedly show that Quirinius was governor of Syria for two distinct periods. In fact, they don't really demonstrate any such thing. We know who the governors of Syria were at that time. In addition, no single person in the Roman Empire served two independent terms of governor in the same province. It is more unlikely that the same person served two independent terms of governor and conducted two independent censuses in the same province during two separated periods, and only one of them was recorded by the historians.

2. Luke 2:2 could be translated as: "This was the census before Quirinius was governor of Syria." or "This registration became most prominent when Quirinius was governing Syria." Both translations have been rejected by Greek language experts. "This census first happened when Quirinius was governing Syria" is the only contextually plausible reading of Luke's Greek. Any other interpretation has convicted Luke of being a talentless and unintelligible author.

3. Since Luke mentioned another census in Acts 5:37, he would have known two independent censuses. However, Luke only recorded Gamaliel's words in Acts 5:35-39. It is Gamliel who

mentioned the census that led to the formation of the Zealot party. The census mentioned by Gamliel should have been the same one recorded by Josephus. It is possible that Luke simply recorded Gamaliel's words without knowing whether or not the census mentioned by Gamaliel was the same as the one he knew.

A straightforward interpretation is that the census in Luke 2:1-2 is the same as the one recorded by Josephus. Therefore, Luke 2:1-2 implies that Yeshua would have been born in 5/6 AD, which was about 10 year difference from his true birth date on 9 March 5 BC (see Chapter 31).

The timeline of Yeshua based solely on Luke's own accounts is self-consistent. According to Luke, Yeshua started to preach the kingdom of God after John the Baptist was in prison (Luke 3:19-23), which was over one year before Yeshua's crucifixion (see Chapter 3). The latest year for Yeshua's crucifixion would have been in 36 AD, the last year of Pilate. So the latest year for Yeshua to start his preaching would have been in 34/35 AD. Since Yeshua was born in 5/6 AD according to Luke, he would have lived for about 29 years when he had started his preaching in 34/35 AD. This is consistent with Luke's direct statement: He began [to be filled with the Holy Spirit] when he was about 30 years old (Luke 3:23).

In ancient times and even in modern China, the age is calculated according to how many new years that have passed from birth. If Yeshua had been born on 2 September 5 AD, which was 20 days from Tishri 1 (September 22), the Jewish new year, he would have been 2 years old on 22 September 5 AD. He would have been 28 years old on 6 September (1 Tishri) 31 AD.

To be consistent with all the accounts of Luke, 33 AD is the only year for Yeshua's crucifixion. Luke 24:21 says that the Sunday afternoon after Yeshua's resurrection was the third day since "these things" happened. These things should have included Yeshua's crucifixion and burial as well as rolling a stone against the door of the tomb. Although Luke did not write down the event of rolling the stone, he should have collected this information. The burial was finished at sunset of the preparation day (Luke 23:54) and rolling the stone should have been finished shortly after sunset (in the beginning part of the next day). According to the day counting method in the time of Yeshua (see Chapter 7), "the third day" from Thursday is the time towards the end of Sunday. The time for Yeshua's appearance to the two believers was indeed toward the end of Sunday (Luke 24:28-29). Therefore, according to Luke's accounts, Yeshua should have been crucified on Wednesday and also on Nisan 14 (the 14th day of the first Hebrew lunar month). In Chapter 7, we have shown that Nisan 14 in 30 AD was on Wednesday and only this year was consistent with the Gospels of both Matthew and John.

From Table IX, we see that Nisan 14 in 33 AD was also on Wednesday. Only this year was consistent with Luke 3:1, which indicates that John the Baptist would have started his ministry in the fifteenth year of Tiberius (between 18 September 28 AD and 17 September 29 AD). Since there were over three years between the beginning of John's ministry and Yeshua's crucifixion, the year of 30 AD for Yeshua's crucifixion contradicts Luke 3:1. To be consistent with all the accounts of Luke, Yeshua would have started his ministry after the fall of 31 AD at the age of 28 years old (or about 30 years old according to Luke 3:23) and be crucified in 33 AD. If this were the case, John the Baptist would have been born in the days of Herod Archelaus (Luke 1:5) rather than Herod the Great. If Yeshua was born in the days of Herod the Great, as recorded by Matthew, he would have been at least 36 years old in the fall of 31 AD, which contradicts Luke 3:23. Therefore, Luke's accounts are self-consistent, but not perfectly accurate compared to the accounts of both Matthew and John. The less accurate accounts of Luke may be due to the fact that he himself did not directly witness Yeshua's nativity, which had taken place about 100 years before he wrote the story.

When Luke wrote the nativity story of Yeshua, he should have collected the following information: 1) John and Yeshua were born in the days of Herod and their birth dates were separated by 6 months; 2) Elizabeth conceived John right after her Husband Zacharias—who was a priest in the division of Abijah—finished his service; 3) Yeshua started his preaching after John was put in prison and when he was about 30 years old; and 4) Yeshua was born in Bethlehem and grew up in Nazareth. But Luke may have missed clear information about which Herod was referred to. So he believed that this Herod would have been Herod Archelaus. Since Luke was an excellent historian and intelligent, the nativity story he wrote must be self-consistent and does not contradict the Roman history and the information he collected.

Table IX: Hebrew Lunisolar Calendar of 33 AD (The first day of each lunar month is indicated with **bold face**. The lunar month's name is on the left side.)

					1	2	3	January
	4	5	6	7	8	9	10	
	11	12	13	14	15	16	17	
(11) Shebet	18	**19**	20	21	22	23	24	
	25	26	27	28	29	30	31	
	1	**2**	3	4	5	6	7	February
	8	9	10	11	12	13	14	
(12) Adar	15	16	17	**18**	19	20	21	
	22	23	24	25	26	27	28	
	1	2	3	**4**	5	6	7	March
	8	9	10	11	12	13	14	
(1) Nisan	15	16	17	18	**19**	20	21	
	21	22	23	24	25	26	27	
	29	30	31	1	**2**	3	4	April
	5	6	7	8	9	10	11	
(2) Iyar	12	13	14	15	16	17	**18**	
	19	20	21	22	23	24	25	
	26	27	28	29	30	1	**2**	May
	3	4	5	6	7	8	9	
	10	11	12	13	14	15	16	
(3) Sivan	**17**	18	19	20	21	22	23	
	24	25	26	27	28	29	30	
	31	1	2	3	4	5	6	June
	7	8	9	10	11	12	13	
(4) Tammuz	14	15	**16**	17	18	19	20	
	21	22	23	24	25	26	27	

	28	29	**30**	1	2	3	4	July
	5	6	7	8	9	10	11	
(5) Av	12	13	14	**15**	16	17	18	
	19	20	21	22	23	24	25	
	26	27	28	**29**	30	31	1	August
	2	3	4	5	6	7	8	
(6) Elul	9	10	11	12	13	**14**	15	
	16	17	18	19	20	21	22	
	23	24	25	26	27	**28**	29	
	30	31	1	2	3	4	5	September
(7) Tishri	6	7	8	9	10	11	**12**	
	13	14	15	16	17	18	19	
	20	21	22	23	24	25	**26**	
	27	28	29	30	1	2	3	October
	4	5	6	7	8	9	10	
(8) Heshvan	11	**12**	13	14	15	16	17	
	18	19	20	21	22	23	24	
	25	**26**	27	28	29	30	31	
	1	2	3	4	5	6	7	November
(9) Kislev	8	9	10	**11**	12	13	14	
	15	16	17	18	19	20	21	
	22	23	24	**25**	26	27	28	
	29	30	1	2	3	4	5	December
(10) Tebet	6	7	8	9	**10**	11	12	
	13	14	15	16	17	18	19	
	20	21	22	23	**24**	25	26	
	27	28	29	30	31			

Error in Luke 23:39-43

Luke records a very famous story about the two criminals who were crucified together with Yeshua in Luke 23:39-43:

⁴⁰Then one of the [two] criminals who were hung blasphemed him, saying, "If you are the Messiah, save yourself and us." But the other, answering, rebuked him, saying, "Do you not even fear God, seeing you are under the same condemnation? ⁴¹And we indeed justly, for we receive the due reward of our deeds; but this man has done nothing wrong." ⁴²Then he said to Yeshua, "Lord, remember me when you come into your kingdom." ⁴³And Yeshua said to him, "Assuredly, I say to you, today you will be with me in Paradise."

This story of Luke contradicts Matthew's and Mark's. Matthew clearly tells us that both criminals reviled Yeshua in Matthew 27:44, **"Even the robbers who were** crucified with him reviled him with the same thing." Mark also said so in Mark 15:32,

> "Let the Messiah, the King of Israel, descend now from the cross, that we may see and believe." **Even those who** were crucified with him reviled him.

In John 19:18, John records that there were **two criminals** who were crucified with Yeshua, one on either side and Yeshua in the center. John did not record the words of the two criminals. Luke also recorded that there were two criminals who were crucified with Yeshua (Luke 23:32). The four Gospels agree on the number (two) of the criminals who were crucified with Yeshua. However, the words of one of the criminals recorded by Luke were completely different from those recorded by both Matthew and Mark.

Luke's account has promoted a theology that a man is saved by faith only, which is in perfect alignment with Pauline Christianity in Romans 10:9-10,

> that if you confess with your mouth the Lord Yeshua and believe in your heart that God has raised him from the dead, you will be saved. For with the heart

one **believes unto righteousness**, and with the mouth confession is made unto salvation.

According to Luke's account, one of the criminals confessed that Yeshua was his Lord, so Yeshua brought him into Paradise. Paul's theology would be in perfect agreement with Yeshua's teachings if Luke's account were reliable.

Therefore, if we believe the accounts of both Matthew and Mark, we have to say that Luke's account of the two criminals should be in error.

CHAPTER
17

Errors in the Book of Acts

In the previous four chapters, we have found some irrefutable errors in the Gospel of Luke. Here we will address some errors in the book of Acts.

Errors in Stephen's quoting the Hebrew Scriptures

Luke recorded Stephen's preaching in Chapter 7 of the book of Acts. There are two errors in Stephen's quoting the Hebrew Scriptures in Acts 7:14-16,

> [14]Then Joseph sent and called his father Jacob and all his relatives to him, **seventy-five** people.[15]So Jacob went down to Egypt; and he died, he and our fathers.[16]And they were carried back to Shechem and laid in the tomb that **Abraham bought** for a sum of money from the sons of Hamor, the father of Shechem.

Acts 7:14 contradicts Genesis 46:27 (Masoretic text), "And the sons of Joseph who were born to him in Egypt were two persons. All the persons of the house of Jacob who went to Egypt were **seventy**." The Masoretic text of Exodus 1:5 also states that there were **seventy**. But these verses in the Septuagint text (Greek translation of the Old Testament) say that there were **seventy-five**, not seventy. In the book: *Perfectly Fulfilled Prophecies and the Destiny of Mankind*, the author shows that the Biblical chronology based on the Masoretic text of the Old Testament has no error. This fact provides strong evidence that the Masoretic text is the most accurate Old Testament. In contrast, the Biblical chronology based on the Septuagint text has an error of over two hundred years. This fact suggests that the Septuagint text should be quite unreliable in particular concerning the numbers. If Stephen had been filled by the Holy Spirit, he would not have made any mistake in quoting the words of God. Quoting the unreliable number in the Septuagint text suggests that Stephen might not have been filled with the Holy Spirit or that Luke may have mistakenly recorded Stephen's words.

Acts 7:16 contradicts Genesis 33:18-20,

> [18]Then Jacob came safely to the city of Shechem, which is in the land of Canaan, when he came from Padan Aram; and he pitched his tent before the city. [19]And he bought the parcel of land, where he had pitched his tent, from the children of Hamor, Shechem's father, for one hundred pieces of money. [20]Then he erected an altar there and called it El Elohe Israel.

Genesis 33:19 clearly tells us that it was Jacob who bought the parcel of land from the children of Hamor, Shechem's father, which is in contradiction with Acts 7:16 which says that Abraham bought it for a sum of money from the sons of Hamor, the father of Shechem. Abraham didn't buy anything in Shechem but the cave of Machpelah (Genesis 23:17).

Two errors in Paul's quoting the Hebrew Scriptures

Luke records the preaching of Paul in Chapter 13 of the book of Acts. There are two errors in quoting the Hebrew Scriptures in Acts 13:20-21,

> [20]After that He gave them judges **for about four hundred and fifty [450] years**, until Samuel the prophet. [21]And afterward they asked for a king; so God gave them Saul

the son of Kish, a man of the tribe of Benjamin, **for forty years**.

According to verse 20, the judges ruled over Israel for about 450 years. This contradicts 1 Kings 6:1, which says, "And it came to pass in the four hundred and eightieth year after the children of Israel were come out of the land of Egypt, in the fourth year of Solomon's reign over Israel, in the month Zif, which is the second month, that he began to build the house of Yehowah." We know that 480 years elapsed between the time when the Israelites came out of Egypt and the time when King Solomon began to build the holy temple.

According to Josephus, the Israelites wandered in the wilderness for 40 years, conquered and divided the land of Canaan for 30 years, were led by King Saul for 20 years (*Antiq.*, bk. 6, 378), by King David for 40 years, and by King Solomon for 4 years before he began to build the temple. Adding all the numbers above yields 134 years. The total length of the judge's reign is calculated to be 346 years by subtracting 134 years from 480 years. Paul's number of 450 years is about 100 years off from the correct number of 346 years. If Paul had been filled with the Holy Spirit, he would have known the total ruling length of the judges.

How did Paul get the length of 450 years? Paul might have gotten the number from the teaching of Pharisees in his time because Josephus a Pharisee stated: "Solomon began to build the temple in the fourth year of his reign, on the second month, which the Macedonians call *Artemisius*, and the Hebrews *Jur*, five hundred and ninety-two (592) years after the exodus out of Egypt." (*Antiq.* bk. 13, 61). Then the total ruling length of the judges is calculated to be 458 years by subtracting 134 years from 592 years. The calculated length of 458 years is indeed close to 450 years, which Paul quoted. But the number of 592 years is incorrect, as shown in *Perfectly Fulfilled Prophecies and the Destiny of Mankind*.

Paul also stated that King Saul reigned for 40 years. We will prove that Saul is unlikely to have reigned for 40 years. Subtracting 154 (134 +20) years from 480 years yields 326 years. This means that the total ruling length of all the judges would have been 326 years if King Saul had reigned for 40 years.

Now we shall check whether Paul's number is compatible with the Scriptures or not. Judges 11:15-27 says,

> [15]"Thus says Jephthah: 'Israel did not take away the land of Moab, nor the land of the people of Ammon; [16]for when Israel came up from Egypt, they walked through the wilderness as far as the Red Sea and came to Kadesh. [17]Then Israel sent messengers to the king of Edom, saying, "Please let me pass through your land." But the king of Edom would not heed. And in like manner they sent to the king of Moab, but he would not consent. So Israel remained in Kadesh. [18]And they went along through the wilderness and bypassed the land of Edom and the land of Moab, came to the east side of the land of Moab, and encamped on the other side of the Arnon. But they did not enter the border of Moab, for the Arnon was the border of Moab. [19]Then Israel sent messengers to Sihon king of the Amorites, king of Heshbon; and Israel said to him, "Please let us pass through your land into our place." [20]But Sihon did not trust Israel to pass through his territory. So Sihon gathered all his people together, encamped in Jahaz, and fought against Israel. [21]And the Lord God of Israel delivered Sihon and all his people into the hand of Israel, and they defeated them. Thus Israel gained possession of all the land of the Amorites, who inhabited that country. [22]They took possession of all the territory of the Amorites, from the Arnon to the Jabbok and from the wilderness to the Jordan. [23]And now the Lord God of Israel has dispossessed the Amorites from before His people Israel; should you then possess it? [24]Will you not possess whatever Chemosh your god gives you to possess? So whatever the Lord our God takes possession of before us, we will possess. [25]And now, are you any better than Balak the son of Zippor, king of Moab? Did he ever strive against Israel? Did

he ever fight against them? **²⁶While Israel dwelt in Heshbon and its villages, in Aroer and its villages, and in all the cities along the banks of the Arnon, for three hundred years, why did you not recover them within that time?** ²⁷Therefore I have not sinned against you, but you wronged me by fighting against me. May the Lord, the Judge, render judgment this day between the children of Israel and the people of Ammon.'"

When Jephthah started to reign over Israel, he sent the messengers to the king of Ammon and said that **Israel had dwelt in Heshbon for three hundred [300] years**. Forty years after coming out of Egypt, the Israelites took Heshbon and spent 30 years on conquering and dividing the land of Canaan before the judges started to rule. Therefore, at the time when Jephthah started to reign, the judges had reigned for 270 years (300 years −30 years).

Judges 12:7-15 further tells us:

> And Jephthah judged Israel **six years**. Then Jephthah the Gileadite died and was buried in among the cities of Gilead. After him, Ibzan of Bethlehem judged Israel. He had thirty sons. And he gave away thirty daughters in marriage, and brought in thirty daughters from elsewhere for his sons. He judged Israel **seven years**. Then Ibzan died and was buried at Bethlehem. After him, Elon the Zebulunite judged Israel. He judged Israel **ten years**. And Elon the Zebulunite died and was buried at Aijalon in the country of Zebulun. After him, Abdon the son of Hillel the Pirathonite judged Israel. He had forty sons and thirty grandsons, who rode on seventy young donkeys. He judged Israel **eight years**. Then Abdon the son of Hillel the Pirathonite died and was buried in Pirathon in the land of Ephraim, in the mountains of the Amalekites.

These verses imply that from the beginning of Jephthah's reign to the end of Abdon's reign, there are 6 years + 7 years + 10 years + 8 years = 31 years. Thus, after Abdon ended his reign, the judges had reigned for 301 years (270 years + 31 years). If King Saul had reigned for 40 years, then the other judges after Abdon would have reigned for 25 years (326 years − 301 years). As seen below, this is incompatible with the Scriptures!

Josephus said that King Saul reigned for 20 years (*Antiq.* bk. 6, ch.14, sect. 9). Since Saul reigned for 20 years, then other judges after Abdon should have reigned for 45 years. As seen below, this is indeed compatible with the Scriptures!

Now we read Judges 13:1, "Again the children of Israel did evil in the sight of Yehowah, and Yehowah delivered them into the hand of the Philistines for **forty years**." This verse is crucial to the construction of the timeline of the judge's period (see Figure 3). This verse tells us that the end of the 40-year period after Abdon was the time when God raised Samuel to deliver all the house of Israel from the Philistines.

About 21 years before God's deliverance, the Philistines attacked Israel and took the ark of Yehowah (1 Samuel 5:1). The ark of Yehowah was in the hands of the Philistines for 7 months (1 Samuel 5:1). Then, "the men of Kirjath Jearim came and took the ark of Yehowah, and brought it into the house of Abinadab on the hill, and consecrated Eleazar his son to keep the ark of Yehowah." (1 Samuel 7:1). "So it was that the ark remained in Kirjath Jearim a long time; it was there **twenty years**, and all the house of Israel lamented after Yehowah." (1 Samuel 7:2). God raised Samuel to deliver the Israelites from the Philistines about 21 years after the Philistines took the ark of God and after Eli died.

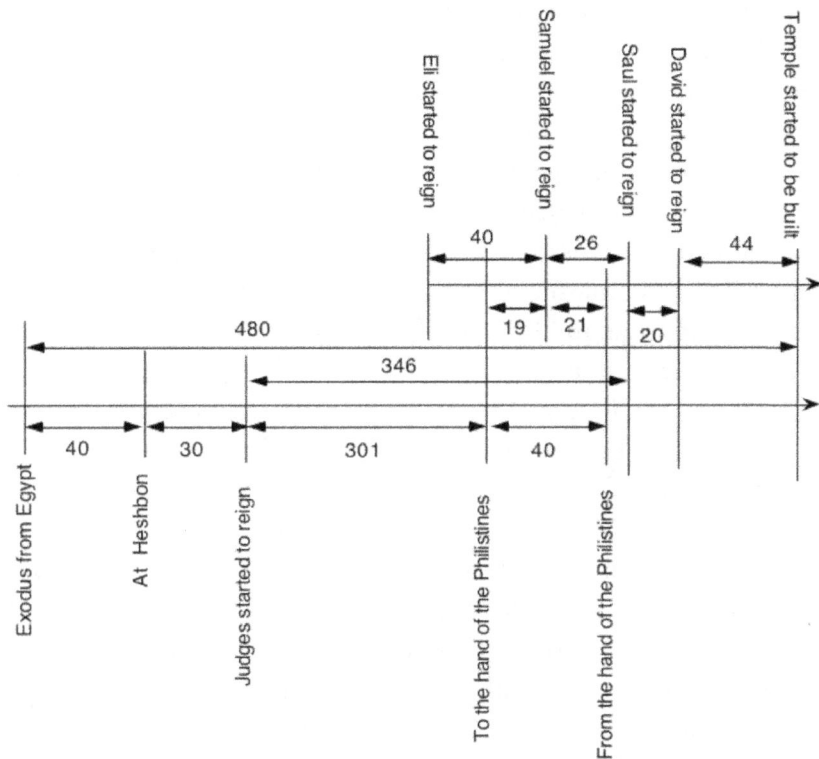

Figure 3: Schematic diagram for the events before the construction of the temple started.

Because Samuel started to reign over Israel after Eli died, he had reigned for 21 years at the time of God's deliverance. At this time, all the judges together had reigned for 341 years (301 years + 40 years). Thus, the total ruling length of all the judges should have been at least 341 years.

As shown above, if Saul had reigned for 40 years, all the judges together would have reigned for 326 years (<341 years), which is impossible. In contrast, since Saul reigned for 20 years, as recorded by Josephus, all the judges together should have reigned for 346 years (>341 years), which is possible. In this case, Samuel should have reigned for an additional 5 years before Saul started his reign. This means that Samuel should have reigned for 26 years over Israel as a judge and prophet.

If Samuel started his reign at the age of 30, he was 56 years old when Saul began to reign. The age of 56 was considered to **be old** at that time, in agreement with the statement of 1 Samuel 8:1, "Now it came to pass when Samuel **was old** he made his sons judges over Israel." Samuel died after Saul had reigned for 18 years (*Antiq.* bk. 6, ch.14, sect. 9), so his lifespan was about 74 years, which is also reasonable.

1 Samuel 13:1-2 says (ASV), "Saul was forty years old when he began to reign; and when he had reigned two years over Israel, Saul chose him three thousand men of Israel whereof two thousand were with Saul in Michmash and in the mount of Beth-el, and **a thousand were with Jonathan in Gibeah of Benjamin**: and the rest of the people he sent every man to his tent."

After Saul had reigned **two years** over Israel, Jonathan the son of Saul should have been at least 21 years old to be qualified as a soldier and army leader. If Jonathan was 24 years old and his younger brother Ishbosheth was 22 years old at that time, then Ishbosheth was 20 years old when Saul started to reign. Since Saul reigned for 20 years, Ishbosheth was 40 years old when Saul died. This is consistent with 2 Samuel 2:10, "Ishbosheth, Saul's son, was **forty years old** when he began to reign over Israel [after Saul died], and he reigned two years. Only the house of Judah followed David." Therefore, Josephus' number for Saul's regnal length of 20 years agrees with the Old-Testament Scriptures while Paul's number is incompatible with the Scriptures.

If Saul begot children at the age of 18, he should have started his reign at the age of about 40 and died at the age of about 60. All these numbers are quite reasonable. If Saul had reigned for 40 years, he would have died at the age of about 80. Then right before Saul and Jonathan were killed, they would not have been like eagles and lions, as King David praised them in his lamentation (2 Samuel 1:23).

Therefore, the errors of Stephen's and Paul's quoting the Hebrew Scriptures indicate that both Stephen and Paul were not filled with the Holy Spirit or that Luke mistakenly recorded their words.

CHAPTER

18

Error in the Second Epistle of "Peter"

The second epistle of "Peter" (Peter II) has been included in the canon of the New Testament. If this book were indeed written by Peter, one of the twelve disciples of Yeshua, there should be no problem with the canonicity of the book. Since its authorship has not been unambiguously proved, it should not be included in the canon of the New Testament.

In order to confirm the authenticity of Peter's authorship for Peter II, it must be proven to have been written prior to Peter's death in about 65-67 AD. Since the letter endorses the Pauline epistles to be as authoritative as the Hebrew Scriptures (2 Peter 3:15), it is impossible for the letter to have been written before 67 AD. Most Biblical scholars agree that the time a New-Testament writer would have referred to another New-Testament writing should have been after 100-150 AD. This implies that this letter should have been written in the second century AD. Thus, Peter the Apostle could not have been the author of Peter II.

Since the book of Revelation has been unambiguously proved to be an inspired book of God (see Chapter 9), anything that disagrees with the teachings in the book of Revelation could not have originated from God, nor from any of Yeshua's twelve disciples. Yeshua must have taught his disciples consistently when he was with them from the beginning. If the disciples were inspired by the same Holy Spirit, they must have had the same doctrine.

The book of Revelation tells us that when Yeshua comes back in the last days he will first establish the millennial kingdom on the earth before the old heavens and earth are completely destroyed (Revelation 20:5-15, 21:1-3). The teaching in Chapter 3 of Peter II contradicts the clear teaching in the book of Revelation. 2 Peter 3:4-13 says:

> [4]and saying, "Where is the promise of His coming? For since the fathers fell asleep, all things continue as they were from the beginning of creation." [5]For this they willfully forget: that by the word of God the heavens were of old, and the earth standing out of water and in the water, [6]by which the world that then existed perished, being flooded with water. [7]But the heavens and the earth which are now preserved by the same word, are reserved for fire until the day of judgment and perdition of ungodly men. [8]But, beloved, do not forget this one thing, that with the Lord one day is as a thousand years, and a thousand years as one day. [9]The Lord is not slack concerning His promise, as some count slackness, but is longsuffering toward us, not willing that any should perish but that all should come to repentance. **[10]But the day of the Lord will come as a thief in the night, in which the heavens will pass away with a great noise, and the elements will melt with fervent heat; both the earth and the works that are in it will be burned up.** [11]Therefore, since all these things will **be dissolved,** what manner of persons ought you to be in holy conduct and godliness, [12]looking for and hastening the coming of the day of God, because of which **the heavens will be dissolved, being on fire, and the elements will melt with fervent heat?** [13]**Nevertheless we, according to His promise, look for new heavens and a new earth in which righteousness dwells.**

This passage tells us (verse 10) that when Yeshua comes as a thief in the night, the heavens will pass away with a great noise, and the elements will melt with fervent heat; both the earth and the works in it will be **burned up.** Verse 12 further says that the heavens will **be dissolved,** being on fire, and the elements will melt with fervent heat. Verse 13 talks about a new heaven and a new earth in which righteousness dwells. In other words, in the days of Yeshua's final return, God will destroy the old heavens and the old earth, and then create a new heaven and a new earth in which the righteous men will dwell.

Therefore, Peter II could not have been written by the true Peter. This is because the doctrine of Peter II about the end times is inconsistent with the teachings in the book of Revelation.

PART

III

PAUL'S APOSTLESHIP
AND DOCTRINE

.

CHAPTER

19

Paul's Apostleship

Paul himself claimed to be an apostle of Yeshua in his 13 epistles except in the epistle to the Hebrews, the author of which was traditionally attributed to Paul. According to the books of Acts, Paul was committed to persecuting the early disciples of Yeshua in the region of Jerusalem before his conversion. When Paul was traveling on the road from Jerusalem to Damascus to arrest Yeshua's believers, the resurrected "Yeshua" supposedly appeared to him. He was blinded by a light from heaven, but after three days his sight was restored by Ananias of Damascus, and he began to preach about the "Messiah." Almost half of the book of Acts records Paul's life and missionary works.

Since Christians believe that the book of Acts is an inspired book of God, they simply believe the story in the book and Luke's claim of apostleship for Paul. Having accepted Paul's apostleship, they naturally believe that his 14 epistles in the New Testament must have been inspired by God.

How do we prove that Paul's own claim of apostleship is true? According to the law, "Whoever is deserving of death shall be put to death on the testimony of two or three witnesses; he shall not be put to death on the testimony of one witness." (Deuteronomy 17:6). Yeshua also said (Matthew 18:15-16), "Moreover if your brother sins against you, go and tell him his fault between you and him alone. If he hears you, you have gained your brother. But if he will not hear, take with you one or two more, that 'by the mouth of two or three witnesses every word may be established.'"

Both Moses and Yeshua have the same teaching concerning the number of witnesses to make a case. Just as a friend would not be qualified to serve as jury, Luke could not be a witness for Paul's apostleship because he was Paul's disciple and friend. Any person mentioned in the book of Acts could not serve as a witness either. Paul's own testimony could not be used to prove his apostleship. In the second epistle of Peter, Peter only called Paul a beloved brother while called himself an apostle of Yeshua. If Peter had endorsed Paul's apostleship, he would not likely have just called Paul a brother while he called himself an apostle of Yeshua. On the other hand, in Chapter 18 we have shown that Peter II was not written by Peter the Apostle. Thus, Peter II could not be used to prove the canonicity of Paul's writings.

Only if the book of Acts were an inspired book of God, could it be used to prove the authenticity of Paul's apostleship. However, we have shown that both the Gospel of Luke and the book of Acts contain serious errors when compared with **the three canonized books: Matthew, John, and Revelation**. Some accounts in Luke's books are also inconsistent with the Old-Testament Scriptures. Moreover, Luke was not a direct disciple of Yeshua and his two books were written over 50 years after Yeshua's crucifixion. Therefore, there is no reliable witness for Paul's apostleship.

Paul used the signs, wonders, and mighty deeds he performed to prove his apostleship (2 Corinthians 12:12). This proof is not tenable either. Yeshua foretold that false prophets would show great signs and wonders to deceive, if possible, even the elect (Matthew 24:24). Yeshua also said (Matthew 7:22-23), "Many will say to me in that day, 'Lord, Lord, have we not prophesied in your name, cast out demons in your name, and done many wonders in your name?' And then I will declare to them, 'I never knew you; depart from me, you who practice lawlessness!'" Yeshua's teaching is consistent with Moses' in Deuteronomy 13:1-5. Both Yeshua and Moses tell us that the signs, wonders, and mighty deeds cannot be used to prove the authenticity of a prophet or an apostle.

In the following chapters of Part III, we will compare Paul's doctrine with the teachings of Yeshua and his disciples. We will also compare Paul's teachings with the Old-Testament Scriptures. From these comparisons, readers can make their own judgment on whether Paul's teachings are inspired by God.

20

Teachings of Yeshua or His Disciples vs Paul

In this chapter, we summarize the teachings of Yeshua and his disciples vs those of Paul, as shown in Table X.

Table X: Teachings of Yeshua and his Disciples vs Those of Paul

Teachings of Yeshua and his disciples	Paul's teachings
1. Jesus said to him, "'You shall love the Lord your God with all your heart, with all your soul, and with all your mind.' This is *the* first and great commandment. And *the* second *is* like it: 'You shall love your neighbor as yourself.' On these two commandments hang all the Law and the Prophets. (Matthew 22:37-40):	1. For **all the law** is fulfilled in **one** word (commandment), even in this: "You shall love your neighbor as yourself." (Galatians 5:14).
2. If you want to enter life, keep the commandants. (Matthew 19:17). Till heaven and earth pass away, one jot or one tittle will by no means pass from the law till all is fulfilled. (Matthew 5:18).	2. Man is justified by faith apart from the deeds of the law. (Romans 4:28). For with the heart one believes unto righteousness, and with the mouth confession is made unto salvation. (Romans 10:10). For all who rely on works of the law are **under a curse.** (Galatians 3:10).

Whoever therefore **breaks** one of **the least** of these commandments, and teaches men so, shall be called **least** in the kingdom of heaven. (Matthew 5:19). All the things that cause to sin and those who **practice lawlessness** will be cast into the furnace of fire at the end of the age. (Matthew 13:41-42). He who **practices righteousness** is righteous, just as Yeshua is righteous. (1 John 3:7). But he who looks into the **perfect law of liberty** and continues in it, and is not a forgetful hearer but a doer of the work, this one will **be bl**essed in what he does. (James 1:25).	Messiah has redeemed us from **the curse of the law**, having become a curse for us. (Galatians 3:13). But now after you have known God, or rather are known by God, how is it that you turn again to the **weak and beggarly** elements, to which you desire again to be **in bondage?** (Galatians 4:9). For on the one hand there is an **annulling** of the former commandment because of its **weakness and unprofitableness, for the law made nothing perfect**; on the other hand, there is the bringing in of a better hope, through which we draw near to God. (Hebrews 7:18-19). But if **the ministry of death, written and engraved on stones [the law of God ministered by Moses]**, was glorious, so that the children of Israel could not look steadily at the face of Moses because of the glory of his countenance, which glory **was passing away**, how will the ministry of the Spirit not be **more glorious?** (2 Corinthians 3:7-8).
3. Yeshua teaches that he comes to fulfill **the law of God** (Matthew 5:11), which hangs on the two commandments of God.	3. Paul teaches that the good deeds of believers fulfill **all the law,** which hangs on the second commandment of God (Galatians 6:2).
4. "Do not call anyone on earth your [spiritual] father, because you have **one Father,** who is in heaven. And do not be called [spiritual] teachers; for **One is your Teacher, the Messiah**. But he who is greatest among you shall be your servant." (Matthew 23:9-10).	4. For though you might have **ten thousand instructors [teachers] in Messiah,** yet you do not have many fathers; for in Messiah Yeshua, **I have begotten you (become your father)** through the gospel. (1 Corinthians 4:15).

Yeshua has never forbidden to call someone one's natural father (Matthew 15:4-5, 19:19).	My children, for whom **I am again in the pains of childbirth** until Messiah is formed in you. (Galatians 4:19). I appeal to you for my son Onesimus, whom **I have begotten** while in my chains. (Philemon 1:10).
5. Yeshua rebukes two of his churches for eating foods sacrificed to idols. But I have a few things against you, because you have there those who hold the doctrine of Balaam, who taught Balak to put a stumbling block before the children of Israel, to eat things sacrificed to idols, and to commit sexual immorality. (Revelation 2:14). Nevertheless I have a few things against you, because you allow that woman Jezebel, who calls herself a prophetess, to teach and seduce My servants to commit sexual immorality and eat things sacrificed to idols. (Revelation 2:20).	5. Paul teaches that believers have a liberty to eat foods sacrificed to idols. According to 1 Corinthians 8:4-13, 10:19-33, Paul teaches (see the interpretations of these verses by his disciples at https://www.revelation.co/2015/07/10/bible-say-meat-sacrificed-to-idols/): Physical idols are really nothing but carved pieces of wood or metal, not some "god" as the pagans believed, and there is really only one true God. Therefore, meat sacrificed to them and then resold is not in any way tainted with evil. Meat is meat, and we need food to live. Therefore, if a person strolls through a meat market, they shouldn't stress about whether the meat had previously been used in some silly idol worship festival. Although a believer does not sin by eating food or meat sacrificed to idols, if it makes a fellow believer more likely to engage in pagan festival feasts, or violate his or her conscience, it then becomes a sin.
6. Yeshua tells us that his eleven disciples who were with him on earth from the beginning will be his witnesses (John 15: 27) and those who believe in him through their word belong to the same fold of sheep and are one in the Father and the Son.	6. Paul claims that only his gospel is true and that anyone (including angels from heaven and twelve apostles) preaching a different gospel from his is accursed (Galatians 1:8-9).

7. John the Apostle declares that only the teachings of the twelve disciples are from God, as seen from 1 John 4:6, "We are of God. He who knows God hears us; he who is not of God does not hear us. By this we know the spirit of truth and the spirit of error."	7. Paul claims that he received his gospel directly from the risen "Messiah" by spiritual revelation, so he does not need to be taught by nor consult with the twelve apostles of Yeshua (Galatians 1:12,17; 2:6).
8. John tells us in Revelation 21:14, "Now the wall of the city [New Jerusalem] had twelve foundations, and on them were the names of the twelve apostles of the Lamb.	8. Paul claims that he is a wise master builder and has laid the foundation, as seen from 1 Corinthians 3:10, "According to the grace of God which was given to me, as a wise master builder I have laid the foundation, and another builds on it. But let each one take heed how he builds on it." Paul admitted that he **was not** one of the twelve apostles of Yeshua (1 Corinthians 15:5-8).
9. John teaches that the body of Yeshua is the temple of God (John 2:21). John also teaches that the Lord Almighty and the Lamb are the temple of the New Jerusalem (Revelation 21:22).	9. Paul teaches that believers are the temples of [God]. Do you not know that you are the temple of God and that the Spirit of God dwells in you? (1 Corinthians 3:16).
10. Yeshua commands his eleven disciples to preach the gospel to all the nations (Matthew 28:19).	10. Paul says that the risen Yeshua commanded him to preach the gospel to the Gentiles and Peter to the Jews (Galatians 2:7-8). Paul's statement even contradicts the account of Luke (Paul's own disciple) in Acts 15:7, "And when there had been much dispute, Peter rose up and said to them: 'Men and brethren, you know that a good while ago God chose among us, that **by my mouth the Gentiles should hear the word of the gospel and believe.**"

11. Yeshua teaches us that the Holy Spirit is the Spirit of Truth, who proceeds from **the Father** (John 15:16). Yeshua also tells his disciples that it is not they who speak, but **the Spirit of your Father** speaking through them (Matthew 10:20). And I looked, and behold, in the midst of the throne and of the four living creatures, and in the midst of the elders, stood a Lamb as though it had been slain, having seven horns and seven eyes, which are the **seven Spirits of God** sent out into all the earth. (Revelation 5:6).	11. Paul teaches that there are two Spirits: The Spirit of the Father and the Spirit of the Son (the Spirit of Messiah). And because you are sons, God has sent **the Spirit of his Son** into our hearts, crying, "Abba! Father!" (Galatians 4:6). You, however, are not in the flesh but in the Spirit, if indeed **the Spirit of God** dwells in you. Anyone who does not have **the Spirit of Messiah** does not belong to him. (Romans 8:9).
12. Yeshua teaches that he is not God and that his Father is greater than him. So he said to him, "Why do you call me good? No one is good but One, that is, God. But if you want to enter into life, keep the commandments." (Matthew 19:17). You have heard me say to you, 'I am going away and coming back to you.' If you loved me, you would rejoice because I said, 'I am going to the Father,' for **my Father is greater than I.** (John 14:28). Yeshua said to her, "Do not cling to me, for I have not yet ascended to my Father; but go to my brethren and say to them, 'I am ascending to my Father and your Father, and to **my God and your God.'"** (John 20:17). [Even the risen Messiah is not God]	12. Paul teaches that the Messiah is the Son of God and equal to God. but has in due time manifested his word through preaching, which was committed to me according to the commandment of **God our Savior**; To Titus, a true son in our common faith: Grace, mercy, and peace from God the Father and **the Lord Jesus Christ our Savior.** (Titus 1:3-4). Looking for the blessed hope and glorious appearance of our great **God and Savior Yeshua Messiah.** (Titus 2:13). Who, being in very nature God, did not consider **equality with God** something to be used to his own advantage. (Philippians 2:6). You, however, are not in the flesh but in the Spirit, if indeed **the Spirit of God** dwells in you. Anyone who does not have **the Spirit of Messiah** does not belong to him. (Romans 8:9). [Messiah is equal to God]

He who overcomes, I will make him a pillar in the temple of **my God**, and he shall go out no more. I will write on him the name of **my God** and the name of the city of **my God**, the New Jerusalem, which comes down out of heaven from **my God**. And I will write on him my new name. (Revelation 3:12). [Even in heaven, Yeshua calls his father his God]	To those not having the [Mosaic] law I became like one not having the [Mosaic] law (though I am not free from **God's law** but am under **Messiah's law**), so as to win those not having the [Mosaic] law. (1 Corinthians 9:21). [God's law is equal to Messiah's law, but different from the Mosaic law]
13. John teaches that the true believers know the Messiah, keep his commandments and word, and walk just as he walked. Now by this we know that we know him, if we keep his commandments. He who says, "I know him," and does not keep his commandments, is a liar, and the truth is not in him. But whoever keeps his word, truly the love of God is perfected in him. By this we know that we are in him. He who says he abides in him ought himself also to walk just as he [Yeshua] walked. (1 John 2:3-6). **Whoever commits sin also commits lawlessness, and sin is lawlessness**. And you know that he was manifested to take away our sins, and in him there is no sin. Whoever abides in him does not sin. Whoever sins has neither seen him nor known him. (1 John 3:4-6).	13. Paul teaches his disciples to walk in the Spirit. The one who is walking in the Spirit is not subject to the law of Moses. All the law is hung on the second commandant of God (Galatians 5:14) rather than on both the first and second commandments of God.

14. Yeshua teaches that the law of Moses is the law of God, which will never pass away till heaven and earth pass away (Matthew 5:17-19; 22:37-40).	14. Paul teaches two laws: the Mosaic law and the law of Messiah (the law of the Spirit). He also claims that the Mosaic law, including the Ten Commandments engraved on the stone, brought curse, bondage, and death, and was abolished while the new law of Messiah is the true law of God (the law of the Spirit), which the believers must obey. (Galatians 3:10,13; 4:9,24-25; Hebrews 7:18-19; 2 Corinthians 3:7-8, 1 Corinthians 9:21; Colossians 2:14).

CHAPTER

21

Two Gospels and Two Laws

In the previous chapter, we have listed Paul's teachings vs those of Yeshua and his disciples. Paul claimed that there was a gospel different from his (Galatians 1:6) and that anyone who preached a gospel other than his was accursed. From the contents of Galatians and Acts, we can see that the fundamental difference between Paul's gospel and the other gospel is related to a question as to whether Yeshua's believers ought to keep the Mosaic law of God. Here, we call Paul's gospel "the grace-only gospel," and the other gospel "the Judaism-like gospel." In the grace-only gospel, there are two laws of God while in the Judaism-like gospel, there is only one law of God (the Mosaic law of God). Paul teaches that the Mosaic law of God was transitory, weak, and even brought curse, bondage, and death. Only the law of "Messiah" (or the spiritual law) invented by Paul would be everlasting and bring life. Before the Pauline law of Messiah came, the the Mosaic law of God had served as a tutor (Galatians 3:25). Thus, Christians would be only subject to the the Pauline law of Messiah and not under the Mosaic law of God . Because Paul did not clearly specify the two different laws in most parts of his writings, most Christians have not recognized Paul's lawless teachings: the Mosaic law of God was abolished by Yeshua who was crucified to redeem those who were under the curse of the Mosaic law. Only by the grace of God, would we be justified by the faith only. Paul says, "Do we then make void the law through the faith? Certainly not! On the contrary, we establish the law." (Romans 3:31). The law Paul refers to in Romans 3:31 cannot be the Mosaic law of God because he himself did not keep the Mosaic law of God but the Pauline law of the "Messiah" (1 Corinthians 9:21). Paul did not uphold the Mosaic law of God that comprises all the commandments of God including the first and great commandment Yeshua mentioned in Matthew 22:37. The Pauline law of the "Messiah" does not include the first and great commandment of God (Galatians 5:14). Paul introduces "the law of Messiah" in 1 Corinthians 9:21 and "the law of the Spirit" in Romans 8:2. Paul teaches that the law of the Spirit has made him free from the [Mosaic] law of sin and death and that he is only subject to the law of Messiah. In contrast, Yeshua teaches that all the law and prophets are hung on the first and the second commandments (Matthew 22:35-40). If "the law of Messiah" were from the true Messiah, why would it be so different from the law of God Yeshua and Moses teach? Below we will compare in detail the two gospels and the two laws.

Two gospels

In Paul's epistles, Paul calls his gospel as "my gospel," and mentions another gospel that was different from his. Paul specifically mentions Yeshua's believers in Jerusalem, led by James and the apostles (Galatians 2:12). This church was established by the twelve apostles of Yeshua and the believers were required to observe the Mosaic law of God—including circumcision of the flesh. In Paul's gospel, a man is justified (or saved) by faith only and the believers are not subject to the Mosaic law of God.

The doctrine of the Judaism-like gospel can be consistently found in the Gospel of Matthew, the Gospel of John, the epistles of John, the epistle of James, as well as in the book of Revelation. The first epistle of John provides a very clear doctrine of this gospel. The other books of Yeshua's disciples also support it.

The Judaism-like gospel comes directly from the twelve apostles of Yeshua who heard, saw, and handled the word of life (Yeshua Messiah) from the beginning (1 John 1:1). They directly saw the life of the Messiah, bore witness of him, and declared to the world that eternal life was with the Father, manifested by His Son Yeshua Messiah (1 John 1:2-4). This message is consistent with John 15:27; 17:20 and Matthew 28:19.

The message of the Judaism-like gospel is as follows:

1. If anyone sins, we have an Advocate with the Father, Yeshua Messiah the righteous. And he himself is the propitiation for our sins, and not for ours only but also for the whole world. (1 John 2:1-2).

2. Now by this we know that we know him, if we keep his commandments. He who says, "I know him," and does not keep his commandments, is a liar, and the truth is not in him. But whoever keeps his word, truly the love of God is perfected in him. By this we know that we are in him. He who says he abides in him ought himself also to walk just as he [Yeshua] walked. (1 John 2:3-6).

3. Whoever commits sin also commits lawlessness, and sin is lawlessness. And you know that he was manifested to take away our sins, and in him there is no sin. Whoever abides in him does not sin. Whoever sins has neither seen him nor known him. (1 John 3:4-6).

4. Little children, let no one deceive you. **He who practices righteousness is righteous, just as he is righteous**. He who sins is of the devil, for the devil has sinned from the beginning. For this purpose the Son of God was manifested, that he might destroy the works of the devil. Whoever has been born of God **does not sin [does not keep sinning]**, for His seed remains in him; and he cannot sin, because he has been born of God. (1 John 3:7-9).

5. Now he who keeps his commandments abides in him [Yeshua], and he [Yeshua] in him. And by this we know that he abides in us, by the Spirit whom he has given us. (1 John 3:24).

6. Beloved, do not believe every spirit, but test the spirits, whether they are of God, **because many false prophets have gone out into the world**. By this you know the Spirit of God: Every spirit that confesses that Yeshua Messiah has come in the flesh is of God, and every spirit that does not confess that Yeshua Messiah has come in the flesh is not of God. And this is the spirit of the

anti-messiah, which you have heard was coming, and **is now already in the world.** (1 John 4:1-3).

7. They [false prophets] **went out from us,** but they were not of us; for if they had been of us, they would have continued with us; but they went out that they might be made manifest, that none of them were of us. (1 John 2:19).

The message of the gospel can be summarized as:

1. We are born of God by believing in Yeshua Messiah who is the Son of God and the propitiation for our sins.
2. Whoever has been born of God does not sin (the present tense in Greek is similar to the present continuous tense in English), for His seed [the Son of God] remains [abides] in him. The Son of God abides in us by the Holy Spirit of the Father sent by the Son.
3. By the Holy Spirit dwelling in us, we can overcome sin and destroy the works of the devil.
4. Sin is lawlessness (breaking the Mosaic law of God). Because the Messiah is sinless [without breaking a single piece of the Mosaic law of God including the dietary law], we all shall keep his commandments and practice righteousness, that is, keep the law of God (the Mosaic law). We all shall be like him when he is revealed (1 John 3:2).

In the Gospels of Matthew and John, Yeshua never teaches that he came to abolish the law of Moses. He teaches in Matthew 5:17-19, "Do not think that I came to destroy the law or the prophets. I did not come to destroy but to fulfil [them]. For assuredly, I say to you, till heaven and earth pass away, one jot or one tittle will by no means pass from the law till all is fulfilled. Whoever therefore breaks one of the least of these commandments, and teaches men so, shall be called least in the kingdom of heaven; but whoever does and teaches them, he shall be called great in the kingdom of heaven."

Here the law Yeshua refers to is definitely the Mosaic law of God, as seen clearly from the several examples of the law Yeshua illustrated in Matthew 5:21-48.

The original Hebrew Matthew 23:2-3 had been mistranslated into all the languages before Nehemia Gordon correctly translated these verses into English in *The Hebrew Yeshua VS The Greek Yeshua* (Hilkiah Press, 2005 and 2006, ISBN 0-9762637-0-X). The English translation from Geek Matthew 23:2-3 is:

> The scribes and the Pharisees sit in Moses' seat. Therefore whatever **they [the** scribes and Pharisees] tell you to observe, that observe and do, but do not do according to their works; for they say, and do not do.

The Shem-Tov's Hebrew Matthew was translated into:

> The Pharisees and the scribes sit in the seat of Moses. Therefore all that **he** [Moses] says to you, diligently do, but according to their reforms (*takannot*) and their precedents (*ma'asim*) do not do, because they talk but they do not do.

To understand what happened, we should compare the Hebrew and Greek versions of the Gospel of Matthew. In the Greek version, Yeshua tells his disciples to obey "all that they [the Pharisees and the scribes] say." In the Hebrew version, his disciples are told to obey "all that he [Moses] says." In Hebrew, there is a tiny difference between "he says" and "they say." There is extra *vav* ו in "they say" compared with "he says." It is interesting that *vav* ו is one of the smallest letters in the Hebrew alphabet, really just a single stroke. The addition of this tiny letter changes Yeshua's instruction to "obey Moses" to his instruction to "obey the Pharisees." Since there is much larger difference between "he says" and "they say" in Greek, the Greek translator may have misread the Hebrew text. This misreading may have been caused by his misunderstanding of Yeshua's words.

If we believe this Hebrew version of the Gospel of Matthew, it is apparent that Yeshua wants his disciples to keep the law of Moses, in agreement with his teaching in Chapter 5 of the Gospel of Matthew.

In contrast, Paul's gospel was obtained through spiritual revelation from the risen "Messiah" who supposedly appeared to him on the road to Damascus according to his own testimony. Since Paul felt that his gospel was inspired directly from the "Spirit" (the risen "Messiah"), he did not need to confer with the flesh and blood [natural men] nor to consult with the twelve apostles in Jerusalem (Galatians 1:16-17). He even claims that only his gospel is true (Galatians 1:8-9) and that he is a wise master builder who has laid the foundation of the doctrine of the gospel (1 Corinthians 3:10).

The message of Paul's gospel is as follows:

1. For all have sinned and fall short of the glory of God. (Romans 3:23).
2. Knowing that a man is not justified by the works of the [Mosaic] law but by faith in Yeshua Messiah, even we have believed in Messiah Yeshua, that we might be justified by faith in Messiah and not by the works of the law; for by the works of the [Mosaic] law no flesh shall be justified. (Galatians 2:16).
3. Messiah has redeemed us from the curse of the [Mosaic] law, having become a curse for us (for it is written, "Cursed is everyone who hangs on a tree"). (Galatians 3:13).
4. which things are symbolic. For these are the two covenants: the one from Mount Sinai which gives birth to bondage, which is Hagar—for this Hagar is Mount Sinai in Arabia, and corresponds to Jerusalem which now is, and is in bondage with her children— but the Jerusalem above is free, which is the mother of us all. (Galatians 4:24-26).
5. But if the ministry of death, **written and engraved on stones,** was glorious, so that the children of Israel could not look steadily at the face of Moses because of the glory of his countenance, which glory **was passing away (transitory),** how will the ministry of the Spirit not be more glorious? (2 Corinthians 3:7-8).
6. For you, brethren, have been called to liberty; only do not use liberty as an opportunity for the flesh, but through love serve

one another. For the entire law is fulfilled in one word: "You shall love your neighbor as yourself." (Galatians 5:13-14).

7. To those without the law I became like one without the law (though I am not outside the law of God but am under the law of Messiah), to win those without the [Mosaic] law. (1 Corinthians 9:21).

8. Do we, then, nullify the law by this faith? Certainly not! Instead, we uphold the law [of Messiah]. (Romans 3:31).

9. You, however, are not in the flesh but in the Spirit [of God], if indeed the Spirit of God dwells in you. Anyone who does not have **the Spirit of Messiah [God]** does not belong to him. (Romans 8:9).

10. And because you are sons, God has sent **the Spirit of his Son** into our hearts, crying, "Abba! Father!" (Galatians 4:6).

The message of Paul's gospel can be summarized as:

1. No one has been righteous under the law of Moses because every human has inherited the original sin stemming from rebellion of Adam and Eve.

2. Yeshua came in a spirit (1 Corinthians 15:46), in the likeness of [hu]man (Philippians 2:7), and in appearance of human (Philippians 2:8) so that only he could be sinless [because he is not a natural man].

3. A man is justified or saved by faith in Messiah only. Christians are not subject to the Mosaic law of God, but to the law of "Messiah," which was invented by Paul.

4. There are two different laws of God. The Mosaic law is the "old" law of God, which served as a tutor and brought curse, bondage, and death. The Pauline law of "Messiah" is the "new" law, which brings life.

5. The law [of "Messiah"] is hung only on the second commandment of God: "You shall love your neighbor as yourself," rather than on both the first and second commandments.

6. The faith upholds the law [of "Messiah"/ "the Spirit"].

7. There are two distinctive Spirits: The Spirit of the Father and the Spirit of the Son. The Spirit of the Son is also called the

Spirit of God (Romans 8:9) because the Son is God in every nature (Philippians 2:6, Titus 1:3-4, Titus 2:13).

8. Both the Father and the Son are God. They are supposed to be equal, but the Son would rather take an inferior position even with no reputation (Philippians 2:6-7).

Two laws

There are two different laws of God according to Paul, corresponding to the two covenants. The first covenant originated from Mount Sinai, ministered by Moses, gave birth to bondage (Galatians 4:24-25), and brought curse (Galatians 3:10) and death (2 Corinthians 3:7). Because the "old" law of Moses was weak and useless and made nothing perfect, the "old" law was annulled and replaced by a better hope (Hebrews 7:18-19), a new and better covenant. The "new" covenant is based on the faith in Messiah only without the deeds of the old law. The law of "the Spirit" or the law of "Messiah" would become the new law. Paul said that he was only subject to the new law (1 Corinthians 9:21).

Paul's own words in 1 Corinthians 9:21 show that he did not keep the law of Moses when he was with the Gentiles. He kept the law of Moses only when he was with the Jews (1 Corinthians 9:20) in order to please them.

Concerning sin, Paul teaches that there is no sin if there is no law of Moses (Romans 4:15). If the law of Moses were abolished, there would be no transgression of the Mosaic law. By this logic, transgressions of the Mosaic law would not lead to sins. On the contrary, Paul teaches that violations of the law of "Messiah" are sins. Who has given Paul such an authority to change the law of God written on the two tablets by God's own finger?

The two laws or the two covenants of God in Paul's gospel contrast with the teachings of Yeshua when he was with his disciples during his 3-year ministry on the earth. In Part I, we have provided plain evidence that Yeshua in the flesh is the true Messiah and the Son of God. In contrast, nobody has clearly identified the true nature of the risen "Yeshua" Paul encountered outside Damascus and in Arabia.

CHAPTER

22

Paul's Teachings vs the Old-Testament Scriptures

In the previous chapters, we have shown many differences between Paul's doctrine and the teachings of Yeshua and his disciples. The differences lead to two different gospels which are related to the most important question as to whether Yeshua's believers should keep the law of Moses in order to enter the kingdom of God. To further clarify this issue, we shall compare Paul's teachings with the Old-Testament Scriptures which have been proved to be inspired words of God in *Perfectly Fulfilled Prophecies and the Destiny of Mankind*.

Here, we compare Paul's teachings with the Old-Testament Scriptures:

1. Isaiah says that the one who eats the unclean fleshes such as swine and mouse will be destroyed by God (Isaiah 66:17) while Paul says that the believers can eat any creature of God (1 Timothy 4:3-5), "forbidding to marry, and commanding to abstain from foods which God created to be received with thanksgiving by those who believe and know the truth. For every creature of God is good, and nothing is to be refused if it is received with thanksgiving; for it is sanctified by the word of God and prayer." Although every creature of God is good, God allows us to eat only clean fleshes. We are not permitted to eat unclean fleshes even if we receive them with thanksgiving and

prayers. Our prayers cannot sanctify unclean fleshes to make them clean.

2. Thus says Yehowah God (Ezekiel 44:9): "No foreigner, uncircumcised in heart or **uncircumcised in flesh**, shall enter My sanctuary, including any foreigner who is among the children of Israel." From chapter 40, Ezekiel describes in detail the millennial temple of God, the city of Jerusalem, and the law of God. Ezekiel 44:9 tells us that in the millennial kingdom of God, the temple of God will be rebuilt and no foreigner, uncircumcised in heart or **uncircumcised in flesh**, shall enter the temple of God. In contrast, Paul teaches that circumcision of the flesh is not required for the Gentile believers. If we were to follow Paul's teaching, we would not be allowed to enter the temple of God to worship Him. What then would the value of our Christian faith be?

3. Yehowah God appeared to Isaac and said (Genesis 26:2-5): "Do not go down to Egypt; live in the land of which I shall tell you. Dwell in this land, and I will be with you and bless you; for to you and your descendants I give all these lands, and I will perform the oath which I swore to Abraham your father. And I will make your descendants multiply as the stars of heaven; I will give to your descendants all these lands; and in your seed all the nations of the earth shall be blessed; **because Abraham obeyed My voice and kept My charge, My commandments, My statutes, and My laws [before Moses issued the law of God to all the Israelites].**" The Hebrew Scriptures clearly tell us that God was pleased with Abraham and blessed him **because Abraham kept His laws** (Genesis 26:4) and was blameless (Genesis 17:2).

   In contrast, Paul teaches that because Abraham believed in Him, it was accounted to him for righteousness. Paul quoted the mistranslated Genesis 15:6 in the Greek Old Testament (LXX) to support his point. Similarly, the Greek translator of the book of James (originally written in Hebrew) mistranslated James 2:23. With this mistranslation, James' quotation of Genesis 15:6 in James 2:23 does not support the conclusion of James 2:24. This mistranslation makes James' argument illogical.

Genesis 15:6 in the interlinear Hebrew-English Bible reads: "And he believed in Yehowah and he accounted it to him for righteousness." There are two possible interpretations to this verse. The first interpretation was given by Paul and the Greek translators of the Old Testament Scriptures. In fact, the translators made a mistake in Hebrew grammar, as pointed out by Dr. Hamilton [*New International Commentary on the Old Testament* (Eerdmans 1990), by Victor P. Hamilton, Vol. 1, page 425].

The second interpretation, which is correct in Hebrew grammar, is "And Abraham believed in Yehowah and Abraham accounted it (Yehowah's faithful word) to Him for righteousness." In other words, because Abraham believed that Yehowah would keep His promise to give him uncountable descendants (Genesis 15:4-5), he attributed Yehowah's faithfulness to His righteousness.

Nehemiah prayed to God in Nehemiah 9:8, "You found his [Abraham's] heart faithful before You and made a covenant with him to give the land of the Canaanites, the Hittites, the Amorites, the Perizzites, the Jebusites, and the Girgashites—to give it to his descendants. **You have performed Your words, for You are righteous**."

Nehemiah 9:8 provides a clear interpretation to Genesis 15:6. Because God found Abraham's heart faithful before him, He accounted him to be righteous and made a covenant with him. This is also consistent with Habakkuk 2:4 (see below). In the same way, because God had performed His words (God's faithfulness), Nehemiah [like Abraham] accounted Him to be righteous. Because Abraham believed that God would perform His words, he accounted Him to be faithful and righteous.

With the correct interpretation of Genesis 15:6, James 2:20-24 can be rephrased as: "But do you want to know, O foolish man, that faith without works is useless? Was not

Abraham our father justified by works when he offered Isaac his son on the altar? Do you see that faith was working together with his works, and by works faith was made perfect? And the Scripture was fulfilled which says, 'Abraham believed God, and he accounted [His faithfulness] to Him for righteousness.' And he was called the friend of God [because Abraham was also faithful and righteous]. You see then that a man is justified by works, and not by faith only." According to James, a man can be justified by his righteous works while faith only without righteous works cannot justify a man. Faith helps us trust in God, obey His words, and do righteous works. God and Messiah will judge men **according to their works** (Revelation 20:13; 22:14; Matthew 25:31-46).

4. Paul misinterpreted Habakkuk 2:4, "But the just shall live by his faith." The Hebrew word "הָאֱמוּנָה (emunah)" means "firmness," "steadfastness," "fidelity," and "faithfulness." In all the English translations for this Hebrew word, only in Habakkuk 2:4, is it translated into "faith" simply because Paul interpreted this word as "faith" to support his doctrine of "salvation by faith only." In fact, Habakkuk 2:5 means that the proud man (the unjust man) with no upright soul acted unfaithfully (deceitfully) or betrayed, which contrasts with the just man who acted faithfully in Habakkuk 2:4. The righteous man shall live because he acts faithfully. God is righteous because he is faithful (Nehemiah 9:8). John also tells us in 1 John 1:9, "If we confess our sins, he is **faithful and righteous** and will forgive us our sins and purify us from all unrighteousness." Therefore, the action of "faithfulness" is essential to "righteousness."

5. Isaiah 42:21 says: "Yehowah is well pleased for His righteousness'sake; He will exalt the law and make it honorable." Psalm 19:7-10 says: "The law of Yehowah is perfect, converting the soul; The testimony of Yehowah is sure, making wise the simple; The statutes of Yehowah are right, rejoicing the heart; The commandment of Yehowah is pure, enlightening the eyes; The fear of Yehowah is clean, enduring forever; The judgments

of Yehowah are true and righteous altogether. More to be desired are they than gold, Yea, than much fine gold; Sweeter also than honey and the honeycomb."

We all know that the law in the Hebrew Scriptures refers to the law of God proclaimed by Moses. When Yeshua quoted the law of God, he also referred to the Mosaic law of God. Psalm 19:7-10 clearly tells us that the Mosaic law of God is perfect, pure, enlightening, true, righteous, more valuable than gold, and sweeter than honey and honeycomb. The law is also eternal, as seen in Psalm 119:44-45, "So shall I **keep Your law continually forever and ever.** And I will walk **at liberty** [rather than bondage], for I seek Your precepts." God will **exalt** the [Mosaic] law rather than abolish it. Yeshua come to exalt the [Mosaic] law by requiring us to keep it even from our hearts and minds. In contrast, Paul teaches that the Mosaic law of God brought curse (Galatians 3:10), bondage (Galatians 4:24), and death (2 Corinthians 3:7). He teaches that the Mosaic law of God is replaced by the law of "Messiah" or the law of "the Spirit" (1 Corinthians 9:21) because the Mosaic law is transitory (Galatians 3:25), weak and unprofitable (Hebrews 7:18-19). The law Paul refers to does not contain the first and the most important commandment of God (Galatians 5:14). In Paul's law of God, the most important commandment of God was excluded.

Paul himself did not keep the Mosaic law of God after his conversion, as seen from his own statement (1 Corinthians 9:19-22): "For though I am free from all men, I have made myself a servant to all, that I might win the more; and to the Jews I became as a Jew, that I might win Jews; to those who are under the [Mosaic] law, as under the [Mosaic] law, that I might win those who are under the [Mosaic] law; to those who are without [Mosaic] law, as without [Mosaic] law (not being without law of God, but under the law of Messiah), that I might win those who are without [Mosaic] law; to the weak I became as weak, that

I might win the weak. I have become all things to [please] all men, that I might by all means save some."

Paul's statement suggests that he acts like a chameleon who changes his behavior with his surroundings. He also commanded his followers to imitate him as he had imitated Messiah (1 Corinthians 11:1). Would Yeshua act like a chameleon and say something like, "I become all things to [please] all people?" Definitely not! Yeshua often offended people when he spoke the truth. Paul never walked with Yeshua but refused to learn anything from the twelve apostles (Galatians 1:17; 2:6-9) who did walk with Yeshua for over three years.

CHAPTER

23

Luke's Accounts vs Paul's Doctrine

In the previous chapters, we have shown Paul's doctrine vs the teachings of Yeshua and his disciples. We have also compared Paul's teachings with the Old-Testament Scriptures. In this chapter, we compare Paul's statements with the accounts of Luke in his two books. Most scholars date the composition of Luke-Acts to around 80-90 AD while some others suggest 90-110 AD. Although Luke was Paul's companion and did not directly witness the life of Yeshua, he may have still honestly written down what he learned from Paul and the other people. Some errors in Luke's accounts, as we discussed in the previous chapters, may have originated from the mistakes in the original sources.

Post-resurrection of Yeshua

Luke records the post-resurrection story of Yeshua in Chapter 24 of the Gospel of Luke. After Yeshua resurrected in the early morning of a Sunday, he first appeared to Peter, then two disciples on the road to Emmaus near the evening of that Sunday, and then to his eleven apostles of Yeshua in the evening of that Sunday (in the beginning of that Monday). Luke recorded the words of the risen Yeshua (Luke 24:46): "Thus it is written, and thus it was necessary for the Messiah to suffer and to rise from the dead the third day."

Luke's account is similar to what Paul states in 1 Corinthians 15:3-8, "For I delivered to you first of all that which I also received: that Messiah died for our sins according to the Scriptures, and that He was buried, and that He rose again the third day according to the Scriptures, and that He was seen by Cephas, then by the twelve. After that He was seen by over five hundred brethren at once, of whom the greater part remains to the present, but some have fallen asleep. After that He was seen by James, then by all the apostles. Then last of all He was seen by me also, as by one born out of due time."

Institution of the Lord's supper

Luke records Yeshua's institution of the Lord's supper in Luke 12:19, "This is my body which is given for you; do this in remembrance of me." But the sentence "do this in remembrance of me" was not recorded in any other Gospel. If Yeshua had indeed instituted the Lord's supper, Matthew and John would have also recorded this commandment.

This account of Luke is very similar to Paul's statement in 1 Corinthians 11:24-25,

> and when he had given thanks, he broke it and said, "Take, eat; this is my body which is broken for you; do this in remembrance of me." In the same manner He also took the cup after supper, saying, "This cup is the new covenant in my blood. This do, as often as you drink it, in remembrance of me."

The two criminals crucified with Yeshua

Luke records the story of the two criminals who were crucified with Yeshua. Luke 23:39-43 says:

> Then one of the criminals who were hung blasphemed him, saying, "If you are the Messiah, save yourself and us." But the other, answering, rebuked him, saying, "Do you not even fear God, seeing you are under the same condemnation? And we indeed justly, for we receive the due reward of our deeds; but this man has done nothing wrong." Then he said to Yeshua, "Lord, remember me when you come into your kingdom." And Yeshua said

to him, "Assuredly, I say to you, today you will be with me in Paradise."

This account of Luke is very different from the accounts of Matthew and Mark who consistently tell us that both criminals mocked Yeshua. But this account of Luke strongly supports Paul's doctrine (Romans 10:9): "that if you confess with your mouth the Lord Yeshua and believe in your heart that God has raised Him from the dead, you will be saved."

A woman anointing Yeshua

The anointing of Yeshua's head and/or feet were recorded in all the four Gospels. The stories in Matthew 26, Mark 14, and John 12 are quite similar, taking place in the same location, the city of Bethany, and a few days before Yeshua's crucifixion. In contrast, the event in Luke 7:31-50 describes a sinful woman who could not have been the woman named as Mary the sister of Martha and Lazarus. Since the host name Simon in Luke's account is the same as that in both Matthew's and Mark's stories, one may argue that the four Gospels should record the same anointing event from different perspectives. Matthew considers this anointing event to be very important, as seen in Matthew 26:13, "Truly I tell you, wherever this gospel is preached throughout the world, what she has done will also be told, in memory of her." If the anointing event in Luke 7:36-50 were different from the most important one recorded in all other Gospels, Luke would have failed to record the most important anointing event Yeshua commanded to be told along with the gospel. If Luke failed to record the most important anointing event all other Gospels recorded, the Gospel of Luke should not be inspired by God. If Luke's anointing event were the same as the one recorded by all other Gospels, why should Luke have recorded the words of Yeshua so different from other authors (Matthew 26:10-13; Mark 14:6-9; John 12:7-8)?

Luke records Yeshua's words in Luke 7:44-47,

> Then he [Yeshua] turned to the woman and said to Simon, "Do you see this woman? I entered your house; you gave me no water for my feet, but she has washed

my feet with her tears and wiped them with the hair of her head. You gave me no kiss, but this woman has not ceased to kiss my feet since the time I came in. You did not anoint my head with oil, but this woman has anointed my feet with fragrant oil. Therefore I say to you, **her sins, which are many, are forgiven, for she loved much. But to whom little is forgiven, the same loves little.**"

Since these words are only recorded by Luke, it is likely that Luke was influenced by Paul to support Paul's doctrine (Romans 5:20): "Moreover the law entered that the offense might abound. But where sin abounded, grace abounded much more."

Paul's conversion and interaction with the apostles in Jerusalem

Luke records Paul's conversion on the way to Damascus and his story after the conversion. According to Luke's account, Paul preached about the Messiah in Damascus immediately after his conversion (Acts 9:19-20). After preaching for many days in Damascus, Paul came to Jerusalem to meet the apostles of Yeshua and stayed in Jerusalem to preach the name of Yeshua (Acts 9:23-30). After Herod Agrippa died in 44 AD, Paul and Barnabas went to Jerusalem to fulfil their ministry there (Acts 12:25). After they returned from Jerusalem, they took John Mark to Antioch (Acts 12:25; 13:1). Afterward, Paul and Barnabas went to Jerusalem again to resolve the conflicting issue of whether it is necessary for Gentiles to be circumcised and keep the law of Moses after their conversion (Acts 15:1-5). The apostles and the elders came together to consider this matter (Acts 15:6). They decided that Gentile believers should not be burdened with circumcision but must astrain from things polluted by idols, from sexual immorality, from things strangled, and from blood (Acts 15:19-20). This is because through many generations Moses had had the preachers in every city read the law of Moses in the synagogues every Sabbath (Acts 15:21).

Luke accounts partially support Paul's statement in Galatians 1:15-19; 2:1-2 if "many days" in Acts 9:23 means "three years" in Galatians 2:1. Paul made an important statement in Galatians 1:15-17,

> But when it pleased God, who separated me from my mother's womb and called me through his grace, to reveal his Son in me, that I might preach him among the Gentiles, I did not immediately confer with flesh and blood, nor did I go up to Jerusalem to those who were apostles before me; but I went to Arabia, and returned again to Damascus.

So Paul's own words tell us that his gospel was revealed directly from the risen "Messiah" possibly in Arabia, and that he did not consult with any man including the apostles in Jerusalem. Only after three years, he went up to Jerusalem to see Peter and James Yeshua's brother and stayed there for 15 days (Galatians 1:18-19).

On the other hand, Luke's accounts partially contradict Paul's statement in Galatians 2:9-10:

> and when James, Cephas, and John, who **seemed to be pillars,** perceived the grace that had been given to me, they gave me and Barnabas the right hand of fellowship, that we should go to the Gentiles and they to the circumcised. They desired only that we should remember the poor, the very thing which I also was eager to do.

According to Luke, the apostles never told Paul and his associates to preach the gospel to the Gentiles while they themselves preached to the Jews only. In contrast, Luke records **Peter's words** (Acts 15:7):

> Men and brethren, you know that a good while ago God chose among us, that **by my mouth** the Gentiles should hear the word of the gospel and believe.

It is clear that God had commanded Peter to preach the gospel to the Gentiles, in agreement with Matthew 28:19 but in contradiction with Paul's statement.

The apostles commanded the Gentiles believers to abstain from foods polluted by idols, things strangled, and blood, and from sexual immorality. The verse in Acts 15:21 may imply that the Gentile believers should keep the law of Moses after they learn the law, just like the Jews who learn it every Sabbath.

On the other hand, Paul tells us (Galatians 2:10) that the apostles only desired Paul and the Gentiles believers to remember the poor. Apparently, Paul did not agree with the commandment of the apostles in Jerusalem. That is why he states that they **seem to be pillars** (Galatians 2:9). He even rebuked Peter of hypocrisy in front of all the others and proclaimed his "sin" to all the believers through the epistle to the Galatians. As discussed in the previous chapters, Paul teaches that the believers can eat foods polluted by idols (as long as they do not cause weak believers to sin) and unclean fleshes (after sanctifying them through prayer and thanksgiving).

Unclean and common animals

Luke records Peter's vision in Acts 9:10-15. In his vison, Peter sees many clean, unclean or common animals descending from heaven down to the earth, and hears a voice from heaven: "Rise, Peter; kill and eat." But Peter says, "Not so, Lord! For **I have never eaten anything common and unclean.**" And the voice speaks to him again, "What God has cleaned you must not call common."

Luke's account appears to suggest that God has cleaned the unclean and common fleshes for us to eat them, which seems to support Paul's teachings on the foods. On the other hand, if Yeshua had taught his disciples that eating the unclean and common fleshes was not against the law, Peter would not have said at this moment: "**I have never eaten anything common and unclean.**" The logical conclusion from Peter's statement is that Yeshua never taught his disciples to eat unclean and common fleshes.

Since the purpose of this vision is to convince him that the Gentiles could also be saved through the blood of Yeshua, Luke's account does not necessarily mean that God has abolished His dietary law. In contrast, this account, if reliable, indicates that Yeshua did not abolish the Mosaic dietary law.

The risen Yeshua: a spirit or flesh?

Luke says that the risen Yeshua is not a spirit but a flesh, as seen from Luke 24:36-43:

> Now as they said these things, Yeshua himself stood in the midst of them, and said to them, "Peace to you." But they were terrified and frightened, and supposed they had seen a spirit. And he said to them, "Why are you troubled? And why do doubts arise in your hearts? Behold my hands and my feet, that it is I myself. Handle me and see, **for a spirit does not have flesh and bones as you see I have**." When he had said this, he showed them his hands and his feet. But while they still did not believe for joy, and marveled, he said to them, "Have you any food here?" So they gave him a piece of a broiled fish and some honeycomb. And he took it and ate in their presence.

Luke clearly tells us that even the risen Messiah is not a spirit but a man with flesh and bones. In contrast, Paul teaches that the last Adam [Yeshua] became a life-giving **spirit** (1 Corinthians 15:46). Paul argues about the nature of a resurrected body in 1 Corinthians 15:35-58. In 1 Corinthians 15:50, Paul explicitly states: "Now this I say, brethren, that flesh and blood cannot inherit the kingdom of God; nor does corruption inherit incorruption." What Paul means is that a natural man with flesh and blood cannot inherit the kingdom of God. Paul further says that a saint who has died will be raised with an incorruptible body in the end times and that a saint who is still alive will be changed into an incorruptible body. The implication of Paul's argument is that a resurrected incorruptible body is just like the risen Messiah who would have an incorruptible spiritual body. According to 1 Corinthians 15:50, the spiritual body does not have natural flesh and blood. The implication of Paul's statement is that Yeshua is simply a life-giving spirit with no human flesh and blood.

CHAPTER

24

Mr. Scott Nelson's Arguments: Paul's Apostleship

In this chapter, we will directly copy some paragraphs written by Mr. Scott Nelson. His current webpage is: https://www.judaismvschristianity. com. Several paragraphs below are directly taken from Mr. Nelson's previous website which is not available now (we made slight rhetorical modifications):

> Now, look at what was said to the church that we know Paul had been involved in... Ephesus. Among the things that Yeshua commended the Ephesian church for doing right, is this quote:
> "I know your works, your labor, and your patience, and that you cannot bear those who are evil. And you have tested those who say they are apostles and are not and have found them liars." (Revelation 2:2)
> Yes, I have no doubts that Yeshua was referring to Paul and his companions, and that his claim of apostleship, as well as his doctrine, were false. Hang in there and consider all the facts with me for a minute. Here are four of them.
>
> 1. Paul's doctrine on the foreknowledge of God is not only groundless (because he had to abuse Scripture to support it), it is blasphemous because it outright accuses God of unrighteousness.

2. We have record of Paul claiming to be an apostle to the Ephesians. "Paul, an apostle of Yeshua by the will of God, To the saints who are in Ephesus." (Ephesians 1:1).
3. We have no record of anyone else claiming to be an apostle to anyone anywhere, not even to the Ephesians.
4. Paul and his doctrine had troubles being accepted in Ephesus.

"And he went into the synagogue and spoke boldly for three months, reasoning and persuading concerning the things of the kingdom of God. But when some were hardened and did not believe, but spoke evil of the way before the multitude..." (Acts 19:8-9).

Remember, this is recorded from Luke's point of view and he believed Paul's doctrine was "the way." Notice that those who rejected Paul are men of the synagogue and not atheists or pagans. If these men had stood up in front of the synagogue and said, "Paul's doctrine is flawed. He is a false apostle, and a liar," Luke would no doubt have seen this as "speaking evil of the way."

If these four reasons are not enough to seriously call into question Paul's status as an apostle there is one more. It is a most interesting quote from Paul's own pen that finally seals the fate of his supposed apostleship. It comes from his second letter to Timothy, written during the same Neronian persecution in which John was given the Revelation. This letter is believed by many scholars to contain the last recorded words of Paul. Here he makes a short statement of lament that seems to have gone unnoticed... the implications of which are devastating to Paul if one is able to hear everything that is being said. Paul makes this statement to Timothy.

"This you know, that all those in Asia have turned away from me." (2 Timothy 1:15).

Asia (all of them) rejected Paul! And when he says, "This you know," it sounds like this must have been relatively common knowledge at that time. Asia is the very place that Yeshua told John to write, where his seven churches were. And they were alive, and obviously had been established for some time. Paul did not say that Asia had rejected Yeshua. Obviously, they hadn't rejected Yeshua if there were thriving churches there that Yeshua wanted to address through John. Instead Paul said that all Asia had rejected him personally. This is also corroborated in the book of Acts where men from Asia accuse Paul of teaching against the law, and bringing an Ephesian friend into the temple.

And when the seven days were almost ended, the Jews from Asia, seeing him in the temple, stirred up the whole crowd and laid hands on him, crying out, "Men of Israel, help! This is the man who teaches all men everywhere against the people, the law, and this place: and furthermore he also brought Greeks into the temple and has defiled this holy place." (For they had previously seen Trophimus the Ephesian with him in the city, whom they supposed that Paul had brought into the temple.) (Acts 21:27-29).

Try to grasp the profound significance of all this. Here we have in the book of Revelation the words of Yeshua commending the Ephesian church for rejecting someone who claimed to be his apostle, while Paul is the only person other than the twelve original apostles to have claimed to be an apostle... and we know that he has made this very claim to this same Ephesian church. At the same time, Paul laments himself of the fact that he has been rejected by them. How could it not be Paul and his associates that Yeshua had commended the Ephesian church for rejecting? Could it be much more obvious? Here are the facts, paraphrased, one more time.

Paul to the Ephesians: "I am an apostle of Yeshua."

The Ephesians to Paul: "No you're not."

Yeshua to the Ephesians: "Well done."

This should at the very least raise serious question about Paul. When we add to this the remaining evidence against his doctrine, as well as the documented fact that he outright lied a number of times (as I will show in the next chapter), we have more than enough reason to do as the Ephesian church and convict Paul of the crime of false impersonation of an apostle.

Yeshua's description of Paul in Revelation was that he was a false apostle, and a liar. Consider his following words.

"He who has an ear, let him hear what the Spirit says to the churches."

Nelson's arguments are relevant if the book of revelation is proved to be the inspired words of God. We have unambiguously proved that this book was written by John the Apostle in the spring of 67 AD and is the true words of God.

CHAPTER

25

Yeshua's Teachings on Anti-messiah

In the previous chapter, Mr. Nelson argues against the apostleship of Paul. If his argument is relevant, one needs to show that the spirit who appeared to Paul is a false messiah (anti-messiah). According to Paul's own statement (1 Corinthians 15:3-8), the resurrected Yeshua appeared to him several years [about 7 years] after he had ascended to heaven [in 30 AD]. According to John, the spirit of the anti-messiah had come when he wrote his first epistle to warn Yeshua's believers (1 John 4:3). The spirit that does not confess that Yeshua Messiah has come in the flesh is the spirit of the false messiah (1 John 4:3). In the previous chapters, we have shown that Paul did not confess that Yeshua had come in the flesh, but in a spirit, in the likeness of human, and in appearance of a man. Then, Paul's "Yeshua" could have been the spirit of the false messiah.

In the Gospel of Matthew, Yeshua prophesizes **where, how, and when** false messiahs will appear to deceive, if possible, even the elect. There are many false messiahs who appear in different times. Yeshua provides a general guideline for identifying false messiahs and false prophets. A false prophet is a person who possesses the spirit of a false messiah and can perform great signs and wonders as well as mighty deeds.

How and where shall the false messiahs appear?

In Matthew 24:23-24, Yeshua foretells his disciples:

> And if anyone says to you, "Look, here is the Messiah!"
> or "There!" do not believe it. For false messiahs and false
> prophets will rise and **show great signs and wonders to
> deceive,** if possible, even the elect. See, I have told you
> beforehand. Therefore if they say to you, "Look, he is **in
> the desert!**' do not go out; or 'Look, he is **in the inner
> rooms!**' do not believe it. For as **the lightning** comes
> from the east and **flashes** to the west, so also will the
> coming of the Son of Man be. For wherever the carcass
> is, there the eagles will be gathered together.

In Matthew 24:5, Yeshua prophesizes that there will be many false
messiahs and false prophets. These false messiahs and false prophets will
rise and **show great signs and wonders to deceive,** if possible, even the
elect. The false messiahs will appear **in the desert (wilderness) and/or
in the inner rooms (secret chambers).**

In contrast, **the true Messiah will come down like thunders and
lightning flashes (since thunders and lightning flashes always come
together just as the eagles gather together wherever the carcass
is).** This is similar to the coming down of Yehowah (or the Angel of
Yehowah), as described in Exodus 19:16, "Then it came to pass on the
third day, in the morning, that there were **thunders and lightning
flashes,** and a thick cloud on the mountain; and the sound of trumpet
was very loud, so that all the people who were in the camp trembled." If
we know how the true Messiah shall come down from heaven, we can
distinguish between the true Messiah and false messiahs.

Luke records Paul's conversion story in Acts 9:3-7,

> As he journeyed he came **near Damascus,** and suddenly
> **a light shone** around him from heaven. Then he fell
> to the ground, and heard a voice saying to him, "Saul,
> Saul, why are you persecuting me?" And he said, "Who

are you, lord?" Then the lord said, "I am Yeshua, whom you are persecuting. It is hard for you to kick against the goads." So he, trembling and astonished, said, "Lord, what do you want me to do?" Then the lord said to him, "Arise and go into the city, and you will be told what you must do." And the men who journeyed with him stood speechless, hearing a voice but seeing no one. Then Saul arose from the ground, and when his eyes were opened he saw no one. But they led him by the hand and brought him into Damascus. And he was three days without sight, and neither ate nor drank.

The "Messiah" Paul encountered came down with **a light shining** around him from heaven. The light blinded the eyes of Paul. There was no thunder. This account of Luke indicates that the "Messiah" did not come down with thunders and lightning flashes. So according to Yeshua's guideline, the "Messiah" Paul encountered is not the true Messiah. In contrast, the true Messiah came down to the earth in the spring of 67 AD with thunders and lightning flashes (see Chapter 9 of the book of revelation).

Paul said to us that the risen "Yeshua" appeared to him outside Damascus (Acts 9:3), in Arabia (Galatians 1:17), and in the barracks (Acts 23:10-11). Arabia is a desert district south of Palestine according to the interlinear Bible. In fact, any region outside Jerusalem is "in the wilderness" according to John (Revelation 12:6; 12:14). Thus, Paul consistently said to us that the "Messiah" appeared to him in the wilderness and in the barracks [in the inner rooms]. According to Yeshua's prophecy in Matthew 24:23-26, if someone says to us that the "Messiah" is in the desert and/or in the inner rooms, we should ignore what he/she says because only the false messiahs appear in the wilderness and/or in the inner rooms. The false messiahs and their false prophets rise and show great signs and wonders to deceive, if possible, even the elect. Since Paul says to us that the "Messiah" appeared to him in the desert and in the inner rooms through the writings of himself and his own disciple (Luke), we should not believe what he says.

When shall the true Messiah appear on the earth?

Yeshua prophesized when he would appear on the earth in the Gospels of Matthew and John. If we know the exact time when the true Messiah is supposed to appear in the world, we can identify the false messiahs from the times of their appearances on the earth.

Yeshua prophesized that the Son of Man would come to the earth when some of his eleven disciples died and some of them were still alive (Matthew 16:28, John 21:22-23). In particular, Yeshua foretells us in John 21:22-23 that he would come to the earth when Peter had died but John was still alive. Yeshua's return in the spring of 67 AD (see Chapter 9) perfectly fulfilled his prophecies in Matthew 16:28 and John 21:22-23.

Yeshua prayed to his Father for his eleven disciples before his crucifixion (John 17). John 17:20-21 clearly indicates that Yeshua prayed specifically for his eleven disciples in Chapter 17 of John. John 17:11 records his prophetic prayer: "Now I am no longer in this world but these [the eleven disciples] are in the world, and I come to you. Holy Father, keep through Your name those whom You have given me, that they may be one as we are." This prophetic prayer implies that Yeshua should not have been in the world while all the eleven disciples were still alive. John 17:11 is consistent with Matthew 16:28 and John 21:22-23, which imply that the Son of Man should have come down to the earth after some of his eleven disciples were not in the world and before all of them left the world.

When did the risen "Yeshua" appear to Paul? The time must have been before 40 AD when King Aretas died according to Paul's own words in 2 Corinthians 11:32, "In Damascus the governor, under Aretas the king, was guarding the city of the Damascenes with a garrison, desiring to arrest me." We also know that James, the brother of John was killed by Herod Agrippa I (Acts 12:2) after Claudius Caesar started to reign in 41 AD (Acts 11:28) and before Herod Agrippa I died in 44 AD (Acts 12:23). James was the first apostle who was martyred between 41 and 44 AD. So Paul's encounter with "Yeshua" happened several years before James one of the eleven disciples was killed. According to Yeshua's own prophecies, he should not have appeared on the earth before 41 AD. This implies that the one appeared to Paul before 40 AD (most likely in 37 AD) should not have been the true Messiah.

How would the true Yeshua have only revealed himself to Paul while all his disciples were still in the world to preach the gospel and bear witness of him? Because Yeshua told this disciples that the Holy Spirit would guide them into all the truth and even speak for them, they should have been able to fulfil all the missions God and Yeshua assigned them to do. Yeshua also assigned his disciples to preach the gospel to the Gentiles before his ascension to heaven (Matthew 28:19). If his disciples had not been able to preach the gospel to the Gentiles even with the help of the Holy Spirit, God would have been unwise and made a terrible mistake in selecting Yeshua's disciples. This is completely impossible!

Was Paul's gospel revealed by a false messiah?

If Paul's gospel was revealed by the risen "Yeshua" who was a false messiah, how could Paul's teachings have come directly from the true Yeshua? Paul's gospel is not from the Holy Spirit either because the Holy Spirit only declares what the true Yeshua says. Paul claims in 2 Corinthians 12:12, "Truly the signs of an apostle were accomplished among you with all perseverance, in signs and wonders and mighty deeds." Paul tried to prove his apostleship by showing signs and wonders and mighty deeds.

Paul should not have used the signs, wonders, and mighty deeds he performed to prove his apostleship. Yeshua foretold that false prophets would show great signs and wonders to deceive, if possible, even the elect (Matthew 24:24). Yeshua also said (Matthew 7:22-23), "Many will say to me in that day, 'Lord, Lord, have we not prophesied in your name, cast out demons in your name, and done many wonders in your name?' And then I will declare to them, 'I never knew you; depart from me, you who **practice lawlessness!**'"

Yeshua's teaching is also consistent with the teaching of Moses in Deuteronomy 13:1-5,

> If there arises among you a prophet or a dreamer of dreams, and he gives you **a sign or a wonder, and the**

sign or the wonder comes to pass, of which he spoke to you, saying, "Let us go after other gods"—which you have not known—"and let us serve them," you shall not listen to the words of that prophet or that dreamer of dreams, for the Lord your God **is testing you to know whether you love Yehowah your God with all your heart and with all your soul. You shall walk after Yehowah your God and fear Him, and keep His commandments and obey His voice, and you shall serve Him and hold fast to Him.** But that prophet or that dreamer of dreams shall be put to death, because he has spoken in order to turn you away from Yehowah your God, who brought you out of the land of Egypt and redeemed you from the house of bondage, **to entice you from the way in which Yehowah your God commanded you to walk.** So you shall put away the evil from your midst.

Both Yeshua and Moses teach us how to recognize a false prophet. No matter how great signs and wonders a prophet can perform, he is a false prophet if he/she has spoken to turn you away from Yehowah your God and to entice you from the way in which Yehowah your God commanded you to walk: keep His commandments and obey His voice, and serve Him and hold fast to Him.

Paul teaches his disciples not to keep the law of Moses. Paul even judges that the Mosaic law of God had brought bondage, curse, and death. He wants to abolish the law of Moses and replace it with the law of "Messiah." He persuades Yeshua's believers to forsake the law of Moses and to follow the law of "Messiah," which even does not include the first and the most important commandment of God (Galatians 5:14; 1 Corinthians 9:21).

Yeshua warns his disciples in Matthew 7:15, "Beware of false prophets, who come to you in sheep's clothing, but inwardly they are ravenous wolves." Paul's teachings appear to be enlightening, encouraging, and helpful from the human perspective. Paul told his disciples that he was persecuted greatly within the church of God for the truth of his gospel because he needed to fight against "false teachers." In the previous chapters, we have shown that Paul's gospel is different from the Judaism-like gospel preached by Yeshua's twelve apostles. Since Paul claims that only his gospel is from God, the "false teachers" Paul refers to should be Yeshua's twelve apostles who **seem to** be the pillars of the church to Paul (Galatians 2:9). According to the Judaism-like gospel, God and the Messiah will judge us according to our works rather than faith only (Revelation 20:13; 22:14; Matthew 25:31-46; 1 John 3:7; James 2:20). In contrast, if we only believe in Paul's gospel: a man is saved by faith only, our salvation may be in risk!

Since Paul admitted that his teachings were rejected by **all** those in Asia (2 Timothy 1:15), he must have been rejected by the church of Ephesus which is in Asia. Yeshua praised the church of Ephesus for their rejection of the teachings of the false apostles (Revelation 2:2) while Paul claimed to be their apostle and stayed there for about 3 years. Only if the Ephesians found Paul a false apostle, they dared to reject his teachings. Therefore, the combined verses of Revelation 2:2 and 2 Timothy 1:15 prove that Paul is one of the false apostles Yeshua refers to. Since the two epistles of Paul to Timothy should have been written around 64-65 AD (https://www.matthewmcgee.org/paultime. html), 1 Timothy 1:3 implies that Timothy may have remained in the church of Ephesus to protect the doctrine of Paul around 64-65 AD and thereafter. As shown in Chapter 9, the book of Revelation was written by John the Apostle in the spring of 67 AD, the time when Timothy may have still remained in Ephesus.

Was Paul martyred for his faith?

Luke's accounts of Paul end with Paul's imprisonment in Rome between 60 and 62 AD (since Porcius Festus was procurator in 59 AD, as verified by the bronze coinage minted by him). Paul's story was unknown after he was free from imprisonment (in 62 AD). It is generally believed that Paul was beheaded by Nero in 67 AD for his faith, but there is no reliable historical evidence for his martyrdom.

Is there any other record of Paul's story after 62 AD? The page at https://en.wikipedia.org/wiki/Costobarus presents an interesting paragraph:

> There is a fringe theory that the Saul in Josephus' writings was the same person as Saul of the New Testament. According to this theory, references to Saul in Acts of the Apostles and some verses of Paul's Epistle to the Romans are believed to reveal connections to the Herodian royal family. In Acts of the Apostles, Saul is named in a list of Christian prophets and teachers in Antioch, following Manaen, who was "brought up with Herod the Tetrarch," but the verse does not clearly connect Saul to Manaen, or to Herod; In the last chapter of the Epistle to the Romans, Paul sends greetings to a man named Herodion, whom he calls a kinsman (Gk: συγγενῆ). However, Herodion is a not uncommon name in the ancient world, and Paul refers to several others as kinsmen in the same chapter. This term likely meant nothing more than that they were also Jewish. If he were a member of the Herodian family, Saul would indeed have been a Roman citizen. His behaviour prior to his conversion, in which he "made havoc for the church" could be seen as reminiscent of that in which Costobar and Saul "were lawless and quick to plunder ... those weaker than themselves," however, the account of the violent behaviour of Costobar and Saul in Josephus would have post-dated Paul's conversion to Christianity by decades.

The last sentence in above passage seems to argue against this fringe theory. However, if Paul [Saul] is a false apostle, the violent behaviour of Josephus' Saul in the 60's of the first century could be a natural continuation of his murderous behaviour before his conversion. Moreover, if Paul is related to the Herodian royal family, there is a good chance for Manaen, a member of the Herodian royal family, to be converted to Paul's Christianity by Paul himself.

According to Josephus (*Wars* bk. 2, ch. 20, sect.1), Cestius Gallus (a Roman senator and general) sent Saul and his friends (at their own desire) to Nero to inform him of heavy losses during the Jewish revolt and to **blame Florus** for kindling the revolt. Saul may have made strong accusation against Florus, which might have caused Nero to rage against him because Florus was appointed to replace Lucceius Abbinus as procurator **by Nero due to his wife Cleopara's friendship with Nero's wife Poppaea**. Nero should have sided with Florus because he launched raids on the temple and Jerusalem to suppress the protests of the Jews against Nero's taxation law. Florus even removed seventeen talents from the treasury of the temple and claimed the money for Nero. Florus' military actions, which indeed prompted a wide and large-scale rebellion, may have been commanded by Nero.

Josephus doesn't say whether or not Saul was executed after he voluntarily went up to Nero to accuse against Florus in the end of 66 AD. The Saul of the New Testament is believed to be beheaded by Nero around the spring of 67 AD while the Saul in Josephus' writings came to Nero in the end of 66 AD to blame Florus (Nero's friend) for kindling the revolt. Since blaming Florus is equivalent to blaming Nero, it is hard to believe that Saul's confrontation with Nero in the end of 66 AD would have had no bad consequence. If Nero had executed Saul because of his accusation against Florus, the two Sauls should have been the same person.

CHAPTER
26

Paul's Christianity

Mainstream Christianity is based on the 14 epistles of Paul, a few Pauline-like epistles, two books of Luke, and less than 10 books of Yeshua's own disciples. Different Christian denominations have different emphases on Paul's doctrine. That is why there are so many (30,000-40,000) Christian denominations. Few denominations only accept the teachings of Yeshua and his disciples. They are called "Churches of Yeshua's Word Only." Even the Jewish Messianic Congregation also considers Paul's epistles to be the inspired words of God although the faith practices of the denomination are different from some teachings of Paul.

The doctrine of the Trinity

Almost all Christian denominations accept the doctrine of the Trinity included in Nicene Creed. Nicene Creed is a statement of belief originally adopted in the city of Nicaea by the First Council of Nicaea in 325 AD. It was amended at the First Council of Constantinople in 381 AD. In Table XI, we compare the original Nicaea Creed and the amended Nicaea Greed. The essential part of the Creed is the doctrine of the Trinity: the Father, the Son, and the Holy Spirit. The Father is God Almighty, Maker of all the things visible and invisible. Yeshua Messiah is the Lord, the only begotten Son of God, the essence of the Father, God of God, begotten but not made, consubstantial with the Father. The Holy Spirit is the Lord and Giver of life, who proceeds from the Father and is with the Father and the Son. He is also worshipped and glorified.

Table XI: The original Nicaea Creed and amended Nicaea Greed (https://en.wikipedia.org/wiki/Nicene_Creed)

First Council of Nicaea (325 AD)	First Council of Constantinople (381 AD)
We believe in one God, the Father Almighty, Maker of all things visible and invisible.	We believe in one God, the Father Almighty, Maker *of heaven and earth, and* of all things visible and invisible.
And in one Lord Yeshua Messiah, the Son of God, begotten of the Father [the only-begotten; that is, of the essence of the Father, God of God,] Light of Light, very God of very God, begotten, not made, consubstantial with the Father; By whom all things were made [both in heaven and on earth];	And in one Lord Yeshua Messiah, the *only-begotten* Son of God, begotten of the Father *before all worlds (æons)*, Light of Light, very God of very God, begotten, not made, consubstantial with the Father; by whom all things were made;
Who for us men, and for our salvation, came down and was incarnate and was made man;	who for us men, and for our salvation, came down *from heaven*, and was incarnate *by the Holy Ghost and of the Virgin Mary*, and was made man;

He suffered, and the third day he rose again, ascended into heaven;	he *was crucified for us under Pontius Pilate, and* suffered, *and was buried*, and the third day he rose again, *according to the Scriptures, and* ascended into heaven, *and <u>sitteth</u> on the right hand of the Father;*
From thence he shall come to judge the quick and the dead.	from thence he shall come *again, with glory*, to judge the quick and the dead; *whose kingdom shall have no end.*
And in the Holy Ghost.	And in the Holy Ghost, *the Lord and Giver of life, who proceedeth from the Father, who with the Father and the Son together is worshiped and glorified, who spake by the prophets.*
	In one holy catholic and apostolic Church; we acknowledge one baptism for the remission of sins; we look for the resurrection of the dead, and the life of the world to come. Amen.

[But those who say: 'There was a time when he was not;' and 'He was not before he was made;' and 'He was made out of nothing,' or 'He is of another substance' or 'essence,' or 'The Son of God is created,' or 'changeable,' or 'alterable'— they are condemned by the holy catholic and apostolic Church.]	

The doctrine of the Trinity is foundational to the faith of mainstream Christians. A simple way to understand the Trinity is that there is one God who eternally exists as three distinct "Persons": the Father, the Son, and the Holy Spirit. Paul refers to the Father as God (Philippians 1:2) and to the Son as God (Titus 1:3-4; 2:13). Luke refers to the Holy Spirit as God (Acts 5:3-4). The teachings of Paul and his disciple suggest that there are three different ways of looking at God or three different roles God plays. On the other hands, Matthew and John clearly tell us that the Father, the Son, and the Holy Spirit are three different "Persons" and that only the Father is God. Mainstream Christians have also cited John 20:28, "And Thomas answered and said to him, 'My Lord and my God!'" to prove that the risen Yeshua is God. In fact, this verse simply shows that Thomas' view on the nature of the Messiah may have been in error because he had not received the Holy Spirit to know all the truth when he said this.

Because Christians consider all 27 books in the New Testament to be the inspired words of God, the doctrine of the Trinity "resolves" the contradiction between Paul's and Yeshua's teachings. That is why the concept of "the Trinity" is too difficult for a normal person to comprehend.

Saved by faith only

The central salvation principle in Paul's gospel is his famous statement (Romans 10:9): "that if you confess with your mouth the Lord Yeshua and believe in your heart that God has raised him from the dead, you will be saved." His salvation principle does not require water baptism and being born again from God.

The second point of Paul's salvation principle is that we are not under the law [of Moses] but under grace. We are justified by faith only (apart from the deeds of the law [of Moses]). Christians are not subject to the Mosaic law.

The third point is that the Mosaic law is abolished through Yeshua's work (nailing it on the cross) because it is transitory, weak, and unprofitable, and because it brings curse, bondage, and death. The Mosaic law is replaced by the law of "Messiah" or the law of "the Spirit." Since there is no law [of Moses], there is no sin (transgression) even if Christians break the Mosaic law. Christians are not subject to the Mosaic law but under the law of "Messiah."

The fourth point is that only faith upholds the law [of "Messiah"/ "the Spirit"]. Paul teaches that if a Christian walks in "the Spirit," [according to the law of "the Spirit"] he/she will not sin. According to Paul, sin is breaking the law of "the Spirit." All the law [of "the Spirit"] is fulfilled in the second commandment of God: "You shall love your neighbor as yourself." (Galatians 5:14). To Paul the second commandment of God is more important than the first commandment of God: "You shall love Yehowah God with all your heart, all your soul, and all your mind." If you please man in all things, you have fulfilled the law of "Messiah." That is why Paul himself practiced this way (1 Corinthians 9:19-22):

> For though I be free from all men, yet have I made myself servant unto all, that I might gain the more. And unto the Jews I became as a Jew, that I might gain the Jews; to them that are under the law, as under the law, that I might gain them that are under the law; To them that are without law, as without law, (being not

without law of God, but **under the law of Messiah,)** that I might gain them that are without law. To the weak became I as weak, that I might gain the weak: **I am made all things to [please] all men**, that I might by all means save some.

Paul would rather please men in all things than keep the Mosaic law of God, which had not been abolished by Yeshua (Matthew 5:17-19).

In several places in the epistle to the Romans (e.g., Romans 1:18-32; 3:31), Paul appears to give us an impression that he does not teach lawlessness. He wrote the epistle to Romans after he was accused of teaching the lawlessness by the Jewish believers (Acts 21:20-21). This may be the reason why he did not clearly teach the lawlessness in his later epistles. Nevertheless, to be consistent with his earlier teachings, the law he talks about is the law that does not include the first commandment of God (Galatians 5:14). Paul listed the lawless deeds in Romans 1:29-31, which is the partial list of breaking the law of Moses. On the other hand, Christians are not required to keep the other parts of the Mosaic law such as keeping the Sabbaths, being circumcised in flesh, and keeping the dietary law. If Paul had taught his disciples to keep the Sabbaths, being circumcised in flesh, and keeping the dietary law, mainstream Christians would have practiced these parts of the Mosaic law. They have broken these parts of the law for about two thousand years!

These parts of the law happen to be included in the first commandment of God but not in the second commandment. Keeping these portions of the law with all our hearts, all our souls, and all our minds is to please and love God only because God is holy and hates everything unholy. The second commandment of God: "You shall love your neighbor as yourself" is a universal law for the entirety of human society. This commandment has been taught and upheld in almost all the cultures in the world. Keeping the second commandment is not sufficient for us to enter the kingdom of God because God's citizens must obey all the law of God with all our strength.

Yeshua came in a spiritual body

Paul teaches that Yeshua came as a spirit, in the likeness of man, and in appearance of a man, as seen from his statements below:

> And so it is written, "The first man Adam became a living being." The last Adam became a **life-giving spirit.** (1 Corinthians 15:46).

> but made Himself of no reputation, taking the form of a bondservant, and coming in **the likeness of men**. And being found in **appearance as a man**, He humbled Himself and became obedient to the point of death, even the death of the cross. (Philippians 2:7-8).

> For what the law [of Moses] was powerless to do in that it was weakened by the flesh, God did by sending His own Son in **the likeness of sinful man,** as an offering for sin. He thus condemned sin in the flesh. (Romans 8:3).

> For all [human flesh] have sinned and fall short of the glory of God [because of the original sin of Adam]. (Romans 3:23).

If Yeshua came in 100% human flesh, he would not have been sinless because all [human flesh] have sinned and fall short of the glory of God according to Paul. If Yeshua were not sinless, he would not be qualified to be the Passover Lamb of God. To resolve this contradiction, Paul had to say that Yeshua did not inherit "original sin" because he was not a natural man with 100% human flesh, but a spirit.

In the same way, Paul argues about the nature of a resurrected body in 1 Corinthians 15:35-58. In 1 Corinthians 15:50, Paul explicitly states: "Now this I say, brethren, that flesh and blood cannot inherit the kingdom of God; nor does corruption inherit incorruption." What Paul means is that a natural man with flesh and blood cannot inherit the kingdom of God. Paul further says that a saint who has died will be raised with an incorruptible body in the end times and that a saint who is still alive will be changed into an incorruptible body. The implication of Paul's argument is that a resurrected incorruptible body is just like the risen "Messiah" who has an incorruptible spiritual body. According to 1 Corinthians 15:50, the spiritual body does not have flesh and blood in contrast to the natural body.

PART

IV

TRUE FAITH IN YESHUA MESSIAH

CHAPTER
27

True Nature of the Messiah

Yeshua himself claimed to be the Son of God, the Son of Man, and the Messiah according to the Gospel of Matthew. The Gospel of John and the book of Revelation tell us that Yeshua is the incarnation of the Word of God who was with God in the beginning even before the creation of the world. To prove Yeshua to be the Messiah, the Gospels and some writings of his disciples must be in perfect agreement with the Old-Testament Scriptures.

The Son of Man

The Messiah must be the Son of Man according to Daniel's vision (Daniel 7:13-14),

> I was watching in the night visions, and behold, one like the Son of Man, coming with the clouds of heaven! He came to the Ancient of Days, and they brought him near before Him. Then to him was given dominion and glory and a kingdom, that all peoples, nations, and languages should serve him. His dominion is an everlasting dominion, which shall not pass away, and his kingdom the one which shall not be destroyed.

The Son of Man came to the Ancient of Days (God the Father) and was given dominion and glory and a kingdom, which is everlasting. All peoples, nations, and languages should serve him. These verses tell us that the Son of Man is the Messiah, who is the King of kings and the Lord of the lords on the earth.

The Son of God

The Messiah must be the Son of God according to Psalm 2:

> [1]Why do the nations rage, and the people plot a vain thing? [2]The kings of the earth set themselves, and the rulers take counsel together, against Yehowah and against His Messiah, saying, [3]"Let us break their bonds in pieces and cast away their cords from us." [4]He who sits in the heavens shall laugh; Yehowah shall hold them in derision. [5]Then He shall speak to them in His wrath, and distress them in His deep displeasure: [6]"Yet I have set My King On My holy hill of Zion." [7]"I will declare the decree: Yehowah has said to me, '**you are My Son, today I have begotten you.** [8]Ask of me, and I will give you the nations for your inheritance, and the ends of the earth for your possession. [9]You shall break them with a rod of iron; You shall dash them to pieces like a potter's vessel.'" [10]Now therefore, be wise, O kings; Be instructed, you judges of the earth. [11]**Serve Yehowah** with fear, and rejoice with trembling. [12]**Kiss the Son,** lest he be angry, and you perish in the way, when his wrath is kindled but a little. **Blessed are all those who put their trust in him**.

Psalm 2:7 tells us that the Messiah is the Son of God. The Son of God will rule the nations with a rod of iron and shall dash the rulers on the earth to pieces like potter's vessel. All the kings and judges of the earth must be wise, be instructed, **serve Yehowah** with fear, rejoice with trembling, and **kiss the Son**. If they do not respect the Son and if his wrath is kindled only a little, they will thus perish. Blessed are all those who put their trust in the Son.

In verse 12, a special Hebrew word "רַב (bar)" is used for "Son." The same Hebrew word is used for "Son" of Man in Daniel 7:13. This Hebrew word is also used in Proverb 31:2 to refer to a son who was the king of Lemuel. This special Hebrew word "bar" may refer to a person who is anointed.

Therefore, the Hebrew Bible teaches us that the titles: the Son of Man, the Son of God, and the Messiah are given to the same being. If Yeshua is the Messiah, he is also the Son of Man and the Son of God. The Gospels of Matthew and John agree with the teachings of the Hebrew Bible. Matthew recorded Yeshua's statement that there is only one teacher the Messiah (Matthew 23:8). John also stated (John 1:17): "For the law was given through Moses, but grace and truth came through Yeshua Messiah." Therefore, only the Messiah is the true teacher and only his interpretation of the Hebrew Bible is truthful.

The Word of God and the Judge of judges

In the Greek Gospel of John, John uses "the god" to refer to the Father and "a god" to the Word of God (John 1:1). The Greek Interlinear Bible of John 1:1 reads: "In the beginning was the Word and the Word was with the god and a god was the Word." The article "the" before god in the Greek text distinguishes the Father from His Son. Since the title of "the god" or capitalized "God" has been given to the Father, His Son cannot be called the god or God, but a god. The Son is God-like and executes all the power on behalf of his Father.

Yeshua has never claimed himself to be the god (God). He said to a rich young ruler, "Why do you call me good? No one is good but One, that is, God. But if you want to enter into life, keep the commandments." (Matthew 19:17). Here, Yeshua directly tells us that he is not God.

He claimed himself to be the Son of Man, the Son of God, and the Messiah. In John 10:30, Yeshua said: "I and my Father are one." Then the Jews accused him of blasphemy because they thought that Yeshua considered himself to be equal to the Father. So, Yeshua cited the Scriptures of the Hebrew Bible to prove that he is the Son of God and can be called a god (John 10:34-36). The judges, who were bestowed by God, could be called gods and the children of God in the Hebrew Bible.

For example, Psalm 82:6 says: "I said: 'you are gods, and all of you are children of the most High. But you shall die like men and fall like one of the princes.'" Here gods refer to judges as inferred from Psalm 82:1, "God stands in the congregation of the mighty; He judges among the gods (the judges). How long will you judge unjustly, and show partiality to the wicked?" We also see that "gods" refer to "judges" in Exodus 21:6, "then this master shall bring him to the gods (the judges). He shall also bring him to the door, or to the doorpost, and his master shall pierce his ear with an awl; and he shall serve him forever."

Therefore, the verses in John 1:1 and John 10:34 consistently tell us that the Word of God is a god (or a judge) who will judge the world justly. Yeshua said, "For the Father judges no one, but has committed all judgment to the Son." (John 5:22). "And He has given him authority to execute judgment also, because he is the Son." (John 5:27).

Yeshua's own words teach us that the Messiah is the Judge of the judges on the earth. He judges the world on behalf of his Father, and he judges according to what he hears from his Father. John 12:48 directly tells us that the word Yeshua has spoken will judge the one who rejects him in the last day. He also said that his word was directly from his Father and that whatever he spoke was just as his father told him. Therefore, he is the Word of God and speaks exactly the same words as what his Father tells him.

The Jews may misunderstand the statement of Yeshua in John 10:30, thinking that he claimed himself to be the same as his Father. In clarifying their misunderstanding, Yeshua in John 10:38 explains the true meaning of his statement: "He and his Father are one." In this verse, he says that the Father is in him and he is in his Father. They are one because his Father's Spirit is in him and they are in perfect union. In John 17:21-23, Yeshua prays that he and all his true believers may be one just as he and his Father are one, and that all his true believers, his Father, and himself may be one. So "one" means "in perfect union" through the same Spirit from the Father. The word "one" in the Gospel of John does not mean "the same" or "equal."

In John 14:28, Yeshua further declares: "My Father is greater than I." He is therefore not equal to his Father. After Yeshua resurrected, he told Mary Magdalene, "Do not cling to me, for I have not yet ascended to my Father, but go to my brethren and say to them, I am ascending to my Father and your Father, and to my God and your God." The resurrected Messiah is still the Son of God and even a brother of his disciples. If the resurrected Messiah were equal to his Father, then God the Father would be our brethren, which makes no sense.

The servant of God

Almost all Christians believe that the prophecy on the sin-bearing servant in Isaiah 53 was fulfilled in Yeshua about 2,000 years ago. This prophecy has been used to prove that Yeshua is the true Messiah. However, many modern Jewish rabbis interpret the sin-bearing servant in Isaiah 53 as the nation of Israel. They believe that Yeshua is not the sin-bearing servant and cannot be their Messiah.

It is impossible for the sin-bearing servant in Isaiah 53 to be the nation of Israel. If the sin-bearing servant in Isaiah 53 were the nation of Israel, how would it be possible for the nation of Israel to be buried with the wicked and with the rich (Isaiah 53:9)? It is obvious that this sin-bearing servant is a single person and does not represent the nation of Israel. In the previous chapters of the book of Isaiah, God calls Israel his servant and witnesses (Isaiah 43:10). Here, the word "servant" has a singular form but represents the people of Israel (plural meaning) because the parallel word "witnesses" has plural form. In Isaiah 53, the sin-bearing servant has a singular form and singular meaning. Similarly, the Hebrew word "seed" has singular form in Genesis 13:16 but plural meaning: descendants. But in Genesis 3:15, the word "seed" has a singular form and singular meaning because the singular pronouns "he" and "his" are used together.

The Prince of God

In Isaiah 49:3, a servant whose name is called Israel is declared. It is this verse that causes the modern Jewish rabbis to misattribute the sin-bearing servant in Isaiah 53 to the nation of Israel or Jacob. This servant Israel cannot refer to Jacob because God had hidden this servant (Isaiah 49:2) until the time of Isaiah while Jacob had been known a long time before Isaiah. At the time of the prophecy, God made this hidden servant known. This servant will bring Jacob back to Yehowah God (Isaiah 49:5), raise up the tribes of Jacob, and restore the preserved ones of Israel (Isaiah 49:6). If this servant were Jacob, how would verses 5 and 6 make sense? This servant will also be the light of the Gentiles and bring the salvation of God to the ends of the earth (Isaiah 49:6).

This servant is also called Israel by God just as many Jews in modern Israel are called "Israel." The same name for multiple persons is very common in many cultures. There are many Joshua's and Peter's in the United States.

Why does God also call this servant Israel? Each Israeli name has a special meaning. For example, Moses called Hosea, the son of Nun, Yehoshua. Hosea means salvation and Yehoshua (Joshua) means "Yehowah is salvation." Yehoshua became a regent of Yehowah on the earth, who led the Israelites and brought them into the promised land of God.

Jacob was called "Israel" after he wrestled with the angel of God. For a meaning of the name Israel, NOBSE Study Bible Name List and BDB Theological Dictionary unanimously go with the verb "הרשׂ," the meaning of which is unsure. NOBSE reads God Strives, and BDB proposes El Persists or El Perseveres. Israel is a compound name of El Sarah, which means "he will rule as God." Alfred Jones thinks that the mysterious verb "הרשׂ" might very well mean "to be princely," and assumes that the name Israel consists of a future form of this verb, which hence would mean to become princely. So Jones interprets the name Israel as "he will be prince with God."

If Israel could mean "he will rule as God" or "he will be prince with God," Israel could be a name of the Messiah who will co-reign with God in the kingdom of God on the earth. The Messiah is the prince of God and will co-reign with God forever. Therefore, the Son of Man, the Son of God, the Messiah, Yeshua, Israel, and the Word of God should all refer to the same being who is the only begotten Son of God.

The sin-bearing servant is the Prince of [new] Israel, who will bear the sins of the tribes of [old] Israel and restore the preserved ones of [old] Israel. Hosea the prophet rebuked the great sins of [old] Israel and prophesized in Hosea 10:15 and 11:1, "Thus, it shall be done to you, O Bethel, because of your great wickedness. At dawn the king of [old]

Israel shall be cut off utterly. For a child Israel, I shall love him, and out of Egypt I shall call my son." These two verses should not be placed in different chapters because they belong to a complete prophecy of God. The verbs "be done," "be cut," and "call" in these two verses are all in the perfect tense while the verb "love" is in the consecutive imperfect tense. The tense in the NKJV of Hosea 10:15 is correct because the perfect tense in Hebrew language can be used as the future tense to express assurance about the action being expressed by the verb. Thus, its use is to emphasize assurance about whatever is being expressed in the sense that the "completeness" of that event is an assured conviction and truth. This is especially true when a prophet of God speaks a prophecy, which must be fulfilled in a future date. That is why the verbs in Isaiah 9:6 are in the perfect tense in Hebrew, but they are changed to the future tense in NKJV. In Hosea 11:1, the verb "love" is in the consecutive imperfect tense, which directly points to the future tense. Then the other verbs in the perfect tense are consistently attributed to the future tense because they are consecutive to the verb "love," which is in the future tense. The same grammatical structure is also found in Isaiah 9:6 where Isaiah prophesies the birth of a child in a future time. In this verse, two verbs are in the consecutive imperfect tense and all the others are in the perfect tense, meaning that all the actions must be taken in a future time.

With the correct tense of Hosea 11:1, we can understand that God will love the new child whose name is also called Israel, and He will also call him out of Egypt. In the time of Hosea, the prophet knew that [old] Israel had been already inflicted by the Egyptians for about 400 years and God had brought them out of Egypt. If the new child Israel in Hosea 11:1 were Jacob, it is meaningless to prophesize something that had already happened. In both verses, Hosea simply prophesizes that the king of [old] Israel shall be cut off completely because of great wickedness while the everlasting Prince whose name is also called Israel shall be called out of Egypt. This prophecy was fulfilled in Yeshua, the Prince of [new] Israel (Matthew 2:15). The Prince of [new] Israel will restore the preserved remnants of [old] Israel and bring God's salvation to the ends of the earth (Isaiah 49:6). God has also made his mouth like a sharp sword (Isaiah 49:2) and he will strike the nations with the sharp sword out of his mouth (Revelation 19:15). He will rule the nations with a rod of iron (Revelation 19:15; Psalm 2:9). Therefore, Hosea and Isaiah both prophesized that the servant of God, whose name is called Israel, would be called out of Egypt, bear the sin of God's people, become the light of the Gentiles, and bring God's salvation to all the nations. Matthew correctly understood the prophecy and attributed this sin-bearing servant to Yeshua Messiah (Matthew 2:15).

The Counselor of God

God's only begotten Son exercises God's power on behalf of his Father. He is the Counselor of the Almighty God and the Prince of peace (Isaiah 9:6).

Isaiah 9:6 has been mistranslated into every language. Here we provide the verse from a Hebrew Interlinear Bible (Scripture 4 All):

> That boy he-is-born to us son he-is-given to us and she-shall-become the chieftainship on shoulder-blade-of him and he-shall-call name-of him one-marvelous one-counseling El masterful Father-of-future chief-of well-being.

When we add punctuation, the verse reads:

> That boy he-is-born to us, son he-is-given to us, and she-shall-become the chieftainship on shoulder-blade-of him, and he-shall-call name-of him **one**-marvelous, **one**-counseling El masterful Father-of-future, chief-of well-being.

If we accept this interlinear translation, we can re-phrase this verse as:

> A boy is born unto us, a son is given unto us, and the government shall be upon his shoulder. And his name shall be called the wonderful, the Counselor of God

Almighty the Everlasting Father, and the Prince of peace.

The phrase "one-counseling El masterful Father-of-future" should mean "the one who will counsel El masterful Father-of-future," that is, "the Counselor of God Almighty the Everlasting Father."

Therefore, the Son is called **"the Wonderful," "the Counselor of God the Father", and "the Prince of peace."** The Son will co-reign with his Father in the everlasting kingdom of God. The Son is not the same as the God Almighty Yehowah. The Son is the Angel (Messenger) of God, who bears the Name of Yehowah. The God Almighty, the Ancient of Days, or Yehowah God is **unbegotten** (Revelation 1:4,8) while the Son is **begotten**. The Father and the Son are not equal, as Daniel tells us in Daniel 7:13-14.

Some rabbis in modern Israel interpret the child in Isaiah 9:6 as Hezekiah king of Judah. No human has ever been called "God Almighty Everlasting Father." If the Messiah who is the King of kings and the Lord of lords on the earth cannot be called "God Almighty Everlasting Father," how could an earthly king have more privilege than the everlasting Prince of God (the Messiah)? The title "God" (meaning the god) is reserved for the heavenly Father only. Because Christians call their Messiah "God Almighty Everlasting Father" due to the mistranslation (misinterpretation) of Isaiah 9:6, the rabbis are angry and mock them for being ignorant. Yet in a similar manner, the rabbis blaspheme God when they refer to King Hezekiah as "God Almighty Everlasting Father." Yeshua declares (Matthew 23:9): "Do not call anyone on the earth your father; for One is your Father, He who is in heaven." Only the Father in heaven is called Everlasting Father. Yeshua also declares that his Father is greater than he (John 14:28). Yeshua's teaching is perfectly truthful, in agreement with John 1:17, "For the law was given through Moses, but grace and truth came through Yeshua."

The Angel of God

Who is the mighty angel of God described in Revelation 10:1-4? The face of the mighty angel was like sun and his feet like pillars of fire (10:1), and a rainbow was on his head. He had a little book open in his hand and cried out with a loud voice like roaring of a lion (Revelation 10:3). When he cried out, seven thunders uttered their voices (Revelation 10:4). In Matthew 17:2, we see that when Yeshua was transfigured into his glorious body, his face did shine as the sun. In Revelation 5:5, the slain Lamb was declared to be the lion of the tribe of Judah. Yeshua prophesized that he would come down to the earth like lightning flashes (Matthew 24:27). Since lightnings always come together with thunders, Revelation 10:4 implies that the mighty angel of God came down with lightning flashes and thunders. From these descriptions, the mighty angel is likely to be Yeshua himself.

How is it possible that Yeshua is the Angel of God? Yehowah God told Moses (NKJV with no modification): "Behold, I send an Angel before you to keep you in the way and to bring you into the place which I have prepared. Beware of Him and obey His voice; do not provoke Him, for He will not pardon your transgressions; for **My name is in Him.** For My Angel will go before you and bring you in to the Amorites and the Hittites and the Perizzites and the Canaanites and the Hivites and the Jebusites; and I will cut them off. ..." (Exodus 23:20-23).

These verses tell us that because the Angel bears the Name of Yehowah God, he is the Regent of God, who acts and speaks on behalf of Yehowah God Himself. That is why the Angel of Yehowah and Yehowah Himself are inter-exchangeable in the five books of Moses. For example, "And **the Angel of God**, who went before the camp of Israel, moved and went behind them; and the pillar of cloud went from before them and stood behind them. So it came between the camp of the Egyptians and the camp of Israel. Thus it was a cloud and darkness to the one, and it gave light by night to the other, so that the one did not come near the other all that night." (Exodus 14:19-20). These verses tell us that the Angel of God went before the Israelites by day in a pillar of cloud to lead the way, and by night in a pillar of fire to give them light. This is in contrast to Exodus 13:21, "And **Yehowah** went before them by day in a pillar of cloud, to lead them the way, and by night in a pillar of fire, to give them light, that they might go by day and by night:" Therefore, **Yehowah Himself and the Angle of God** did the same things for the Israelites.

Who does bear the Name of Yehowah? Moses called Hoshea (meaning salvation), the son of Nun, Yehoshua (Numbers 13:16). The name of Yehoshua (Joshua) is the compound name of Yehowah and Hoshea, which means "Yehowah is Salvation." Yehoshua the son of Nun was a man and a leader of the Israelites. Yehoshua cannot be the Angel of God because he did not go before the Israelites by day in a pillar of cloud to lead the way, and by night in a pillar of fire to give them light. Yeshua is the shorter version of Yehoshua. Yeshua the son of Jozadak (Ezra 3:2) should not have been the Angel of God either. The name of the Messiah is called Yeshua because he will save his people from their sins (Matthew 1:21). Since the name of the Messiah bears the Name of Yehowah, he should be the Angel of God mentioned in the books of Moses. If this is true, no one in the Hebrew Bible directly saw Yehowah God Himself, but His Angel who bears His Name. That is why Yeshua said, "No one has seen God **at any time**. The only begotten Son, who is in the bosom of the Father, he has declared Him." (John 1:18). Yeshua also said, "All the things have been delivered to me by my Father, and no one knows the Son except the Father, nor does anyone know the Father except the Son, and **the one to whom the Son wills to reveal Him**." (Matthew 11:27). Therefore, Yeshua's own words confirm that the Angel of God in the Old Testament is actually the Son of God who bears the Name (Yehowah) of his Father. The Son of God spoke and acted in the Name of his Father in the Old Testament and came in the flesh in the Name of his Father in the New Testament.

Because the Angel of God fully represents God, he speaks and acts with the same authority as God. In ancient China, the messenger of an emperor also spoke and acted with the same authority as his emperor. Whoever knew the identity of the messenger had to bow down to him because he was like the emperor.

The capitalization of the words such as "Angel", "He", "His", and "Him" in these verses implies that the NKJV translators have referred to the Angel (Messenger) of God as the Son of God. Therefore, the author of this book is not the only one who has identified the Angel of God in the Old Testament as the only begotten Son of God in the New Testament.

One can identify the Angel of God as Yeshua Messiah from Revelation 22:6-7. In Revelation 22:6-7, the angel said to John: "These words are faithful and true. And the Lord God of the holy prophets sent the angel of Him to show His servants the things which must shortly take place. Behold, I am coming quickly! Blessed is he who keeps the words of the prophecy of this book."

From verse 22:6, we see that God sent His angel to show His servants—things which must shortly take place. The angel also said to John (verse 22:7), "Behold, I am coming quickly!..." In this verse, "I" must refer to the angel who talked to John and was one of the seven angels who had the seven bowls (Revelation 21:9). Who is coming quickly? It is the angel of God who is coming quickly. It is Yeshua Messiah who is coming quickly. In fact, the words recorded in Revelation 22: 9-16 are all from the angel of God. From the contents of these words, it is apparent that the angel must be Yeshua Messiah.

Therefore, the mighty Angel in the book of Revelation is Yeshua himself. This conclusion is further supported by the verse: "And I will give power to my two witnesses, and they will prophesy one thousand two hundred and sixty days, clothed in sackcloth." (Revelation 11:3). Since the mighty Angel gives power to **his** two witnesses who are the two olive trees and the two lampstands before the God of the earth, he must have great power and authority. No other angel in the Hebrew Bible has authority and power comparable to the Angel of Yehowah who bears His Name and executes all His authority. Yeshua the Son of God was given all authority in heaven and earth after he resurrected (Matthew 28:18) and was restored to his original glory before the world was created (John 17:5). Yeshua also declared that all the things the Father has are his (John 16:15). The Son of God has the authority to send the Holy Spirit (the Spirit of the Truth) from the Father to his disciples to testify of him (John 15:26) and to guide his disciples into all truth (John 16:13). Therefore, only the Son of God has such a great authority to give power to **his** two witnesses.

Who are the two witnesses of the mighty Angel? When Yeshua was transfigured into his glorious body, Moses and Elijah also appeared to three disciples of Yeshua (Matthew 17:3). This implies that Moses and Elijah are the two witnesses of Yeshua. The two witnesses in the book of Revelation should also be Moses and Elijah because they will perform miracles (Revelation 11:5-6) similar to those performed by Moses and Elijah in the past and because Yeshua stated that Elijah would come in a future time (Matthew 11:14). The future time for Elijah to come should be right before the great day of Yehowah in the end times, which was prophesized in Malachi 4:5, "Behold, I will send you Elijah the prophet before the coming of the great and **dreadful day** of Yehowah." The great and dreadful day of Yehowah (probably the third woe in the book of Revelation) will take place after the 7th trumpet and the second woe. The two witnesses sent by the mighty Angel of God will prophesize 1260 days before the 7th trumpet sounds (Revelation 11). One of the witnesses, Elijah, will be sent by Yehowah Himself according to Malachi 4:5. The apparent contradiction between Malachi and Revelation can be naturally resolved if the mighty Angel of God is Yeshua himself who has received all the power and glory from his Father after his resurrection. Yeshua has the authority to send the Spirit of Truth from his Father to his disciples after he sat on the right-hand side of his Father. Therefore, the mighty Angel of God must be Yeshua himself in order for Moses and Elijah to be his witnesses.

28

Yeshua Messiah: Recognized by Few Jews

Rabbis in the first century AD and in modern Israel have missed an important prophecy about two advents of the Messiah. Yehowah God declares in Zechariah 9:9-10,

> [9]Rejoice greatly, O daughter of Zion! Shout, O daughter of Jerusalem! Behold, your king is coming to you; He is just and having salvation, lowly and riding on a donkey, A colt, the foal of a donkey. [10]I will cut off the chariot from Ephraim And the horse from Jerusalem; The battle bow shall be cut off. He shall speak peace to the nations; His dominion shall be from sea to sea, And from the River to the ends of the earth.

In verse 9, Zechariah prophesizes the first advent of the Messiah. At his first advent, he was humble, riding on a colt to enter Jerusalem. He was just and brought salvation. This was fulfilled in Yeshua when he was riding on a colt to enter Jerusalem on 10 Nisan 30 AD as the Passover Lamb of God. He is the Judge of judges but was judged and slain because of the sins of God's people.

In verse 10, Zechariah prophesizes the final advent of the Messiah. At his final coming, he will judge the nations and reign with his Father forever.

Between the first and final advents of the Messiah, he returned in the spring of 67 AD (see Chapter 9). His return in 67 AD was prophesized by Yeshua himself in Matthew 10:23, Matthew 16:28, and John 21:22-23. Because these Jewish rabbis do not understand these multiple advents before his final return to rule on the earth, most of them have not recognized Yeshua as their Messiah.

They will eventually recognize Yeshua as their Messiah, as prophesized in Zechariah 12:10-14:

> And I will pour on the house of David and on the inhabitants of Jerusalem the Spirit of grace and supplication. And they will look on the one whom they pierced. Yes, they will mourn for him as one mourns for his only son, and grieve for him as one grieves for a firstborn. In that day there shall be a great mourning in Jerusalem, like the mourning at Hadad Rimmon in **the plain of Megiddo**. And the land shall mourn, every family by itself: the family of the house of David by itself, and their wives by themselves; the family of the house of Nathan by itself, and their wives by themselves; the family of the house of Levi by itself, and their wives by themselves; the family of Shimei by itself, and their wives by themselves; all the families that remain, every family by itself, and their wives by themselves.

The Hebrew Interlinear Bible for Zechariah 12:10 (with added punctuation) reads: "And I will pour on the house of David and on the inhabitants of Jerusalem the Spirit of grace and supplication, and they will look toward whom they pierced. Yes, they will mourn for him as one mourns for his only one and grieve for him as one grieves for a firstborn." In most English versions, "me" is added before whom, which makes the crucified Messiah identical to Yehowah God. The added "me" does not make any sense because in the latter sentences, the third-person pronoun "him" is used to refer to the one whom they pieced. Only in the Contemporary English Version and God News Translation, is "the one" instead of "me" added before "whom."

The Messiah is the true Prophet whom Moses foretold in Deuteronomy 18:17-19:

> And Yehowah God said to me: "What they have spoken is good. I will raise up for them a prophet like you from among their brethren, and will put My words in his mouth, and he shall speak to them all that I command him. And it shall be that whoever will not hear My words, which he speaks in My name, I will require it of him."

When the true Prophet spoke the words on behalf of Yehowah God, God's people should have listened to him. However, they did not hear his words but instead condemned him unjustly to the cruelest punishment of crucifixion (being pieced through). In contrast, a false prophet should not live and deserve condemnation of being pierced through. That is why Yehowah God declares that (Zechariah 13:3) a false prophet shall not live and be pierced through by their parent in that day when everything is judged righteously. For a lesser offense, a false prophet might be permitted to live and punished with his arms being pierced. His remaining life will be shameful, as stated in (Zechariah 13:6): "And one will say to him [the false prophet], 'What are these wounds between your arms?' Then he will answer, 'I was wounded in the house of my friends.'" In fact, he is wounded in his own house by his parent due to his false prophecy in the name of God. To cover the great shame of being a false prophet, he would rather tell a lie.

Some modern Jewish rabbis misunderstand Chapters 12 and 13 of the book of Zechariah. They argue that since a false prophet should be punished with being pierced through, Yeshua's crucifixion suggests that he would have been a false prophet. This argument appears reasonable on the surface. In fact, the Messiah the true Prophet was pierced unjustly by his own people. It was the mistake of his own people who unjustly pierced the true Prophet. We have shown in Part I that Yeshua's own prophecies were perfectly fulfilled, which proves that he is the true Prophet foretold by Moses. The pierced Messiah will be recognized by

God's people after God pours out the spirit of grace and supplication on them in the end times.

Yeshua the sin-bearing servant of God (also called Israel) was judged unjustly due to the sins of God's people, as clearly prophesized in Isaiah 53. Most Jews have missed this crucial point for over 2,000 years. They have not learned from the history of their severe punishments by God. They should have asked the questions as to: 1) why God did not accept their offerings between 30 and 70 AD after they crucified Yeshua in 30 AD; 2) why the holy temple and the holy city were destroyed and over 1 million Jews were killed in 70 AD—exactly 40 years after Yeshua's crucifixion; 4) why the Islamic Dome of the Rock was sitting near the holiest temple site; and 5) why 6 million Jews were killed by the Nazis during the second world war.

The greatest iniquity God's people have committed is their rejection of Yeshua, His only begotten Son. The Son of God is the Shepherd and the Companion of Yehowah God (Zechariah 13:7). He is in the bosom of the Father (John 1:18) from the beginning (John 1:1). Zechariah 13:8 prophesized that Yehowah God would strike the Shepherd, and His sheep would be scattered. This prophecy was fulfilled in Yeshua and his disciples (Matthew 26:31; John 16:32). Because the Shepherd was judged unjustly and suffered most severely for the sin of God's people, Yehowah God intended to turn his hand upon His inferior sheep. Like their Shepherd, the inferior sheep shall also suffer greatly to be refined like gold and silver (Zechariah 13:8-9) before they go back to their holy land. This prophecy was fulfilled perfectly in the second world war when about 6 million Jews were killed by evil Nazis (see Chapter 27 of the book: *Perfectly Fulfilled Prophecies and the Destiny of Mankind*).

When the Dome of the Rock started to be built in 688 AD, the Jews were almost completely driven out of the holy city and became powerless. At this time, they still did not understand why God treated them so harshly. They were in the wilderness for 1260 years before they were brought back to the holy land in 1948 AD, as prophesized in Daniel 12:7 and Revelation 12:6. There is only one possible explanation: Yeshua is the true Messiah who was crucified for the sin of God's people in 30 AD. Daniel's 70-week prophecy has been perfectly fulfilled in Yeshua (see Chapters 4 and 5).

Because the Jewish rabbis do not believe Yeshua to be the Messiah, they misinterpreted Daniel's 70-week prophecy. Within their interpretation, Daniel's 490 years (70 weeks) is referred to the time span between the first and the second destructions of the holy temple. With this interpretation, the date for the first destruction of the holy temple would have been in 421 BC, which was off by 166 years compared with the true date (587 BC). Because of this mistake, the Jewish year in 2020 AD would be the 5780th year from the creation of Adam, which is off by 210 years compared to the true 5990th year.

CHAPTER
29

Should We Worship the Messiah?

Yeshua has clearly said that he is not God (Matthew 19:17). He also explicitly tells us that his Father is greater than him (John 10:29; John14:28). In Chapter 27, we show that Yeshua Messiah is the Son of God, the Son of Man, the Word of God, the Prince of God, the Counselor of God, and the Servant of God.

An important question arises as to whether the Messiah should be worshipped. In the book of Revelation, in all the verses describing the heavenly worships, only God Almighty is worshipped. The Lamb receives power and riches and wisdom and strength and honor and glory and blessing (Revelation 5:12, Matthew 28:18). In Revelation 5:13-14, John records one of the heavenly worships (Aramaic version): "And I heard the whole creation, that is in heaven and on the earth and under the earth and that is in the sea, and all that is in them, saying to Him who sits on the throne and to the Lamb … Blessing, and honor, and praise, and dominion, forever and ever! And the four beasts were saying, Amen. And the elders fell down and worshipped." Verse 14 does not clearly tell us whom the elders worshipped. But from the previous verses, we see that only God sat on the throne and the Lamb stood in the midst of the elders (Revelation 5:6). Therefore, the elders worshipped God who sat on the throne. Although the elders and four living creatures fell down before the Lamb, John did not say that they worshipped him. Their protraction in this verse could simply show their homage to the Lamb who is worthy of receiving honor and glory and blessing. In Revelation 22:8, John fell down to worship before the feet of the Angel who showed all these things to him, but the Angel [Yeshua] said to him (Revelation 22:9): "You do not do that. For I am a fellow worker of you, of your brethren, of the prophets, and of those who keep the words of this book. Worship God."

In verse 8, John not only fell down but also worshipped the Angel, as the text clearly states. Why did John worship the Angel? This is because John finally realized that this Angel was actually Yeshua Messiah, his Lord and Teacher after the Angel told him that he would come quickly in the previous verses (Revelation 22: 6-7): "These words are faithful and true. And Yehowah God of the holy prophets sent His angel to show His servants the things which must shortly take place. Behold, I am coming quickly! Blessed is he who keeps the words of the prophecy of this book." It is Yeshua who said, "Behold, I am coming quickly!"

When Yeshua was with disciples right after his resurrection, he told them that he was going to come back when John was still alive and after Peter had died (John 21:22-23). A while ago John did not recognize the mighty Angel to be Yeshua himself because his appearance was very different from that of the risen Yeshua in the flesh.

After John recognized the Angel as Yeshua, he fell down to worship him. But Yeshua told him not to do so because he was also a servant of God, as clearly seen from John 20:17 and Matthew 28:10 as well as from Isaiah 49-53. Here, Yeshua explicitly addresses the problem of John's worship possibly because many believers (including his disciples) at that time may have worshipped the Messiah in church congregations. By correcting John, Yeshua teaches his believers to worship the Father only.

When the resurrected Messiah revealed himself to the Mary's, they held him by the feet and worshiped him (Matthew 28:9). Yeshua did not directly correct their action but instead said to them: "Do not be afraid. Go and tell **my brethren** to go to Galilee, and there they will see me." Yeshua told them that he was **the brethren of his disciples**, implying that he considered himself to be the fellow servant of his disciples. When his disciples saw the resurrected Messiah, they also worshipped him (Matthew 28:17) but Yeshua did not correct them. Even before he was crucified, he was worshipped by those in the boat when he calmed down the wind (Matthew 14:33). Yeshua did not correct their action of worship either.

Before Yeshua resurrected, he was a man in the flesh. According to the law, no man shall be worshipped. But because Yeshua came in the Name of his Father and executed all the authority on behalf of his Father, he could accept worship. In the Old Testament, the Angel of God also accepted worship because he represented God Himself. After Yeshua resurrected, he received all authority from the Father (Matthew 28:18). Yeshua says in John 16:7, "If I depart [from the world], I will send him [the Holy Spirit] to you." Yeshua further says, "Whatever you ask the Father in my name, He will give you." (John 16:23). "He [The Holy Spirit] will glorify me, for he will take of what is mine and declares to you." (John 16:14). These verses tell us that the Holy Spirit comes to the world and speaks Yeshua's words when Yeshua is with his Father in heaven.

When Satan asked Yeshua to worship him, Yeshua answered: "Away with you, Satan! For it is written, 'you shall worship Yehowah your God, and **Him only** you shall serve." According to Yeshua and the law, we shall worship and serve Yehowah God only.

Yeshua also teaches in John 4:22, "The truth worshipper will **worship the Father** in spirit and truth." Here, Yeshua narrows our worship toward the Father only and addresses our premier problem of our worship.

Only Yehowah God deserves worship because He is the LORD (Master) of all in heaven and on the earth. Although the Messiah is the Lord of lords and the King of kings on the earth and is above all other angels in heaven, he is still under his Father (John 14:28). He is the Angel of Yehowah God in the books of Moses and the Servant of Yehowah God in the book of Isaiah. Psalm 2:11-12 also instructs us to serve and worship Yehowah God only and to kiss (honor) the Son. Only God whose Name is called Yehowah deserves worship according to Yeshua's instruction and the law.

In Revelation 22:3, we are told: "And there shall be no more curse, the throne of God and throne of the Lamb shall be in it, and His servants shall serve **Him** (God)." Although the Lamb has his own throne, God's servants shall **serve God only** because this verse clearly says, "serve Him" rather than "serve Them."

In Revelation 20:4, we are also told: "And I saw thrones, and they sat on them, and judgment was committed to them…." Who will sit on the thrones to make judgment? Yeshua says unto them in Matthew 18:28: "Verily I say unto you, that you who have followed me, in the regeneration when the Son of man shall sit on the throne of his glory, you also shall sit upon twelve thrones, judging the twelve tribes of Israel." These thrones are the twelve thrones of Yeshua's disciples. The disciples have their thrones to judge the twelve tribes of Israel. In a similar manner, the Lamb has his own throne to rule over all the nations on the earth on behalf of his Father. In other words, the Messiah will co-reign with the Father in the everlasting kingdom of God. Since the Messiah is the Prince of God and the Counselor of God, his role in God's kingdom may be like Joseph in Egypt.

CHAPTER

30

True Faith in Yeshua Messiah

We have proved that Yeshua is the Messiah, the Son of God, the Son of Man, the Word of God, the Lamb of God, and the Angel of God.

Yeshua was born on Nisan 1 (March 9) of 5 BC (see Chapter 31). He started his earthly ministry in the spring of 27 AD and ended his ministry in the spring of 30 AD. He was crucified on April 6 of 30 AD and resurrected on April 9. He had twelve disciples and one of them, Judas, betrayed him. He lived with them for about three years, teaching them about the words of God, the kingdom of God, and eternal life.

Yeshua's words and deeds were recorded in the Gospel of Matthew, the Gospel of John, and the book of Revelation. Only these books were written by his direct disciples who followed him from the beginning of Yeshua's ministry. These books do not contradict each other, and all the numerical prophecies of Yeshua recorded in these books were perfectly fulfilled. Furthermore, all the teachings of Yeshua in these books are consistent with the Old-Testament Scriptures. For these reasons, these three books should be the inspired words of God. Therefore, our Christian faith must be consistent with the law of Moses, the words of the true prophets in the Old Testament, and all the words of Yeshua in the Gospel of Matthew, the Gospel of John, and the book of Revelation. The teachings in the epistles of John and James should also be the inspired words of God because they agree with the teachings of these three books.

How to be saved?

Yeshua directly told Nicodemus (John 3:5): "Most assuredly, I say to you, unless one is born of water and the Spirit, he cannot enter the kingdom of God." Yeshua's statement indicates that there are two necessary conditions for entering the kingdom of God: 1) he/she must be born of water, that is, he must be baptized in water; and 2) he/she must be born of the Spirit, that is, he must have received the Holy Spirit. By believing and receiving Yeshua as the Son of God, he is born of God (John 1:12-13).

1 John 2:1-2 says: "if anyone sins, we have an Advocate with the Father, Yeshua Messiah the righteous. And he himself is the propitiation for our sins, and not for ours only but also for the whole world." We must first repent and be baptized in the name of Yeshua for the remission of our sins. We then receive the Holy Spirit after the baptism.

John further tells us in John 3:15-17:

> that whoever believes in him **should not** perish but have eternal life. For God so loved the world that He gave His only begotten Son, that whoever believes in him **should not** perish but have everlasting life. For God did not send His Son into the world to condemn the world, but that the world through him **might be** saved.

In fact, the above English translation is not very accurate. From the Interlinear Greek-English Bible, we obtain more accurate translation:

> that whoever believes in him **may** not perish but **may** have eternal life. For God so loved the world that He gave His only begotten Son, that whoever believes in him should not perish but **may** have everlasting life. For God did not send His Son into the world that he **might** condemn the world, but that the world through Him **might** be saved.

These passages tell us that believing in Yeshua is a necessary condition for eternal life, but not a sufficient condition.

John also teaches us in the following passages:

> Now by this we know that we know him, if we keep his commandments. He who says, "I know him," and does not keep his commandments, is a liar, and the truth is not in him. But whoever keeps his word, truly the love of God is perfected in him. By this we know that we are in him. He who says he abides in him ought himself also to **walk just as he [Yeshua] walked**. (1 John 2:3-6).

> Whoever commits sin also commits lawlessness [breaking the Mosaic law], and sin is lawlessness. And you know that he was manifested to take away our sins, and in him there is no sin. Whoever abides in him does not sin. **Whoever sins has neither seen him nor known him.** (1 John 3:4-6).

> Little children, let no one deceive you. **He who practices righteousness is righteous, just as he is righteous**. He who sins is of the devil, for the devil has sinned from the beginning. **For this purpose the Son of God was manifested, that he might destroy the works of the devil. Whoever has been born of God does not sin, for His seed remains in him; and he cannot sin, because he has been born of God.** (1 John 3:7-9).

These passages teach us that we do not sin (the present tense of "do not sin" in Greek means "do not keep on sinning" in English) because we have been born of God. Since the Son of God has destroyed the works of the devil, we can overcome sin and keep the commandants of God if we abide in Yeshua and walk just as he walked. If we keep on breaking the law of God, we are unrighteous and cannot enter the kingdom of God. If we walk in the light as he is in the light, we have fellowship with one another, and the blood of Yeshua Messiah cleanses us from all sin. If we are overcome by sin occasionally, we must confess our sin and repent. Then God will forgive our sin because He is faithful and righteous (1 John 1:9).

Only if we keep the commandants of God, can we be the children of God (Revelation 12:17; 14:12; 22:14). Only if we have true faith in Yeshua Messiah, can we have the power to keep commandants of God and enter the kingdom of God.

The salvation principle taught in the Gospel of John, the epistles of John, and the book of Revelation is also consistent with the teaching in Matthew 19:16-22,

> [16]Now behold, one came and said to him, "Good Teacher, what good thing shall I do that I may have eternal life?" [17]So he said to him, "Why do you call me good? No one is good but One, that is, God. But if you want to enter into life, keep the commandments." [18]He said to Him, "Which ones?" Yeshua said, "'You shall not murder,' 'You shall not commit adultery,' 'You shall not steal,' 'You shall not bear false witness,' [19]'Honor your father and your mother,' and, 'You shall love your neighbor as yourself.'" [20]The young man said to him, "All these things I have kept from my youth. What do I still lack?" [21]Yeshua said to him, "If you want to be perfect, go, sell what you have and give to the poor, and you will have treasure in heaven; and come, follow me." [22]But when the young man heard that saying, he went away sorrowful, for he had great possessions. [25]When His disciples heard it, they were greatly astonished, saying, "Who then can be saved?" [26]But Yeshua looked at them and said to them, "With men this is impossible, but with God all things are possible."

In the above passage, Yeshua tells us that if we want to enter into eternal life, keep the commandments of God, in particular, the Ten Commandments. The rich young man had not kept all the commandments because he was unwilling to follow Yeshua's step to love God with all his heart, all his soul, and all his mind. The rich man broke the first and the most important commandment because he loved the worldly things more than he loved God and because he would rather serve money than God. That is why Yeshua said: "It is easier for a camel to go through the eye of a needle than for a rich man to enter the kingdom of God." (Matthew 19:24).

Yeshua further told his disciple (Matthew 19:26): "With men this [entering into the kingdom of God] is impossible, but with God all things are possible." The meaning of this verse is: We cannot enter the kingdom of God with our own effort, but if we are born of God by believing in the Son of God and being baptized in water, we can keep the commandments of God and enter the kingdom of God.

Yeshua also teaches that if we break the least commandment of God, we will be called the least in the kingdom of God (Matthew 5:19). This implies that if we do not keep the Sabbaths, breaking this important commandant, we may be denied entry to the kingdom of God.

Has the law of God been abolished by Yeshua?

In Matthew 5:17-20, Yeshua says:

> Do not think that I came to destroy the law or the prophets. I did not come to destroy but to fulfill. For assuredly, I say to you, till heaven and earth pass away, one jot or one tittle will by no means pass from the law till all is fulfilled. Whoever therefore breaks one of the least of these commandments, and teaches men so, shall be called least in the kingdom of heaven; but whoever does and teaches them, he shall be called great in the kingdom of heaven. For I say to you, that unless your righteousness exceeds the righteousness of the scribes and Pharisees, you will by no means enter the kingdom of heaven.

It is clear that Yeshua did not come to destroy the law but to make it full (the Greek word "pléroó" means "make full"). How did Yeshua make the law full? In Matthew 5: 21-48, Yeshua teaches us to keep the law of God from our inner hearts. He gave some examples to demonstrate how to keep the commandments of God in our hearts. He wants us to be sinless in both heart and behavior, making the law full and honorable. Yeshua's teaching is consistent with Isaiah 42:21, "Yehowah is well pleased for His righteousness sake; He will **exalt** the law and make it honorable." The Father God wants to **exalt** the law and make it honorable, and Yeshua came to make it full or exalt it.

The prophet Ezekiel also declares in Ezekiel 36:26-27, "I will give you a new heart and put a new spirit within you; I will take the heart of stone out of your flesh and give you a heart of flesh. I will **put My Spirit within you** and **cause you to walk** in My statutes, and you will **keep** My judgments and **do** them." Through the salvation work of Yeshua, we receive the Holy Spirit of God, who helps us **keep** the law of God more fully and honorably.

Should we keep the Sabbaths?

Most Christians misunderstand Matthew 5:17, thinking that we do not have to keep the law of God because Yeshua has fulfilled it and kept it for us. If this understanding were correct, why did Yeshua say: "Whoever therefore **breaks** one of the least of these commandments, and teaches men so, shall be called least in the kingdom of heaven." Here "**breaking**" refers to our own action of not keeping the law. If we break one of the least of these commandments, we will be called the least in the kingdom of heaven. Keeping the weekly Sabbaths is one of the important commandments of God. Since breaking one of the least commandments makes us the least in the kingdom of heaven, we may not even be allowed to enter the kingdom of heaven if we do not keep the Sabbaths.

Yeshua's teaching is consistent with those of the prophets of God. Isaiah declares in Isaiah 56:1-7:

> Thus says Yehowah: "**Keep** justice, and **do** righteousness, For My salvation is about to come, And My righteousness to be revealed. Blessed is the man who **does** this, and the son of man who **lays hold on** it; Who **keeps from defiling the Sabbath**, and keeps his hand from doing

any evil." Do not let the son of the foreigner who has joined himself to Yehowah speak, saying, "Yehowah has utterly separated me from His people"; Nor let the eunuch says, "Here I am, a dry tree." For thus says Yehowah: **"To the eunuchs who keep My Sabbath, and choose what pleases Me, and hold fast My covenant, even to them I will give in My house and within My walls a place and a name better than that of sons and daughters; I will give them an everlasting name that shall not be cut off.** "Also the sons of the foreigner who join themselves to Yehowah, to serve Him, and to love the name of Yehowah, to be His servants—**Everyone who keeps from defiling the Sabbath, and holds fast My covenant—Even them I will bring to My holy mountain, and make them joyful in My house of prayer**. Their burnt offerings and their sacrifices will be accepted on My altar; **For My house shall be called a house of prayer for all nations."**

Yehowah God wants us to keep the Sabbath holy in any period. If Yeshua had taught us not to keep the Sabbath, he would have been a false prophet. In contrast, Yeshua teaches that he is the Lord of the Sabbath and that the Sabbath is for man, not man for the Sabbath. According to Yeshua, the Sabbath is set for human, in agreement with words of Yehowah in Isaiah 56:1-7. If the foreigners (Gentiles) keep the Sabbath, but not defile them, they will be given a place and a name better than those of God's chosen people. There is no place in the Hebrew Scriptures nor in the words of Yeshua, which says that the day of the weekly Sabbaths has been changed from the seventh day to the first day of a week and that the Gentile believers do not have to keep the Sabbaths.

Should the Gentile believers keep the dietary law of Moses?

Another important question arises as to whether the Gentile believers should keep the dietary law of Moses. Yeshua never abolished the dietary law. In the story of eating bread with unwashed hands, Yeshua did not teach that we could eat the unclean foods prescribed by Moses. What Yeshua teaches is that to eat with unwashed hands does not defile a man (Matthew 15:20). If Yeshua had taught his disciples to eat unclean food, he would have been against the teaching of Isaiah in Isaiah 66:14-17:

> [14]When you see this, your heart shall rejoice, and your bones shall flourish like grass; The hand of Yehowah shall be known to His servants, and His indignation to His enemies. [15]For behold, Yehowah will come with fire and with His chariots, like a whirlwind, to render His anger with fury, and His rebuke with flames of fire. [16]For by fire and by His sword Yehowah will judge **all flesh**; And the slain of Yehowah shall be **many**. [17]"Those who sanctify themselves and purify themselves, to go to the gardens after an idol in the midst, **Eating swine's flesh and the abomination and the mouse, shall be consumed together**," says Yehowah.

A more accurate English translation for Isaiah 66:17 is,

> "**Those** who sanctify themselves and purify themselves in the gardens after idol in the midst, **those** who eat swine's flesh and the abomination and the mouse, shall be consumed together," says Yehowah.

In the last days, Yehowah will judge **all flesh** (verse 16), including His own people and the Gentiles. He will consume those who are the idol worshippers and those who eat swine's flesh and the abomination and the mouse (verse 17). Thus, Yehowah did not abolish the dietary law. That is why Yeshua said: "till heaven and earth pass away, one jot or one tittle will by no means pass from the law till all is fulfilled (made full)." What Yeshua means that any part of the law delivered by Moses will never pass away till heaven and earth pass away.

Should we be circumcised in the flesh?

Almost all Christians believe that the Gentile believers are not required to be circumcised in the flesh, and that if we would try to keep the law [of Moses] we would lose our salvation (Galatians 5:1-6). In the Gospels, Yeshua himself did not teach about the requirement of flesh circumcision. But Ezekiel the prophet of God clearly teaches us that even foreigners are required to be circumcised both in the flesh and the heart in order to enter the temple of God in the millennial kingdom of God (Ezekiel 44:6-9).

The law of circumcision in the flesh has not been abolished by God. This is because circumcision in the flesh is the sign for the **everlasting** covenant between God and descendants of Abraham. Foreigners must also be circumcised in the flesh in order to live among them. This can be seen from Genesis 15:1-14:

> When Abram was ninety-nine years old, Yehowah appeared to Abram and said to him, "I am Almighty God; walk before Me and be blameless. And I will make My covenant between Me and you, and will multiply you exceedingly." Then Abram fell on his face, and God talked with him, saying: "As for Me, behold, My covenant is with you, and you shall be a father of many nations. No longer shall your name be called Abram, but your name shall be Abraham; for I have made you a father of many nations. I will make you exceedingly fruitful; and I will make nations of you, and kings shall come from you. And I will establish My covenant between Me and you and **your descendants after you in their generations**, for an **everlasting** covenant, to be God to you and your descendants after you. Also I give to you and your descendants after you the land in which you are a stranger, all the land of Canaan, as an **everlasting** possession; and I will be their God." And God said to Abraham: "As for you, you shall keep My covenant, **you and your descendants after you**

throughout their generations. This is My covenant which you shall keep, between Me and you and your descendants after you: **Every male child among you shall be circumcised**; and you shall be circumcised in the flesh of your foreskins, and it shall be **a sign of the covenant between Me and you**. He who is eight days old among you shall be circumcised, every male child in your generations, he who is born in your house or bought with money from **any foreigner who is not your descendant. He who is born in your house and he who is bought with your money must be circumcised**, and My covenant shall be **in your flesh for an everlasting covenant**. And the uncircumcised male child, who is not circumcised in the flesh of his foreskin, that person shall be cut off from his people; he has broken My covenant."

Abraham is the father of the nation of Israel. The Gentile believers are adopted as the descendants of Abraham by circumcision in the flesh, which is **the sign of the everlasting covenant** between God and all the descendants of Abraham.

Only Paul teaches that circumcision in the flesh is not required for salvation. The decision of the Jerusalem council concerning the requirement of flesh circumcision was recorded in Acts 15. James and Peter appeared to agree that the Gentile's believers are not required to be circumcised in flesh. There are two possible explanations for this: 1) Luke did not honestly record the decision of the Jerusalem council; 2) The apostles and elders in Jerusalem were misled by Paul who declared how many miracles and wonders God had worked through them among the Gentiles (Acts 15:12-13). We believe the second explanation because Yeshua prophesizes in Matthew 24:24, "For false messiahs and false prophets will rise and show great signs and wonders to deceive, if possible, even the elect." Paul used his wonders, signs, and mighty deeds he performed to prove his apostleship (2 Corinthians 12:12). Paul's argument sounds very reasonable to most people and has misled many people and even the elect.

The Holy Spirit might have reminded James and the elders of Yeshua's forewarning, causing them to reverse their decision. This can naturally explain why James was very hard on Paul on his last visit to Jerusalem. James and the elders in Jerusalem said to Paul (Acts 21:20-25),

> "You see, brother, how many myriads of Jews there are who **have believed**, and they **are all zealous for the law**; but they have been informed about you that you teach all the Jews who are among the Gentiles to **forsake Moses,** saying that they **ought not to circumcise their children nor to walk according to the customs.** What then? The assembly must certainly meet, for they will hear that you have come. Therefore do what we tell you: We have four men who have taken a vow. Take them and be purified with them, and pay their expenses so that they may shave their heads, and that **all may know that those things of which they were informed concerning you are nothing, but that you yourself also walk orderly and keep the law.** But concerning the Gentiles who believe, we have written and decided [that they should observe no such thing, except] that they should keep themselves from things offered to idols, from blood, from things strangled, and from sexual immorality."

The words of James and the elders in the Jerusalem church tell us that Jewish believers are required to keep the law of Moses including circumcision in flesh. Gentile believers were commanded not to break the very important parts of the Mosaic law. This time, they did not say that circumcision in flesh was not required for the Gentile believers. The sentence inside the brackets in verse 25 exists only in few versions of the Bible (e.g., NKJV). This suggests that this sentence may have been added by someone to match the previous council decision. Their silence on this issue may imply that the Gentile believers should start with keeping the essential parts of the law and then keep more parts of the law after they learn the law every Sabbaths.

Should we eat the things sacrificed to idols?

There is another important issue about eating things sacrificed to idols. The law forbids eating things sacrificed to idols. Yeshua reinforced this law in the church in the book of Revelation. Yeshua says in Revelation 2:14,

> "But I have a few things against you, because you have those who hold the doctrine of Balaam, who taught Balak to put a stumbling block before the children of Israel, to eat things sacrificed to idols, and to commit sexual immorality."

He says again in Revelation 2:20,

> "Nevertheless I have a few things against you, because you allow that woman Jezebel, who calls herself a prophetess, to teach and seduce My servants to commit sexual immorality and eat things sacrificed to idols."

Most Christians believe that as long as they have strong faith in the Messiah, they could eat anything including unclean food and even the food sacrificed to idols. This is because Paul argued that an idol is nothing in the world compared with the only God we believe. This argument sounds very reasonable to most people, but eating foods sacrificed to idols are forbidden by God. This is the commandment of God and we should keep it independent of whether or not an idol has power. God's law is the truth (Psalm 119:160) and eternal (Psalm 119:44-45): "So shall I keep Your law continually forever and ever. And I will walk at liberty, for I seek Your precepts."

True or false prophet?

We should only believe the true prophets of God like Yeshua, Moses, Isaiah, Ezekiel, Daniel, and Jeremiah. There are also some false prophets and teachers, who lead us to break the law of God, which is perfect and everlasting. Both Yehowah and Yeshua have never abolished any part of the law. Law breakers cannot enter the kingdom of God as Yeshua declares in Matthew 7:21-23: "Not everyone who says to me, 'Lord, Lord,' shall enter the kingdom of heaven, but he who does the will of my Father in heaven. Many will say to me in that day, 'Lord, Lord, have we not prophesied in your name, cast out demons in your name, and done many wonders in your name?' And then I will declare to them, 'I never knew you; depart from me, you who **practice lawlessness!**'"

If anyone teaches you not to keep the Mosaic law of God (practicing lawlessness) no matter how much work and wonder he has done in the name of Yeshua, he is a false prophet and Yeshua never knows him. Similarly, Moses also teaches us how to test a false prophet in Deuteronomy 13:1-5:

> If there arises among you a prophet or a dreamer of dreams, and he gives you a sign or a wonder, and the sign or the wonder comes to pass, of which he spoke to you, saying, 'Let us go after other gods'—which you have not known—and let us serve them,' you shall not listen to the words of that prophet or that dreamer of dreams, for Yehowah your God is testing you to know whether you love Yehowah your God with all your heart and with all your soul. You shall walk after Yehowah your God and fear Him, and keep His commandments and obey His voice, and you shall serve Him and hold fast to Him. But that prophet or that dreamer of dreams shall be put to death, because he has spoken in order to turn you away from Yehowah your God, who brought you out of the land of Egypt and redeemed you from the house of bondage, to entice you from the way in which Yehowah your God commanded you to walk. So you shall put away the evil from your midst.

This teaching of Moses here is the same as Yeshua's in Matthew 7:21-23. Even if someone gives you a sign or a wonder, and the sign or the wonder comes to pass, but if he seduces you to break the law of God and/or to serve other gods, he is a false prophet and must be condemned.

In contrast, Yeshua is the true Prophet. He also gave us signs or wonders, and the signs or the wonders came to pass. But his teachings are always consistent with the law and the Scriptures in the Hebrew Bible. He always teaches us to serve the Father God only and keep His Commandments with all our hearts, all our souls, and all our minds. He always speaks the words only the Father commands him to say.

In Deuteronomy 18:15-22, Moses tells Israelites:

> "Yehowah your God will raise up for you a Prophet like me from your midst, from your brethren. Him you shall hear, according to all you desired of Yehowah your God in Horeb in the day of the assembly, saying, **'Let me not hear again the voice of Yehowah my God, nor let me see this great fire anymore, lest I die.'** And Yehowah said to me: 'What they have spoken is good. I will raise up for them a Prophet like you from among their brethren, and will put My words in His mouth, and He shall speak to them all that I command him. And it shall be that whoever will not hear My words, which he speaks in My name, I will require it of him. But the prophet who presumes to speak a word in My name, which I have not commanded him to speak, or who speaks in the name of other gods, that prophet shall die.' And if you say in your heart, 'How shall we know the word which Yehowah has not spoken?' when a prophet speaks in the name of Yehowah, if the thing does not happen or come to pass, that is the thing which Yehowah has not spoken; the prophet has spoken it presumptuously; you shall not be afraid of him."

Yeshua spoke in the name of his Father and made several prophecies, which were proved to be fulfilled perfectly (see Chapters 7-9). Therefore, Yeshua must be the true Prophet foretold by Moses. God will judge us for not listening to the true Prophet.

CHAPTER

31

Birthday of Yeshua Messiah

On December 25, Christians around the world gather to celebrate Yeshua's birthday. Was Yeshua Messiah really born on December 25? If not, when was the exact date of his birth? Although the Scriptures do not directly tell us the exact birthday of Yeshua, can we identify it? Great efforts have been made to obtain the exact birthday of Yeshua for about 2,000 years, no consensus has been reached so far. Here, we attempt to determine the true birthday (9 March 5 BC) of Yeshua from the Gospels of Matthew and John as well as from the astronomical and historical records.

Yeshua's birth on Nisan 1

In order to identify the true birthday of Yeshua, we need to find hints from the Scriptures. In the previous chapters, we have proved that Yeshua is the Messiah, the Son of God, the Son of Man, the Word of God, the Passover Lamb of God, the Angel of Yehowah God who bears the Name of Yehowah. He is the Regent of Yehowah God, speaking and acting on behalf of Yehowah.

Matthew cited the Hebrew Bible, saying, "Behold, a virgin (young woman) shall be with child, and shall bring forth a son, and they shall call his name Emmanuel, which being interpreted is, God with us." (Matthew 1:23). Matthew tells us that the birth of Yeshua signifies "God is with us" or "God dwells among us."

The apostle John states in John 1:14, "And the Word became flesh and dwelt among us, and we beheld his glory, the glory as of the only begotten of the Father, full of grace and truth." John also declared that the Word was with God from the beginning (John 1:1). He speaks and acts exactly according to what his Father tells him. "No one has seen God at any time. Only the begotten Son, who is in the bosom of the Father, has declared Him." (John 1:18). The Son of God appeared to Moses as the Angel of God, who bears the Name of Yehowah (Exodus 23:20-23). The Angel of God is the same as the Word of God because he speaks the Word of God on God's behalf and with the same authority of God. The Son of God became flesh and directly appeared to the Israelites on behalf of his Father. This is the most direct signature of "God's dwelling among us."

Moses also told us that the tabernacle (the simple tent-sanctuary) was the portable earthly meeting place of God with the children of Israel from the time of the exodus of Egypt. The tabernacle is the symbol of "God dwelling among us" in the time of Moses (Exodus 25:8) and in the eternal kingdom of God (Revelation 21:3).

Since both the tabernacle and the incarnated Son of God (the Messiah) symbolize the dwelling of God among us, setting up God's tabernacle in the time of Moses should have been a foreshadow of the Messiah's birth. God instructed Moses, "On the first day of the first month (Nisan 1) shall you set up the tabernacle of the tent of the congregation. And you shall put in it the ark of the testimony, and cover the ark with the veil." (Exodus 40: 2-3). "And it came to pass in the first month in the second year, on the first day of the month, that the tabernacle was raised up." (Exodus 40:17). Moses indeed set up the tabernacle on Nisan 1. This provides a strong hint that Yeshua should have been born on Nisan 1 if he is the true Messiah and his name is called Emmanuel.

When should Yeshua have been conceived if he was born on Nisan 1? We can find a hint from the starting time of building the tabernacle. In the third month—according to Jewish sage, the first day of that month (Exodus 19:1, NIV) marks the time more explicitly, that is, 45 days after the exodus from Egypt on the first Passover (Nisan 15). Moses spent one day on the mountain (Exodus 19:3), one day returning the people's answer (Exodus 19:7-8), three days of preparation, making the whole time 50 days from the first Passover to the promulgation of the law (Ten Commandments) and the establishment of God's covenant with the Israelites. Hence on the Feast of Pentecost, that is, in the sixth day of the third Hebrew lunar month (Sivan 6), the covenant of God with the Israelites was established. After God made the covenant, He called Moses out of the midst of a cloud and Moses went up into the mountain in the seventh day of the third lunar month (Exodus 24:16-18). It was on the 7th day of the third month, Moses went up into the mountain and was instructed by God to build the tabernacle.

From the promulgation of the law on the day of Pentecost (14 June 1457 BC) to setting up the tabernacle on the next Nisan 1 (31 March 1456 BC), there were 290 days, which is close to the duration of a woman's pregnancy in the ancient time (in ancient China, the normal pregnancy lasted about 10 lunar months from the time of conception, that is, about 295 days). Since the power of the Spirit of God made Virgin Mary conceive Yeshua, the conception should have also taken place on Pentecost, the very day the almighty God selected for the promulgation of His law.

Yeshua is not only the Messiah but also the Passover Lamb of God. According to the Hebrew Bible, the Passover lamb must be one year old, implying that a Passover lamb must be born in the month of Nisan. Therefore, Yeshua must have been born on Nisan 1 in order for him to be both the Messiah and the Passover Lamb of God.

Messiah's birth on Nisan 1 (March 9) of 5 BC

The account of Matthew about Yeshua's nativity gives us a hint that he must have been born before Herod died, "Now when Yeshua was born in Bethlehem of Judea in the days of Herod the king, behold, there came wise men from the east to Jerusalem." (Matthew 2:1). It has been generally accepted that Herod died in the spring of 4 BC. In Chapter 2, we have unambiguously proved that Herod indeed died near the end of March 4 BC.

According to the law, a prophet must be at least 30 years old. Ezekiel was called to be the prophet of God in the 30th year of his life (Ezekiel

1:1). Since Yeshua was also the prophet Moses foretold (Deuteronomy 18:18), he must have been at least 30 years old when he began to minister and speak the words of God. In Chapter 3, we have shown that Yeshua was declared to be the Lamb of God by John the Baptist on Nisan 10 of 27 AD and called his disciples on Nisan 11 of 27 AD (April 6). If he was born on Nisan 1 of 5 BC, he was 31 years old when he started to minister on Nisan 11 of 27 AD.

Nisan 1 of 5 BC was on March 9 according to the astronomical new-moon data and the rules for the Hebrew lunisolar calendar (see Table XII). If Yeshua was indeed born on 9 March 5 BC, his birthday should be consistent with the star of Bethlehem recorded by Matthew (2:1-12). If Yeshua was born on 9 March 5 BC, Yeshua should have been conceived on the Feast of Pentecost of 6 BC, which was on May 23. From 23 May 6 BC to 9 March 5 BC, there were 291 days.

The star of Bethlehem

The star of Bethlehem is recorded in Matthew 2:1-12:

> [1]Now after Yeshua was born in Bethlehem of Judea in the days of Herod the king, behold, wise men from the East came to Jerusalem, [2]saying, "Where is He who has been born King of the Jews? For we have seen his star in the East and have come to worship Him." [3]When Herod the king heard this, he was troubled, and all Jerusalem with him. [4]And when he had gathered all the chief priests and scribes of the people together, he inquired of them where the Messiah was to be born. [5]So they said to him, "In Bethlehem of Judea, for thus it is written by the prophet: [6]'But you, Bethlehem, in the land of Judah, are not the least among the rulers of Judah; For out of you shall come a ruler who will shepherd My people Israel.'" [7]Then Herod, when he had secretly called the wise men, determined from them what time the star appeared. [8]And he sent them to Bethlehem and said, "Go and search carefully for the young child, and when you have

found him, bring back word to me, that I may come and worship him also." ⁹When they heard the king, they departed; and behold, the star which they had seen in the East went before them, till it came and stood over where the young child was. ¹⁰When they saw the star, they rejoiced with exceedingly great joy. ¹¹And when they had come into the house, they saw the young child with Mary His mother, and fell down and worshiped him. And when they had opened their treasures, they presented gifts to him: gold, frankincense, and myrrh. ¹²Then, being divinely warned in a dream that they should not return to Herod, they departed for their own country another way.

The account in the Gospel of Matthew describes how the Magi saw a star which they believed to herald the birth of the Messiah-King of Jews and how they followed the star to find the child and presented their gifts to him.

The star of Bethlehem has been mythical and unrelated to a real astronomical phenomenon. Here, we show that the star of Bethlehem was a new sword-like star near α-*Altair*, which was observed by the Chinese astronomers in the second Chinese lunar month of 5 BC, which was between March 9 and April 7.

There are several characteristics of the star of Bethlehem recorded in Matthew's Gospel. The characteristics are as follows:

1. It should be a star which had newly appeared. The best candidate should be a bright nova or supernova.
2. The star was seen in the east by the Magi in the time of the Messiah's birth (Matthew 2:2). When they came to Jerusalem and were sent to Bethlehem by Herod, the star in the east went ahead of them during their journey to Bethlehem, which is due south of Jerusalem. This implies that the star slowly moved through the sky from the east to the south during traveling of the Magi from their country to Jerusalem.

3. The star "stood over" Bethlehem. Matthew 2:9 records that the star "went ahead of them and "stood over" the place where the child was." According to Matthew, the star, as viewed from Jerusalem, "stood over" Bethlehem.

4. The Magi should have arrived in Bethlehem after Mary the mother of Yeshua was ceremonially clean. This should have been at least 40 days after she gave birth to the male child (Yeshua) according to Leviticus 12:1-4: "If a woman has conceived, and borne a male child: then she shall be unclean seven days; as in the days of her customary impurity shall she be unclean. And in the eighth day the flesh of his foreskin shall be circumcised. And she shall then continue in the blood of her purification three and thirty days; she shall touch no hallowed thing, nor come into the sanctuary, until the days of her purification be fulfilled."

A "comet"-like star observed by the Chinese astronomers meets the above characteristics. It was newly formed and "stood over" in the sky. The phrase "stood over" or "hung over" was uniquely applied to describe a comet in ancient literature. For example, Josephus stated: "a star, resembling a sword, stood over the city." (*Wars*, bk. 6, ch. 5, sect. 3). We have shown that he refers to a long star (extending 37 degrees) observed also by the Chinese astronomers on 29 July 65 AD. This star appeared for 56 days according to the Chinese record. Unlike a Halley comet that travels in the sky about 2-5 degrees per day, the long star does not change its position in the sky. Although the ancient Chinese astronomers did not clearly distinguish between a long star (possibly bright nova or supernova) and a comet, the detailed descriptions of their sky behaviors (e.g., position and brightness) were different. Josephus also made the distinction between a sword-like star and a comet, both of which were observed before the Jewish war that started in April of 67 AD (*Wars*, bk. 6, ch. 5, sect. 3).

A sword-like star for the Messiah appears to be foretold in the Hebrew Bible in Numbers 24:15-19 (Balaam fourth Oracle): "And he took up his oracle, and said, Balaam the son of Beor has said, and the man whose eyes are open has said: He has said, who heard the words of

God, and knew the knowledge of the Most High, who saw the vision of the Almighty, falling into a trance, but having his eyes open: I shall see him, but not now: I shall behold him, **but not near: there shall come a star out of Jacob, and a scepter shall rise out of Israel**, and shall crush the forehead of Moab, and destroy all the children of Sheth. And Edom shall be a possession, Seir also shall be a possession for his enemies; and Israel shall do valiantly. Out of Jacob shall come he that shall have dominion, and shall destroy him that remains of the city."

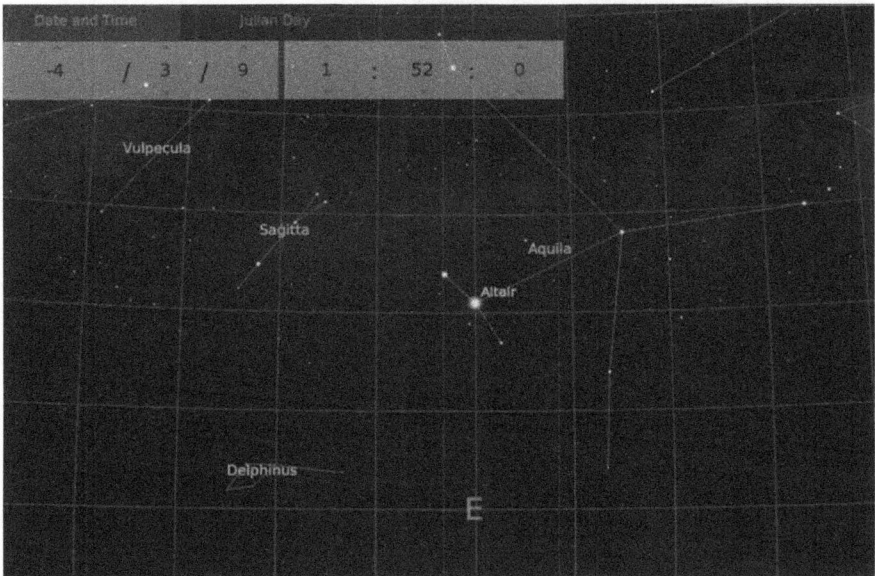

Figure 4: Sky view from Baghdad on 9 March 5 BC, as predicted from the Stellarium Program. The position of α-*Altair* at 1:52 was at 90 degrees, due east of Baghdad.

The Oracle foretold that a star would come out of Jacob and a scepter would rise out of Israel in far future to have dominion over the nations. Here, the second sentence essentially repeats the first sentence to imply that a new star resembling a scepter will come out of Israel. The new star resembling a scepter (sword) is the star of the Messiah who will rule the nations with a rod of iron and with a sharp sword in his mouth. Therefore, a long star resembling a sword should be the best candidate for the star of Bethlehem.

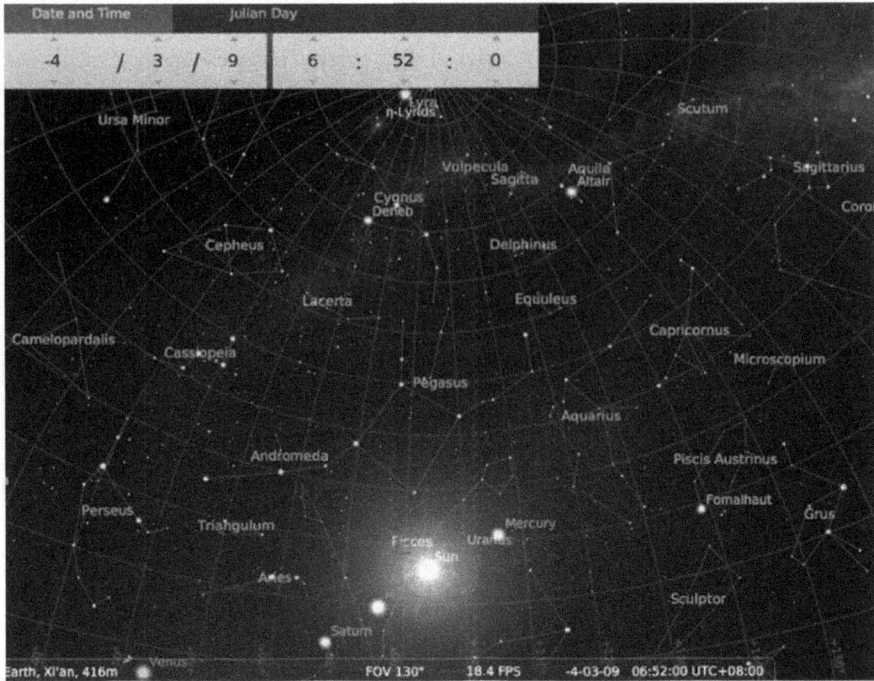

Figure 5: Predicted sky view from Xi-An, China on 9 March 5 BC. The position of α-*Altair* at 6:52 was at about 150 degrees, south-east of Xi-An.

The Chinese chronicle (in *Qian Han Shu*) recorded: "In the second year of the reign period of Jian-Ping, second month, a *hui-xing* (comet) appeared in *qian-niu* for more than 70 days."

This record tells us that during the interval between March 9 and April 7 of 5 BC (the second Chinese month), a comet was visible for more than 70 days near α-*Altair*. Although *hui-xing* refers to a comet, it could also refer to a bright nova. For example, both the Chinese and European astronomers used the word "comet" to describe the supernova of 1572 AD. Since the "comet" did not move in the sky, it must be a long star resembling a sword.

In Figures 4 and 5, we show the predicted sky views on 9 March 5 BC, which were observed from Baghdad (close to Babylon) of Iraq and from Xi-An (the capital city of Eastern Han Dynasty) of China, respectively. The sky views are predicted from the Stellarium Program. The position of α-*Altair* at 1:52 on March 9 of 5 BC was due east of Babylon (see Figure 4). If the comet-like star appeared near α-*Altair* at

1:52 Babylon time, it was seen in the direction of due east (the cardinal compass point is at 90 degrees), in agreement with Matthew 2:2. The Jerusalem time was at 0:52 on 9 March 5 BC, which was on Nisan 1. The Xi-An time was at 6:52 on 9 March 5 BC, which was the first day of the second Chinese month. The position of α-*Altair* seen from Xi-An was at about 150 degrees, south-east of Xi-An (see Figure 5). The comet-like star near α-*Altair* should have been visible in China at this time because it was about 20 minutes before sunrise. The comet-like star could have been seen in China on any clear day of the second Chinese month if the new star appeared for 70 days and was first seen at 0:52 Jerusalem time on 9 March 5 BC, the time when Yeshua was born.

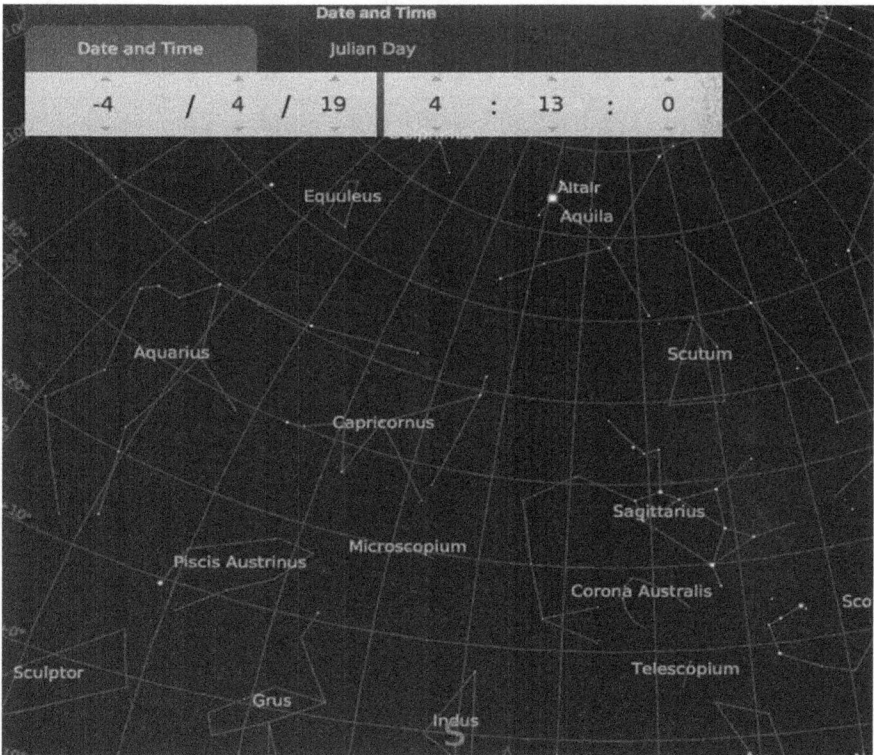

Figure 6: Predicted sky view from Jerusalem on April 19 of 5 BC. The position of α-*Altair* at 4:13 was at 180 degrees, due south of Jerusalem.

After the Magi saw the star in the east on March 9, they may have immediately left Babylon for Jerusalem. How long did they take to travel from Babylon to Jerusalem? The distance is about 900 miles if they traveled through the Fertile Crescent. If they rode on their donkeys, they should have been able to travel 25 miles per day comfortably. So it is reasonable that the Magi took about 6 weeks from first sighting the star until their arrival in Jerusalem.

Table XII: Hebrew Lunisolar Calendar of 5 BC (The first day of each lunar month is indicated with **bold face**. The lunar month's name is on the left side.)

							1	January
	2	3	4	5	6	7	8	
(11) Shebet	9	**10**	11	12	13	14	15	
	16	17	18	19	20	21	22	
	23	*24*	25	26	27	28	29	
	30	31	1	2	3	4	5	February
(12) Adar	6	7	8	**9**	10	11	12	
	13	14	15	16	17	18	19	
	20	21	22	*23*	24	25	26	
	27	28	29	1	2	3	4	March
(1) Nisan	5	6	7	8	**9**	10	11	
	12	13	14	15	16	17	18	
	19	20	21	22	*23*	24	25	
	26	27	28	29	30	31	1	April
(2) Iyar	2	3	4	5	6	7	**8**	
	9	10	11	12	13	14	15	
	16	17	18	19	20	21	*22*	
	23	24	25	26	27	28	29	
	30	1	2	3	4	5	6	May
(3) Sivan	**7**	8	9	10	11	12	13	
	14	15	16	17	18	19	20	
	21	22	23	24	25	26	27	
	28	29	30	31	1	2	3	June
(4) Tammuz	4	5	**6**	7	8	9	10	

	11	12	13	14	15	16	17	
	18	19	**20**	21	22	23	24	
	25	26	27	28	29	30	1	July
(5) Av	2	3	4	**5**	6	7	8	
	9	10	11	12	13	14	15	
	16	17	18	**19**	20	21	22	
	23	24	25	26	27	28	29	
(6) Elul	30	31	1	2	3	**4**	5	August
	6	7	8	9	10	11	12	
	13	14	15	16	17	**18**	19	
	20	21	22	23	24	25	26	
(7) Tishri	27	28	29	30	31	1	**2**	September
	3	4	5	6	7	8	9	
	10	11	12	13	14	15	**16**	
	17	18	19	20	21	22	23	
	24	25	26	27	28	29	30	
(8) Heshvan	1	**2**	3	4	5	6	7	October
	8	9	10	11	12	13	14	
	15	**16**	17	18	19	20	21	
	22	23	24	25	26	27	28	
(9) Kislev	29	30	**31**	1	2	3	4	November
	5	6	7	8	9	10	11	
	12	13	**14**	15	16	17	18	
	19	20	21	22	23	24	25	
(10) Tebet	26	27	28	29	**30**	1	2	December
	3	4	5	6	7	8	9	
	10	11	12	13	**14**	15	16	
	17	18	19	20	21	22	23	
(11) Shebet	24	25	26	27	28	**29**	30	

On 19 April of 5 BC, six weeks after Yeshua was born, the position of α-*Altair* at 4:13 was at 180 degrees, due south of Jerusalem (see Figure 6). This is consistent with Matthew's account (Matthew 2:9). The six

weeks were still well within the period (10 weeks) of visibility of the Chinese comet-like star. The Magi should have been able to see the star in the early morning when the sky was clear. If they rode on their donkeys and traveled to the west, they should not have been able to see the star even if the sky was clear in the morning. If the Magi arrived in Jerusalem on 18 April 5 BC and the sky was not clear, they could not have seen the comet-like star when they left Jerusalem for Bethlehem in the early morning of April 19. Due to a possible divine interference, the sky may have suddenly become clear around 4:00 am to allow the Magi to see the star in the due south of Jerusalem. Since both Bethlehem and the star were due south of Jerusalem, the comet-like star appeared to "hang over" Bethlehem to the eyes of the Magi.

This new comet-like star is indeed the best candidate for the star of Bethlehem described in the Gospel of Matthew. Is it significant that the star was born near α-*Altair*. We know that α-*Altair* is the brightest star in the constellation of *Aquila* and the 12th brightest star in the night sky. The ancient Babylonians called α-*Altair* the eagle star. The ancient Chinese called it *Niu Lang Xing* (the oxherd star). In the vision of Ezekiel, he saw the appearance of the glory of Yehowah God. Within it there came the likeness of four living creatures (Ezekiel 1:5) and each one had four faces, one like the face of a man, one like the face of a lion, one like the face of an ox, and one like the face of an eagle (Ezekiel 1:10). His vision tells us that eagle is one of the four perspectives of the likeness of the glory of Yehowah God. This is also consistent with Exodus 19:4, "You have seen what I did unto the Egyptians, and how I bore you on eagles' wings, and brought you unto myself." Since there were four eagle faces in the vision of Ezekiel, Yehowah God carried the Israelites on the wings of eagles (plural form) and brought them into Himself. Therefore, we may assign α-*Altair* into the Star of the Father and the new sword-like star into the star of the Messiah.

CHAPTER

32

Daniel's Prophecy: The Last Half of the 70th Week

In Chapters 4 and 5, we have unlocked the major part of Daniel's prophecy on the 70 weeks in Daniel 9:24-27. Here, we discuss the prophecy on the last half of the 70th week. Before we do this, we repeat the verses of Daniel 9:26-27 below (our modified English translation based on Interlinear Bible):

> [26]And after the sixty-two weeks messiah shall be cut off, but not to himself; And he shall destroy the city and the sanctuary with the coming prince. The end of it shall be with a flood, and till the end of the war desolations are determined. [27]And he shall confirm a covenant with many for one week; but in the middle of the week he shall cause sacrifice and offering to fail. And on the extremity of abominations, [it shall] be desolated even until the consummation. And [that] being determined is poured out on [the one] being desolated.

In Chapter 5, we proved that the 70th week started on 11 Nisan 27 AD. The Messiah was crucified on 14 Nisan 30 AD, which was in the middle of the 70th week. Thus, the crucifixion of Yeshua in 30 AD confirmed the prophecy in the first part of Daniel 9:26. The second part of verse 26 means that to the Messiah himself, he was not actually cut off. He was not cut off because he resurrected 3 days and 3 nights after his crucifixion. The resurrected Messiah went back to heaven and sat on the right-hand side of his Father on the Feast of Pentecost of 30 AD. The third part of verse 26 tells us that the Messiah would destroy the city and the sanctuary with the coming prince. Yeshua himself also prophesied the destruction of the temple and the city when he was with his disciples. God gave the Jews a grace period of 40 years hoping for their repentance at the preaching of His only begotten Son. Since they did not repent, God poured out His wrath to His people and destroyed the temple and city in 70 AD. We also know that Yeshua received all authority from his Father after his resurrection (Matthew 28:19). Therefore, it was the Messiah and God who destroyed the temple and the city because of their unrepented sins and evil works. Josephus also said that it was the divine wrath of God that led to the destruction of Jerusalem and the holy temple.

In the first half of the 70th week, Yeshua confirmed the covenant with many and caused sacrifices and offerings to fail (cease) in the middle of the week. He finished God's work of salvation within about three years. He then ascended to heaven on 6 Sivan (26 May) 30 AD and the clock of the 70th week was paused. The total length of his ministry in his first advent was 1143 days (see Chapter 3). In his final advent, the clock of the 70th week may be re-initiated on 6 Sivan 2027 AD, on the feast day of Pentecost. From 6 Sivan (12 May) 2027 AD to 1 Nisan (25 March) 2031 AD (when the Messiah and God shall start to reign), 1413 days will elapse. The 1413 days can be calculated from the Julian day number JD 2461537 for 12 May 2027 AD and JD 2462950 for 25 March 2031 AD. This should be the second half of the 70th week during which the Messiah will finish God's work of judgment and ultimate salvation. Since 1143 days +1413 days = 2556 days = 7365.143 days, the time for the entirety of the 70th week is indeed very close to 7 solar years (2556.7 days). A difference of less than one day could be due to the fact that we do not know exactly the starting and ending hours of the two periods and that we do not consider the very short time of his work in 67 AD (see Chapter 9).

A schematic diagram in Figure 7 summarizes Daniel's 70 weeks (490 years). The two dashed lines in the Figure indicate two gap-periods: two weeks and 1,997 years. The second dashed line started on the feast day of Pentecost in 30 AD and will end on the feast day of Pentecost in 2027 AD, which spans 1,997 years.

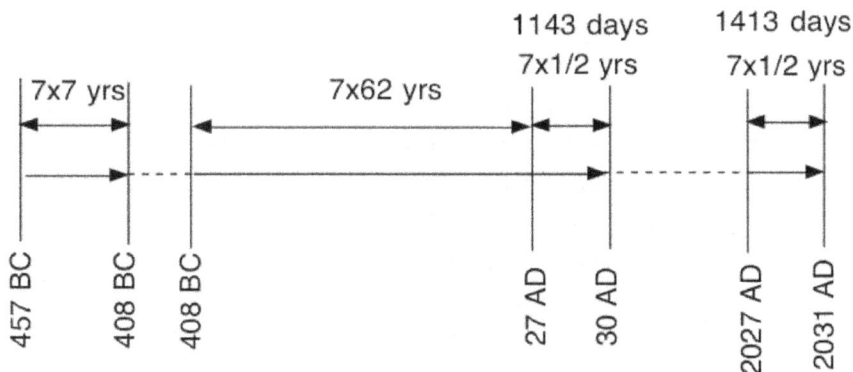

Figure 7: Schematic diagram of the prophetic 70 weeks (490 years) of Daniel.

The prophetic 490-year period started from 1 Nisan (26 March) 457 BC, which was exactly on the Vernal Equinox (at 6:50) and will end on 1 Nisan (25 March) 2031 AD, which is 4 days after the Vernal Equinox (at 21:47 on March 20, the beginning of March 21 in the Hebrew calendar). God appointed the exactly 490 solar years to accomplish His work of salvation and judgment. 490 is a complete number, as suggested by Yeshua in Matthew 18:21-22, "Then Peter came to him and said, 'Lord, how often shall my brother sin against me, and I forgive him? Up to seven times?' Yeshua said to him, 'I do not say to you, up to seven times, but up to seventy times seven.'" Seven appears to be a complete number to Peter, but seventy times seven [490] is the true complete number to Yeshua. In Chapter 4 of the book: *Perfectly Fulfilled Prophecies and the Destiny of Mankind*, the author shows that a complete cycle of Enoch's solar calendar is also 490 years.

Yeshua spends a total of exactly 7 solar years on the earth to finish the work of God's salvation and judgment (the 70th week). Within the 7 solar years, he spent 1,143 days on the earth to finish the work of God's salvation about 2,000 years ago and will spend 1,431 days on the earth to finish the work of God's judgment.

The new year of Gentile's kingdoms such as Babylonian, Persian, and Greek kingdom starts from Nisannu 1 (the first day of the first month) in the Babylonian lunisolar calendar. The first new year of the Messianic kingdom will start from Nisan 1 of 2031 AD in the Hebrew calendar. Yehowah God and the Messiah will co-reign over the world for 1,000 years. During the millennium kingdom of God, all flesh will come to Jerusalem to worship God from one Sabbaths to another and from new moon to another (Isaiah 66:23). The Gentile survivors (spared by God) must come to Jerusalem to worship God and keep the Feast of Tabernacles every year (Zechariah 14:16).

The people of God in Jerusalem will live a long and happy life (Isaiah 65:22-23). Even a sinner may live over one hundred years (Isaiah 65:20). Sinners will be struck down by God and their corpses will be thrown into the Gehenna and become abhorring to all flesh (Isaiah 66:24). In the millennium kingdom, there will still be death, crying, weeping, and punishment.

After the millennium kingdom, God will make new heaven, new earth, and new Jerusalem (Revelation 21:1-2, Isaiah 65:17-18). God will wipe away every tear from their eyes; there will be no more death, nor sorrow, nor crying, nor pain (Revelation 21:4, Isaiah 65:18-19). The new heaven and new earth will never pass way (Isaiah 66:22) and the saints dwelling in the new Jerusalem shall serve God and co-reign with Him forever and ever (Revelation 22:1-5).

INDEX OF SCRIPTURES

Symbols

1 Corinthians 3:
    10 130, 139
    16 130
1 Corinthians 8:
    4-13 129
1 Corinthians 9:
    19-22 146, 173
    20 141
    21 132, 133, 135, 140, 141,
        146, 165
1 Corinthians 10:
    19-33 129
1 Corinthians 11:
    1 147
    24-25 149
1 Corinthians 15:
    3-8 148, 160
    5-8 130
    35-58 154, 175
    46 140, 154, 175
    50 154, 155, 175, 176
1 John 1:
    1 135
    2-4 135
    9 145, 204
1 John 2:
    1-2 136, 202
    3-6 132, 136, 203

1 John 3:
    2 137
    4-6 132, 136, 203
    7 128, 166
    7-9 136, 203
    24 136
1 John 4:
    1-3 137
    3 160
    6 130
1 Kings 6:
    1 113
1 Samuel 5:
    1 116
1 Samuel 7:
    1 116
    2 116
1 Samuel 8:
    1 118
1 Samuel 13:
    1-2 118
1 Timothy 1:
    3 166
1 Timothy 4:
    1-3 xii
    3-5 142
2 Corinthians 3:
    7 141, 146
    7-8 128, 133, 139
2 Corinthians 11:
    32 163

2 Corinthians 12:
 12 xiv, 126, 164, 210
2 Peter 3:
 4-13 120
 15 119
 15-16 xii
2 Samuel 1:
 23 118
2 Samuel 2:
 10 118
2 Timothy 1:
 15 157, 166

A

Acts 1:
 3 21
 21 90
Acts 5:
 3-4 172
 35-39 104
 37 104
Acts 7:
 14 111
 14-16 111
 16 112
Acts 9:
 3 162
 3-7 161
 10-15 153
 19-20 151
 23 152
 23-30 151
Acts 11:
 28 163
Acts 12:
 2 163
 23 163
 25 151
Acts 13:
 1 151
 20-21 112

Acts 14:
 4 xiii
 14 xiii
Acts 15:
 1-5 151
 6 151
 7 152
 12-13 210
 19-20 151
 21 151, 153
Acts 19:
 8-9 157
Acts 21:
 20-21 174
 20-25 211
 27-29 158
Acts 23:
 10-11 162

C

Colossians 2:
 14 133

D

Daniel 7:
 13 181
 13-14 179, 187
Daniel 9:
 24 37
 24-25 26
 24-27 227
 25 34
 26 37, 75
 26-27 60
 27 34, 36
Daniel 12:
 4 40
 9-10 39, 40
Deuteronomy 13:
 1-5 xiv, 126, 164, 213
Deuteronomy 17:

6 125
Deuteronomy 18:
   15-22 214
   17-19 194
   17-22 73
   18 218
Deuteronomy 19:
   15 xiv

E

Ephesians 1:
   1 157
Exodus 1:
   5 111
Exodus 12:
   3 14
Exodus 13:
   21 188
Exodus 14:
   19-20 188
Exodus 19:
   1 216
   3 216
   4 226
   7-8 217
   16 161
Exodus 21:
   6 182
Exodus 23:
   20-23 188, 216
Exodus 24:
   16-18 217
Exodus 25:
   8 216
Exodus 40:
   2-3 216
   17 216
Ezekiel 1:
   1 218
   5 226
   10 226

Ezekiel 4:
   1-3 41
   1-6 41
   4-5 41
Ezekiel 8:
   3 62
Ezekiel 36:
   26-27 206
Ezekiel 44:
   6-9 209
   9 143
Ezra 1:
   1-4 27
Ezra 3:
   2 189
   10-11 28
Ezra 4 28
Ezra 4:
   6 28
   6-23 28
   11-12 28
   21 28
   23 29
   24 28
Ezra 6:
   15 28
Ezra 7:
   6 29
   6-26 27
   8 30
   9 32
   14 29
   18 29
Ezra 9:
   9 29

G

Galatians 1:
   8-9 129, 139
   9 xii
   12 130

15-17 152
15-19 152
16-17 139
17 130
18-19 152
Galatians 2:
1 152
1-2 152
6 130
7-8 130
9 153
9-10 152
12 135
16 139
Galatians 3:
10 127, 133, 141, 146
13 128
25 134
Galatians 4:
6 131, 140
9 128
24 146
24-25 141
24-26 139
Galatians 5:
1-6 209
13-15 140
14 127, 132, 135, 146, 165,
173, 174
Genesis 3:
15 183
Genesis 13:
16 183
Genesis 15:
1-14 209
4-5 144
6 143, 144
Genesis 17:
2 143
Genesis 23:
17 112

Genesis 26:
2-5 143
4 143
Genesis 33:
18-20 112
19 112
Genesis 46:
27 111

H

Habakkuk 2:
4 144, 145
5 145
Hebrews 7:
18-19 128, 133, 141, 146
Hosea 10:
15 184
Hosea 11:
1 184, 185

I

Isaiah 9:
6 185, 186, 187
Isaiah 42:
21 145, 206
Isaiah 43:
10 183
Isaiah 49:
2 183, 185
3 183
5 184
6 184, 185
Isaiah 53:
4-6 36
8 36
9 183
10 36, 37
11 37
12 37
Isaiah 56:
1-7 206, 207

Isaiah 65:
    17-18 230
    18-19 230
    20 230
    22-23 230
Isaiah 66:
    14-17 208
    17 142, 208
    22 230
    24 230

J

James 1:
    25 128
James 2:
    20 166
    20-24 144
    23 143
    24 144
Jeremiah 32:
    6-15 77
John 1:
    1 181, 182, 195, 216
    12-13 202
    14 216
    17 181
    18 189, 195, 216
    28 47
    28-51 47
    29 47
    29-34 14
    29-36 14
    35-42 15
    43 48
    43-51 15
John 2:
    1 15, 48
    1-2 47
    1-11 14
    7-11 16
    13 14

19-21 15
    20 62, 63
    21 130
John 3:
    5 202
    15-17 202
    19 48
John 4:
    22 199
    31-38 22
    35 23
John 5:
    22 182
    27 182
John 6:
    4-14 18
John 10:
    29 197
    30 181, 182
    34 182
    34-36 181
    38 182
John 11:
    55 19
John 12:
    48 182
John 14:
    28 131, 182, 187, 199
John14:
    28 197
John 15:
    16 131
    27 129
    27 22, 90, 135
John 16:
    31-32 92
    32 195
John 17:
    11 163
    20 135
    20-21 22

21-23 182
John 19:
    14 49
    18 109
    31 49
    40 49
John 20:
    1 51
    10 94
    14-17 21
    17 131, 198
    19 21, 94
    19-20 94
    21-23 94
    24 94
    28 172
John 21:
    1-23 94
    14 94
    21-23 72
    22-23 163, 193, 198
Jonah 1:
    17 44
Jonah 2:
    1-10 45
Judges 11:
    15-27 114
Judges 12:
    7-15 115
Judges 13:
    1 116

L

Leviticus 12:
    1-4 220
Luke 1:
    5 106
Luke 2:
    1-2 103, 105
    1-4 101
    2 104

Luke 3:
    1 106
    1-3 98
    19-23 105
    23 105, 106
Luke 7:
    31-50 150
    36-50 150
    44-47 150
Luke 12:
    19 149
Luke 23:
    32 109
    39-43 108, 149
    54 52, 105
Luke 24 93
Luke 24:
    1 96
    3 96
    4 96
    21 105
    28-29 106
    36-43 154
    45-46 95
    46 148

M

Malachi 4:
    5 191
Mark 14:
    27 94
Mark 15:
    32 109
Matthew 1:
    21 189
    23 215
Matthew 2:
    1 217
    1-12 218
    2 219, 223
    9 220, 225

15 185, 186
20-23 102
Matthew 3:
    1 37
Matthew 4:
    1-2 15
Matthew 5:
    11 128
    17 206
    17-19 133, 137, 174
    17-20 205
    18 127
    19 128, 205
    21-48 205
    21-48 138
Matthew 7:
    15 165
    21-23 213
    22-23 xiv, 126, 164
Matthew 10:
    16-23 61
    20 131
    23 72
Matthew 11:
    14 191
    27 189
Matthew 12:
    38-40 ix, 44, 46
    38-41 42
    40 48
Matthew 13:
    41 59, 60
    41-42 128
Matthew 14:
    1-12 19
    13-21 19
    33 198
Matthew 15:
    4-5 129
    20 208
Matthew 16:

27 72
28 72, 163
Matthew 17:
    2 188
Matthew 18:
    15-16 125
    16 xiv
    21-22 229
    28 200
Matthew 19:
    16-22 204
    17 127, 131, 181, 197
    19 129
    24 205
    26 205
Matthew 20:
    1-16 46
    16 xiii
    18-19 45, 46
Matthew 22:
    35-40 127, 135
    37-40 133
Matthew 23:
    2-3 138
    8 181
    9 187
    9-10 128
    37-39 42
Matthew 24:
    1-2 42
    4-5 56, 58
    6-14 56
    15-20 56
    21-22 57
    23-24 161
    23-28 57
    24 164, 210
    26-31 62
    27 188
    29 50
    29-31 58

32-34 58
34 55, 59
36 39
Matthew 25:
31-46 145, 166
Matthew 26:
13 150
31 94, 195
31-32 92
32 21
Matthew 27:
9-10 76, 79
44 109
45 49, 50
45-50 49
57 46, 49
62-66 49
63 45, 46
Matthew 28:
1 51
2 52
2-3 54
5 52
9 21, 198
10 21, 198
16 21, 93, 94
16-17 94
17 198
18 190, 197
18-20 94
19 130, 135, 153, 164, 228
19-20 22
Micah 5:
2 102

N

Nehemiah 1:
1-3 29
3 29
Nehemiah 2 29
Nehemiah 2:

1-6 27
7-8 27
Nehemiah 6:
15 30
Nehemiah 9:
8 144
Numbers 13:
16 189
Numbers 24:
15-19 220

P

Philippians 1:
2 172
Philippians 2:
6 131, 141
6-7 141
7 140
7-8 175
8 140
Proverb 15:
8 36
Proverb 31:
2 181
Psalm 2 180
Psalm 2:
7 180
9 186
11-12 199
Psalm 19:
7-10 145, 146
Psalm 40:
6-8 36
Psalm 82:
1 182
6 182
Psalm 119:
44-45 146, 212
160 212

R

Revelation 1:
  4,8 187
  9 63
  10-11 67
Revelation 2:
  2 156, 166
  14 129, 212
  20 129, 212
Revelation 3:
  3 39, 40
  12 132
Revelation 5:
  6 131, 197
  12 197
  13-14 197
Revelation 10:
  1 67
  1-2 62
  1-3 63, 187
  3 188
  4 188
Revelation 11 191
Revelation 11:
  2 62, 63, 67
  3 190
  5-6 191
Revelation 12:
  17 204
Revelation 14:
  12 204
Revelation 19:
  15 186
Revelation 20:
  4 200
  5-15 120
  13 145, 166
Revelation 21:
  1-2 230
  1-3 120
  3 216

  4 230
  9 190
  14 130
  22 42, 130
Revelation 22:
  1-5 230
  3 199
  6-7 198
  6-7 190
  8 197
  9 198
  9-16 190
  14 145, 166, 204
Romans 1:
  18-32 174
  29-31 174
Romans 3:
  23 139, 175
  31 134, 140, 174
Romans 4:
  15 141
  28 127
Romans 5:
  20 151
Romans 8:
  3 175
  9 131, 140, 141
Romans 10:
  9 150, 173
  9-10 109
  10 127

T

Titus 1:
  3-4 131, 141
Titus 2:
  13 131, 141, 172

Z

Zechariah 8:
  19 6

Zechariah 9:
9-10 192
Zechariah 11:
12-13 79
13 79
Zechariah 12:
10 193
10-14 193

Zechariah 13:
3 194
6 194
7 195
8 195
8-9 195
Zechariah 14:
16 230